ON
BRAND

SHAPE YOUR NARRATIVE.
SHARE YOUR VISION.
SHIFT THEIR PERCEPTION.

ON
BRAND

ALIZA LICHT

AUTHOR OF *LEAVE YOUR MARK*

UNION
SQUARE
& CO.

NEW YORK

UNION
SQUARE
& CO.

NEW YORK

ISBN 978-1-4549-4906-0 (hardcover)
ISBN 978-1-4549-4908-4 (ebook)

For information about custom editions, special sales, and premium
purchases, please contact specialsales@unionsquareandco.com.

Printed in the United States of America
2 4 6 8 10 9 7 5 3 1

unionsquareandco.com

Interior design: Gina Bonanno
Cover design: Elizabeth Mihaltse Lindy
Cover art: Shutterstock.com

To David, Jonathan, and Sabrina, nothing matters more than you.
Thank you for always letting me dream big.

To my mom, Madelaine, who instilled the importance of having a
confident voice and made sure I had one.

In loving memory of my dad, Michael, whose personal brand always
stood for generosity and kindness.

TABLE OF INSPIRATION

Part Three
SUSTAIN YOUR BRAND

CONCLUSION

My Reputation Doesn't Matter . . .
Said No One Ever

I don't love the word *expert*, but *guru* is way worse, don't you think? There are very few people in the world who actually are experts. But the individuals who brand themselves as such know that in this ever-changing and competitive world, we must all become adept at marketing ourselves.

While the digital age gave those who opted in the means to amplify themselves, the hybrid and often virtual landscape we now work in proves that having a personal brand is no longer a choice; it's a requirement. There's no unsubscribe button. To succeed, we must have the means to convey who we are no matter what the medium. A strong personal brand sets you apart from the pack and secures your professional longevity—because what you do today may not be what you do tomorrow.

Your personal brand ensures that your name gets dropped in rooms you're not in. It allows you to capture opportunities others haven't even heard of yet. It puts you in a position to win because the people around you know the value you add. Why? Because you're in control of your narrative, and you've done a stellar job conveying your worthiness consistently, clearly, and with integrity, every time you show up.

I hate to say it, but without a personal brand, you're flying on a trapeze without a net. Now more than ever, it can influence the opportunities presented to you *or* handed to someone else. We've all seen it happen—someone less deserving gets awarded an opportunity over someone else more worthy and possibly even more talented. Because it's not just about your abilities, it's also about who you are, who you know, and *their* perception of you.

I've spent more than two decades immersed in the business of shaping perception. In my early years at high-fashion magazines, I observed how influence and taste are cultivated. When I moved to the corporate PR side, I learned what it takes to build a brand with cultural impact and longevity. I've worked with some of the most prestigious luxury brands and have been on some of the best marketing and communications teams in the fashion industry. As each year passed, my responsibilities and reputation grew in kind. I became a key stakeholder, working on the front lines of brand positioning, creating relevancy, building awareness and, later, fostering innovation.

Growing up, I was raised to have a confident voice and, throughout my career, supported by mentors to use it. That characteristic has consistently earned me a seat at the table, with the ability to assuredly explore and share my ideas, no matter how unconventional they might be and regardless of who is in the room.

In 2009, one such idea catapulted me from my traditional role in public relations to the Wild West of social media. This singular concept would alter my career trajectory forever. Before the creator economy even existed, I plunged into an emerging world, becoming a social media pioneer in the fashion industry and one of the first examples of a fashion *influencer*, even though we didn't know that word at the time.

I created an anonymous social media personality for my former employer of which I was the sole voice (and later, the face) and organically built a highly engaged cross-platform community of over 1.5 million followers (*which was huge in the early days of brands on social media*). I taught myself the building blocks of what it takes to authentically tell a brand's story online and foster a passionate fan base around it. When I was revealed as the person behind the persona, the news generated more than 230 million media impressions, including a full-page feature story in the *New York Times*.

But I never imagined that the same tactics and marketing principles I had applied to my corporate work for years would later be pivotal in rebranding myself. In doing so, I evolved from a corporate employee to someone with a multimedia personal brand that includes two books, a podcast, speaking engagements, newsletters, a private online community, and a creative brand marketing and digital strategy consultancy. It didn't happen overnight, and it took hard work, consistency, and passion. The good news: I'm about to share all my insider strategies with you.

Let me be clear, though; while I love a good outfit more than most, this is not a fashion book. But my learnings come from an industry built on image. We are selling it. We make you crave it. You consume it.

I don't care whether you're a marketer, coach, artist, banker, athlete, consultant, entrepreneur, writer, lawyer, doctor, teacher, influencer, actor, server, bartender, administrative assistant, cashier, student, or unemployed. Simply having the skills to do a particular job doesn't cut it anymore. Of course you need to have the credentials. That should go without saying. But more than that, no matter what you do professionally, you need your own, clearly defined personal brand to cut through the noise and set you apart. Or, more specifically, to put you in a position to be chosen or recommended for whatever plum opportunity you're after.

Creating a personal brand is not about being famous or becoming an influencer unless that's something you strive to be. It's about communicating who you are, what you align with, and what you do well. It's about providing value to the people around you. It's about getting the credit you deserve and everything that comes with that.

Your personal brand doesn't necessarily need to live online, but having a strategic digital presence will strengthen your position. Nevertheless, it absolutely needs to exist in the real world. How you present yourself, build social capital, and exude executive presence is directly proportional to your success. True talent is delivering the message that you intend with refinement. Standing out in a sea of competition and becoming known for what you do best are the by-products of well-crafted communication and repetition.

I'm going to assume that you've picked up this book because you want to be seen, change how people perceive you, or maybe even change how you view yourself. Perhaps you have no idea and need to figure it out. Either way, you're looking to define your personal brand to help drive what you're trying to achieve. Maybe you're just curious as to what this personal brand hype is about.

If you're new to the concept of a personal brand, welcome! You may have never thought about it before, but fun fact, you already have some version of one. **It starts with what makes you, you.** The impression others have of you stems from how you tell your story and express your unique combination of personality, experience, and skills. It lies in both the spoken and unspoken, and in your mannerisms, energy, and attitude, whether in person, online, in the media, or by word of mouth. It's your visual identity and the things you choose to surround yourself with. It's what people think you do, who you are, and what you stand for. Saying something is **on brand** for you means that it aligns with you aesthetically or in concept. People's perception of you becomes their reality of you, whether you like it or not. Your personal brand is a powerful tool that, if mishandled, can cause harm. *Hello, cancel culture.*

But it can also take you to the highest heights if managed strategically. The best thing is, it's personal! No two people are alike, and with that comes the opportunity to design your brand by shaping your narrative, sharing your vision, and shifting their perception. Think couture, *baby,* because this thing must be tailored to perfection.

WHAT BRINGS YOU HERE?

In theory, everything you say and do should be on brand for you. Your communication and actions should support the image you want to convey. But first, you need to know why you're here. Many roads can lead you to want to create or better communicate your personal brand or change perception.

Your motivation might be that you're looking to become more notable in your industry, or perhaps you're in the early stages of your career and want to build for the future. You might be someone lacking the gravitas needed to lead, or maybe you're excellent at what you do but don't seem to get the credit for it. You could have been passed over for a promotion or, worse, been laid off or fired. If you're an aspiring entrepreneur, you might be trying to transform your side hustle into a company or position yourself to investors. You could be a content creator looking to get to the status of influencer or crushing your career but never thought to build a presence online. You might want to pivot but don't know how to reshape your story. You could also be someone who needs to get back in touch with the value you bring because somehow you've lost that confidence. No matter your current situation, if you do what I'm suggesting, **this book will change how you view yourself and how others perceive you.**

Because personal branding is essential for everyone, I'll share advice and scenarios geared toward various career stages, no matter the industry. Don't limit yourself to what you professionally identify as today. Tomorrow might be a new reality for you. The possibilities are endless, and with this book, you'll be prepared for each of them.

I'll guide you on how to start, where you might need improvement, and explain the path you need to take to reach your full potential. You'll finish this book knowing exactly how to position yourself and be able to tackle the areas below that every person needs to maximize their personal brand.

MY 10 COMMANDMENTS OF PERSONAL BRANDING

In this book, you will learn how to:

1. Analyze your brand's current state and focus on what you want to be known for.

2. Lay your foundation with a website, an all-star LinkedIn page, and a compelling bio.

3. Nail your elevator pitch, tell your story, and communicate your wins strategically.

4. Establish your brand at work, earn social capital, and cultivate authentic relationships.

5. Become a captivating speaker and presenter.

6. Craft a social media strategy and build an online presence.

7. Manage your reputation, learn PR 101, and survive cancel culture.

8. Establish your signature look and visual identity.

9. Understand your value and negotiate what you're worth.

10. Overcome imposter syndrome, step into your power, and rebrand yourself.

I know it sounds like a lot and may feel overwhelming, but I will hold your hand every step of the way. Sometimes my words might feel like tough love, but you can't do this if you're not self-reflective. You also won't succeed if you don't believe you can. Whatever baggage you're bringing to this book, I can help you. There is more out there for you. But you need to be willing to put in the time and the thought process. **I can't create your personal brand for you. You must craft it; to do that, you need to be clear on your intention.**

Whatever your reason for picking up this book, I commend you for investing in yourself and being open to the possibilities. I've lived the advice and methods I'm about to share, and they work. But first, take yourself out of the box you've mentally put yourself in. There's no "I can't." There's no "I don't." There's no "I'm not." Remove the labels you've assigned yourself. Erase the self-judgment that's held you back.

Too many people have chastised themselves to me for not having done this sooner. They berate themselves for "not being good at this." News flash: you can't be bad at something you didn't even try. By reading this book, you are willingly shifting your mindset. When you allow yourself to get out of your own way, you'll be amazed at what can happen.

Why do this, you might ask? Because your career is likely to go in many different directions, and no matter what, I bet you have aspirations greater than where you are today. You may have forgotten them, but this book will peel back those layers and expose the dreams you've been scared to wish for out loud. So go ahead and turn the page and permit yourself to say, "What if?" Because what lies ahead is an opportunity to rediscover yourself. And for some of you, maybe for the first time.

It's true our world is more uncertain than ever. We can, however, control how we communicate, the ways in which we connect, the energy we give off, and what we choose to align with. We all need to be ready for anything, and whatever you can do to protect yourself from the changes around you, the better off you'll be. To successfully pivot at any given point requires that instead of putting all your efforts into one company, role, and title, you must have that same intention for yourself. With *On Brand*, I invite you to step into your new role as Chief Brand Officer of YOU.

PART ONE
Craft Your Brand

1

Nice to Meet You, I'm Aliza

If you've stumbled upon this book because the title or the cover caught your eye, please allow me to introduce myself. I'm someone who pivoted long before it was trendy to do so. Having studied neurobiology and physiology in college and completed several premed internships, I was on the path to becoming a plastic surgeon . . . or so I thought. In my junior year, I realized that the reality of working day in and day out in a hospital was not going to bring me joy. But do you know what did? Fashion. Growing up in my bedroom that was wallpapered with high-fashion editorials from *Vogue*, *Harper's Bazaar*, and the like, I knew that my destiny laid in those glossy pages. I decided to listen to that feeling in my gut that screamed yes to fashion! and no to surgical masks (*ironic, I know*). After graduation, I applied for an internship at several top fashion magazines and got lucky with a stint in the accessories department at *Harper's Bazaar*. Talk about taking a chance on an unknown kid with no experience! They gave me my first opportunity, and I am forever grateful.

My career started in the very coveted fashion closet. Imagine striving to end up in a closet? But this was no ordinary closet. Rows of designer shoes and bags and trays of fine jewelry told me that I had made the right move tossing my Bachelor of Science degree by the wayside. It was the late '90s in Fashion, and I could not have started at a more epic time.

I made it my business to be the person to turn on the lights at the office in the morning and turn them off as the last one to leave at night. I was determined to make an impression. I tried to anticipate my boss's needs and took pride in everything I did, down to plucking the dust bunnies out of the shoes. I knew that as much as what I was doing was mundane and manual, thousands of people would have killed for my internship. It was my first behind-the-scenes glimpse into how influence is created. The editors at *Bazaar* informed you of what you wanted to wear next season. This was still in the heyday of fashion magazines, and I was fortunate enough to experience it all.

My hard work paid off, and my internship supervisor's recommendation landed me my first job, at *Marie Claire* magazine, where I continued to train my eye and love for all things luxury fashion. After two years, I felt I was worthy of a promotion, but that was sadly not in the cards. I decided to broaden my horizons and look beyond the four walls I was in. As an assistant accessories editor, I spoke to public relations people, aka PR people, all day. They were the people from whom I borrowed accessories samples to photograph for the magazine. By closely watching what they did on the other side, I felt I could take on that position without having the technical experience. I was right, and in 1998, I started working in PR at DKNY, an NYC-based sister fashion brand to Donna Karan New York, founded by designer Donna Karan.

At DKNY, the irony was that I was back in the accessories closet. It was almost the identical job, just on the opposite end of the spectrum. I had gone from being the person who requested accessories from the fashion houses to the fashion house who hoped that the magazines would call requesting accessories to shoot. We didn't use email back then, so I would call editors on their LANDLINE (for those of you too young to know what that is, it's a phone that's attached to a wall via a phone cord) and pitch our products. "Hi, this is Aliza from DKNY" became my calling card. After a while, when relationships were farther along, I graduated to "Hi, it's me." That was the gold standard.

As the years passed, my responsibilities expanded. I would have never believed that I'd spend 17 years there, but that's what happened. Eventually, I became senior vice president of global communications overseeing both Donna Karan New York and DKNY. My job entailed everything from ensuring that our clothing and accessories were featured in fashion magazines, producing the runway shows every season, and dressing celebrities for the red carpet. Award season was my Super Bowl. But 11 years into my journey at the company, we were faced with an exciting new opportunity. The world of social media was upon us, and though most brands had Facebook pages by that time, in particular for the fashion industry, an online presence was still somewhat uncharted territory.

In a marketing meeting one day, our team was contemplating joining Twitter and what that would mean for the brands. As the senior vice president of global communications, I was always considering the ramifications of communications gone wrong. Since both the founder and the brand name was Donna Karan, I was concerned that if we made the Twitter handle @donnakaran (*Donna Karan New York was too long*), people would assume the person, Donna Karan, was tweeting. We didn't want to add any ancillary words to it either because you don't mess with an established brand.

I tried to conjure up another idea, and this one came easily. We would create a character to be the voice of the Twitter handle. It would be represented by a fashion illustration, and no one would need to know this character's name. *Gossip Girl* (the original TV series) was all the rage at the time, and the idea of anonymity seemed like the perfect solution. But we had to come up with a narrative, and that's when I suggested that we use the filter of public relations as the lens through which we would tell our story. DKNY PR GIRL was born on Twitter in May 2009, and our legal team decided that only one person would be permitted to tweet anonymously—and that person would be me.

You might be asking yourself why this is significant to this book or to my career journey, and that's where even I never would have dreamed what would happen or how it could be. I started tweeting every day, testing the waters. As a company, we all held hands and agreed that the person behind the Twitter handle would remain a secret. It just seemed easier that way. We wouldn't need to explain who DKNY PR GIRL was, and to be honest, in my mind, I was playing with paper dolls. The sketch that we used as the profile picture was a fashionable cartoon character of a girl, and without my knowledge, the first designer who drew it decided to use my picture as the inspiration for the illustration. I didn't object. She was an exaggerated version of me and unrealistic enough not to give away my secret; it also seemed fitting for the world I was trying to create. I would use my career to fabricate her life, and that's how we would market our brands. The bio was simple: "I'm your well-placed fashion source bringing you the behind-the-scenes scoop from inside Donna Karan New York & DKNY and my life as a PR girl living in NYC." My concept here was "don't share the brand, live the brand," and so I did.

CREATING DKNY PR GIRL'S PERSONAL BRAND

To be clear, I wasn't thinking about personal branding back then. I had never even heard of it, but what I did intuitively know from my work helping to build awareness for the company was that defining a brand's DNA and creating a brand filter is where you start. In this case, the brand had its DNA all set. Donna Karan had built not one but two incredible brands with global reach and recognition. I was clear on what they stood for and the reasons they were created in the first place. You might ask why that's meaningful, and it's because when you endeavor to build brand recognition, you need a strong foundation, and that begins with authenticity. Every founder will tell you that there's a specific problem they're trying to solve, and it's likely their own personal problem.

So I put pen to paper and decided to create a brand filter for DKNY PR GIRL. First and foremost, she was all about fashion, so I would change her outfit every month. I worked with Dallas Shaw, an amazing illustrator, to sketch her monthly looks. And boy did we have fun with it. One month, I would put her in the Garden of Eden, picking forbidden (aka chic!) shoes off a tree; another month, she was on a yacht living her best life. Changing her Twitter avatar generated buzz and engagement every time. But then there was the issue of brand voice. Donna Karan herself was the voice of Donna Karan New York (the luxury label), but DKNY didn't really have one. I decided to contemplate what that voice could be.

If you imagine a funnel in which all decisions are put through, the top of the funnel is wide and narrows as you go down. Identifying these guardrails would help me decide how DKNY PR GIRL would speak and the way in which I wanted the public to view her.

In my mind, I wanted her to be all these things:

What would she talk about? What would she not talk about? I knew she had to be your best girlfriend, the kind of friend who tells you the truth even when you don't want to hear it. She was sassy yet kind, accessible and friendly, but also aspirational. I took a bit of *Gossip Girl's* Serena and mixed her with Blair (yup, there was a bit of snark at times too), putting my own spin on how she spoke. It was second nature to me because I knew that her voice was also my natural voice. I was that friend to those who knew me well, always with the person's best interests at heart, but as direct as they come.

I also didn't want to overtly sell anything. Instead, I wanted to live up to the bio and give people an authentic, fly-on-the-wall view into our fashionable world. Brands were precious with themselves at the time (many still are) and showing what happened behind the scenes wasn't really done. Everything was externally perfect, and no one knew the inner workings of how things came to be. I wanted to expose all of that, albeit understanding that I was still a publicist, and I wasn't going to air anything inappropriate. What I could share, though, was the reality of my world. Things didn't always go to plan, and disclosing the drama and stress of my role would be intriguing for people who had no idea what went on inside the world of fashion PR.

The strategy worked, and we all kept this secret for two years—the identity of the person behind DKNY PR GIRL— watching the account grow in both size and visibility. DKNY PR GIRL took on a life of her own, and at 380,000 followers on Twitter alone (which was a lot back then), she had become a pop culture star, leading the way fashion brands would embark on social media. Some have even credited her as being one of the first fashion influencers, a phrase that we didn't know at the time. I was tweeting upward of 100 times a day, live tweeting the red carpet for award season and TV shows like *Gossip Girl*, *Revenge*, and *Scandal*. DKNY PR GIRL had become a social fixture that people began to feel attached to. By 2011, the secret became too much to bear, and we decided to reveal the person behind the popular handle. The news sent shock waves worldwide, resulting in more than 230 million media impressions. The mystery was way bigger than I knew. The *New York Times* covered the story as a full-page article titled "PR Girl Revealed as PR Executive." The secret was out, and the news was everywhere.

Being DKNY PR GIRL allowed me to share my voice in a remarkable way. The joy I felt connecting with people around the world was intoxicating. I had expanded to Tumblr and Instagram, garnering a community of more than 1.5 million people organically. DKNY PR GIRL had inspired several products and packaging. She had her own stamp of editor's picks on the DKNY website and often guest-blogged with industry partners like Bergdorf's—a brand that didn't even sell the clothing collection. The Twitter account had clout, and it grew to 530,000 followers. The "PR Girl" persona was even a suggested Halloween costume one year—all you had to do was wear a chic dress and hold a giant cup of coffee, ha!

Twitter back then was a special place. It's hard to imagine that now, but the friendships we formed were real—and for me, those relationships still exist today. Social media gave me a new way to network. It also provided a new medium to begin to share my personal passions.

Along the way of me tweeting and blogging about fashion shows and celebrity dressing, I found myself trying to mentor, using my platform to educate aspiring PR professionals on the business of communications. After all, PR was in the name. Mentoring became a regular occurrence, and I started to become known for the advice I was giving out. On Twitter, I would tweet under #PR101 or #Life101. I was storytelling in a way that brought the DKNY brand along for the ride, but in a noncommercial way. On my blog, I'd tackle career and workplace topics and creatively tie them back to fashion in interesting ways. I was writing so much long-form copy that the kind people at Tumblr definitely thought I was using their platform incorrectly. I had a lot to say, and I leveraged these online outlets to say it. I had no idea who was paying attention.

LEAVING MY MARK

In 2013, I was sitting in my office at DKNY when my phone rang. On the other end of the line was a girl named Amanda Englander, a stranger who was following DKNY PR GIRL. She was an editor at a publishing house who was reading my work across platforms and pitched me the idea of writing a book. I was utterly freaked out. How could I write a book with a full-time job and as a mom of two little kids? What on earth would I write about? Who would even read it? I politely declined her offer, but she was (*and still is*) really good at her job (*she's responsible for this book too!*). Like a dog with a bone, she kept on me, trying to convince me that it wouldn't be that hard since I already tweeted 100 times a day. I remember her saying, "Just think how many words that is!" She gave me carte blanche on the topic.

I was scared. Though I said no at first, I also knew that combatting my fear was precisely why I had to do it. *Final score: Aliza 1, Fear 0.* When I came to terms with writing my first book, I knew I wanted it to serve a purpose. I decided to write a career mentorship and pay forward what I had learned along my journey. The cover would feature a coffee cup stained with my signature red lip to symbolize my way of grabbing coffee with everyone who DMed me on Twitter asking for career advice. My focus was on professional development, but then there was the story of creating DKNY PR GIRL, a brand that I'd built within a brand.

Leave Your Mark: Land your dream job. Kill it in your career. Rock social media. was published in May 2015, almost exactly six years to the day that I started tweeting as DKNY PR GIRL. Drawing on invaluable lessons from my own life experience, I shared my story, complete with personal advice and inspiration, no matter what industry you work in. The book is geared toward aspiring young professionals with a strong focus on how to land your dream job, succeed in your career, and, of course, rock social media. It is all the things they never teach you in college on how work actually works, filled with insider tips that can only come from experience. I like to think of myself as the reader's best friend and knowledgeable guide to the working world, where personal and professional lines are blurred and a strong sense of self is required.

When *Leave Your Mark* was published, I had a glamorous book party in New York City and then went on a press tour to the UK and Canada. I was so excited about the response to the book, but back at the office, the ground was shifting under my feet. . . .

In January of that same year, our new CEO appointed two new co-creative directors and a new chief image officer to DKNY. This was a massive change for the company, and we had no choice but to embrace it. It was an enormous transition from the core team that had created DKNY and worked there for decades.

Months later, and after my glitzy book tour was over, coming back to the office was a bit of a buzzkill. While I loved my job, I'd been doing it for so long. Sitting at my desk felt a little like "been there, done that." I started to fantasize about what my life might be like if I didn't work there anymore. I played all the versions of the what-if game. But everyone at the company felt like family, and there was no way I'd leave them and my fantastic team. Until one day I was summoned to lunch with our CEO and Patti Cohen, my boss and mentor. I had no idea what we'd discuss, but it felt ominous. Why was our CEO coming? Was I being fired?

I will never forget that lunch as long as I live. We went to an Italian restaurant off Fifth Avenue and Sixtieth Street. It started off well enough, but I knew why I was there within minutes. The CEO shared that they had been doing research to understand the state of the DKNY brand, and it turned out that DKNY PR GIRL, the social media personality of which I was both the voice and the face, no longer aligned with the new direction they wanted to take the brand.

Donna Karan herself always referred to DKNY as the "pizza" to Donna Karan New York's "caviar." It was downtown versus uptown. It was the energy and spirit of New York, and because of this, I was able to take creative liberties and ideate a character I believed personified DKNY—one that would resonate with people. Though I was spot-on in my assumption, DKNY PR GIRL's penchant for sequins and bows in combination with her "girl on fire" attitude was in clear contrast to the new intended

DKNY brand, which was cool kid, minimalist, and starker in every way.

The CEO conveyed the need to create space for the new creative directors to make their own mark, and DKNY PR GIRL stood in the way of that. I was stunned and asked if I was being fired. The answer was no, but DKNY PR GIRL sure was.

Then she asked me to delete the accounts. . . .

Mic drop.

Hearing those words was a forceful punch to my gut. This was my baby. I dedicated myself to it 24/7 on top of my regular day job in communications. But more than that, DKNY PR GIRL was beloved by the community. As much as I didn't want to admit it, though, I knew the CEO was right. DKNY PR GIRL had become too big, and if the new creative directors were going to have a fair shot at media success, she needed to go.

I pulled myself together, fighting back the tears that were obviously there. Six years of passionate work went into creating that social media presence. I was proud of what DKNY PR GIRL had become, and the idea of deleting her was devastating. I was too emotional to go back to the office that afternoon.

Sometimes the universe has a way of pushing you in the direction it wants you to go. Here I was in my job after the launch of my book, fantasizing about what it might be like to do something on my own, yet I would never have resigned. But the end of DKNY PR GIRL was all I needed to convince myself that my position there needed to come to an end. I loved connecting with people around the world, and I didn't want this job without DKNY PR GIRL. In truth, they probably knew that, too, and were waiting for me to pull the trigger.

But that wasn't all that happened. Later that same month, Patti stepped down from the company and Donna Karan soon after. This news, combined with the demise of DKNY PR GIRL and the fact that I knew deep down that I wanted to pursue something new for myself, gave me the courage to resign. Since I wasn't trying to get another corporate job, I offered to finish out the rest of the year, especially since fashion week was coming. In August, I worked with an outside PR agency to craft the press release announcing that DKNY PR GIRL was over. The media ran with it, and the community felt the blow too. Headlines ran globally, generating millions of impressions. Here are some of my favorites:

FROM *THE HOLLYWOOD REPORTER*

Sad Times: DKNY PR Girl Is No Longer a Thing
DKNY's social media channels are no longer handled by the popular online personality. The times they are a-changin'.

FROM *PRWEEK*

End of a Twitter era as DKNY PR Girl account is no more
The handle had a half-million followers by the end of its run.

FROM *MASHABLE*

Farewell, DKNY PR Girl: The fashion brand breaks with its sassy mascot

FROM *HELLO!* MAGAZINE

DKNY erases all social media posts

My last DKNY runway show was the debut of the new co-creative director's first DKNY collection. I produced it with my team with the same dedication and gusto that we always did. While my head was completely in the game, my heart wasn't. My career at DKNY would soon be over and a new day was dawning.

NEW YEAR, NEW ME

On the first Monday in 2016, I woke up with my newfound freedom. Not having a job after 17 years at one company was a foreign feeling. My life had been the same for so long. How many times had I ridden the 6 train and switched to the N/R at Fortieth Street and Seventh Avenue? How often had I taken the elevator at 550 Seventh Avenue, one of the most iconic fashion buildings in New York City? How many times had I introduced myself as Aliza from DKNY, or someone had introduced me as DKNY PR GIRL? An accurate count was impossible.

On that morning, my view was different. Nothing was the same. It was exciting but also uncomfortable. I had to remind myself of the mantra I had written in *Leave Your Mark*: **"If change doesn't hurt a little, it's not change."**

It was so much easier dishing out that advice than taking it. I needed a major rebrand. I had spent almost two decades helping to build relevance for these brands. I had to discover what was now on brand *for me*. With DKNY PR GIRL, I had created a brand within a brand from scratch.

Surely, I could do it again for myself?

2
Focus on What You Want to Be Known For

W/e all lose touch with ourselves sometimes. The afterglow of DKNY PR GIRL and those millions of media impressions had dimmed. My book launch had died down. There was so much buzz, and now it all felt so quiet. I had to move on and needed to tap back into the secret sauce that got me to that point in my career in the first place. I was successful before DKNY PR GIRL. I had a covetable job and was respected by my peers and industry, yet I was starting to question my purpose and lose my confidence. Leaving a role can do that, especially a high-profile one.

Life was different when I started working at Donna Karan International. People stayed in their roles for years, and doing something beyond your day job was rare. If there were side hustles, no one spoke about them. I certainly didn't have one. You worked at one company and your job title became your identity. Then you went home at the end of the day and lived your personal life.

A quick recap for those of you who weren't there in those early years. Forget about online anything. I know for some of you this sounds impossible to imagine, but people didn't know where you were all the time. We didn't document our every move. Our friends (and bosses) would leave us twenty-minute voicemail messages that we'd have to play over and over to make sure we hadn't missed anything. If you were lucky enough to have a cell phone, texting meant punching the keypad to spell out the letters you needed to make a cohesive sentence. This was how we communicated.

Today it's nearly impossible to disconnect from work, friends, and family. We have passions and side hustles beyond our day job. Back then, we were all one-note and far too dependent on our jobs and the security they made us feel. I say "we" because I wasn't alone. My mistake? Because I never thought about my future beyond that one company, I didn't even meet with outside recruiters! I was naive and too comfortable. The only advantage I had later on was my early opportunity to build a personality on social media and the foresight to recognize that a social presence was going to be important.

> **Pro Tip:** Don't make a company your identity, even if you own it. And never give away the trademark to your name! Founders can be removed.

Being known as DKNY PR GIRL certainly had its benefits, but **I'd created a personal brand for something that I didn't own.** What's more, I got so absorbed in it that I never thought to create my own social media channels until years later. The identity overshadowed me as an individual and became how I was known in social circles. Now it was time to rebrand myself in both the work I did and how I positioned myself.

I needed to answer the following questions:

1. Who was I without my lofty executive title at an LVMH-owned major American fashion brand?

2. Who was I without DKNY PR GIRL and those millions of followers?

3. What did I want to be known for now?

Though I didn't have those answers yet, I was clear that I needed to make my name matter in a new way. I also knew . . . *wait for it* . . . that I didn't want to do PR anymore. I had done it all already, and the idea of pitching the media on behalf of another brand after the wonderful career I'd had with Donna Karan felt so wrong to me.

I needed to turn the tables on myself and get advice from someone I admired. So I reached out to Ross Martin.

I met Ross in 2014 when I attended PTTOW!, a weekend-long conference founded by Roman Tsunder, in California. PTTOW! is called the "TED event of the marketing world" and describes itself as "an invite-only, member network and summit for CEOs, CMOs, and Cultural Icons who are shaping our culture." I went alone to represent DKNY. I knew no one. I immediately bonded with a woman named Jamie Gutfreund, who introduced me to her friend Ross.

Today, Ross is the cofounder and president of Known, an award-winning modern marketing company. Ross's work has benefited the likes of Lady Gaga, Malala, Netflix, Citi, Google, and many, many more. Back then, though, he worked at Viacom (now called Paramount), leading the portfolio's global marketing priorities, including MTV and Nickelodeon, to name a few. He was also the founder of Scratch, an internal "black ops" group working on top-secret projects. Ross was very interesting to me. He was a mix of familiarity (*like every guy I went to high school with on Long Island*) but also a bit mysterious and eccentric.

He graciously accepted a meeting, and in a world that's so transactional, where everyone's time is scarce, I had nothing to offer. (P.S. It's staggering to see how many people immediately peace out when they think you're not of the same status anymore. While I'm happy to say I didn't experience this ghosting, it doesn't mean that I didn't worry about it.)

Pro Tip: The biggest gift you can give anyone is to continue to be there for them after they leave a big role.

I went to Ross's office to meet him. I was nervous. When I think about marketing and the standards that brands employ to define who they are, what they stand for, and how they communicate, Ross is one of the best in the business. If anyone could help me focus on what was next, he could.

The conversation with Ross was everything I needed to hear to move forward. Of course, being DKNY PR GIRL was how Ross knew me, but he reminded me that what I had created was just one noteworthy example out of an incredible, nearly two-decade-long career. The skills I'd acquired were still mine; now I just had to apply them to something else.

Having Ross as a sounding board meant the world to me. I will digress here to say that **one of the best things you can do is surround yourself with people who see a better version of you than you even see for yourself.** It's a meeting I will never forget.

MAKING THE PIVOT

I wasn't looking for another job and I didn't want to do PR, so my rebrand needed to transition me from a corporate PR executive and famous social media personality to an author and creative brand marketing and digital strategy consultant. (I purposely added the word *creative* because IMO not every marketer is also a creative.) Because my natural default setting is branding, I was immediately like, "I need a company name! I need a logo!" Never mind I had no plan beyond that. I love thinking of names. I honestly think the best job in the world belongs to the person who names lipsticks or nail polishes. Who wouldn't want to do that?! Well, David, my husband, sort of crushed that fun. Because while I was sitting around contemplating what I wanted to call my new company, without telling me, he had already filed the LLC. When that official document came in the mail, I was shocked. My initial reaction was: "How could he do that without me? It's my decision!" Then, when I opened the document and read LEAVE YOUR MARK LLC, I felt stupid. It made so much sense! You might be thinking, "Duh, that's obvious," but it wasn't to me.

Sometimes you have to name something to make it feel real. Or at least that's how I start to feel like something is actually happening. I was so conditioned to being a corporate executive with a title, that without it I felt a bit naked. Of course, the joke was that I was the same person the day before when I still had the title. David filing for that official LLC and naming it LEAVE YOUR MARK made me realize, for the first time, that it could be more than a book. That might seem silly, but it wasn't a given to me. LEAVE YOUR MARK could provide the foundation I needed to start again. It was my brand. I just had to see it.

Pro Tip: Assess what brand assets you already have to work with and how they can be expanded.

Don't be too impressed, though. The imposter syndrome always has a way of rearing its ugly head. I had a "company," but what was my title? I'm quite certain that a man in this instance would have immediately printed a business card with CEO on 32-point cardstock. I couldn't say CEO with a straight face, let alone write it anywhere. Truth be told, I did play around with it on Canva, my favorite branding site. Every time I saw those three letters, though, I got incredibly uncomfortable. CEO of what, exactly? Talk about smoke and mirrors. I wouldn't let myself do it. It made me feel like a fraud. Instead, I opted for Founder & President. I reasoned here that I was the founder of a book (*so a check mark for accuracy there*), and President just meant that I was the boss of an LLC. It felt better.

What came next was the visual branding of it all, and this is another area that I love working on. Creating a logo made my company feel legit. Posting it on social media and sharing that I was going to start consulting with my network under my new company name made it official.

That internal struggle with calling myself CEO was invisible to the public. My network only saw the end result, which appeared buttoned-up and intentional, even if it was just a shell in reality.

Pro Tip: People only know what you tell them.

Start-up founders do this all the time. They have an idea but no real company. They package the dream and sell you what it could be if you're smart enough to invest early. Sometimes they believe their own dream and hype so much that they oversell it and can't deliver. Similarly, I was building a dream a little ahead of where I was. (*OK, fine, a lot ahead of where I was.*) I didn't have a road map or a plan, but doesn't everybody need to do that in some way? We are all chasing aspirations and running just a little behind.

I don't believe in three- or five-year plans. I'm not saying they aren't valuable; I just think that so much changes as you go. I prefer to set small and somewhat reachable goals and chip away at them. In this case, I'd need to catch up to the logo I'd designed. One day, though, you do catch up, and what felt like the impossible is suddenly your reality. Having the courage to build the plane while you're flying is really what everyone must have the stomach to do. It's not easy, and it takes time—and when I say *time*, I mean years.

> **Pro Tip:** It's better to start and learn as you go than waste time seeking perfection.

But then there was another hurdle. While I might have believed that the official creation of LEAVE YOUR MARK LLC and a logo was the start of a new consulting career in creative brand marketing and digital strategy, the areas I wanted to focus on now, that's not what people associated me with. I was well-known for being a publicist. But that wasn't going to work in my favor if I no longer wanted to do public relations. How was I going to rectify having my career so tied to PR when I didn't want to do that anymore?

My experience was broader than just public relations, and all the skills I'd developed over the years proved that. But unless someone was reviewing my resume, it would be up to me to make sure that people understood that. The only challenge was, how do you undo what's been documented all over the internet? How do you change the way people view you when you've been known for something for so long and when Google tells a different story?

> **Pro Tip:** Start by changing the way you view yourself.

Since I had no job, my new priority was networking with as many people as I could. Morning power breakfasts, midmorning quick coffees, networking lunches, afternoon catch-up teas, and evening drinks and dinners with business friends—I swear I'd never had more food or beverages in my life. (*For the record, it was exhausting and expensive.*) But I used these meetings as an opportunity to do some PR on my own reputation. Funny, no?

As I was making connections old and new in my newfound noncorporate life, I made it a point to correct people anytime I heard those two letters (*PR*) come out of someone's mouth. If I had a dollar for every time someone said to me, "I'll let you know if I hear of any PR consulting gigs." But my response was always "Oh, I don't actually do PR anymore. I'm focusing on creative brand marketing and digital strategy now."

Pro Tip: Strategically and consciously build a bridge between your past and your future.

I was conditioning people to understand the new direction I wanted to go in. The other important thing to model here is that in reshaping how people thought of me, I was also planting seeds. By sharing what I wanted to do and what I could do, I enabled people to think of me if any opportunities in these new areas I wanted to work in came their way. Part of making people understand this was also speaking about things in the past tense.

I made sure to update my social media bios accordingly, leading with "Creative Brand Marketing and Digital Strategist." I didn't want to erase the legacy of DKNY PR GIRL, but instead, I put it at the end and added the word *former* in front of it. If character count was limited, I wrote "ex–DKNY PR GIRL."

I wanted to be known as a marketer, not a PR girl. While I loved being a PR girl, I needed to commit to the rebrand.

When you do PR as long as I had, you learn that what you tell people is what they know. What's the headline of your press release? People can't absorb volumes of information, so thinking in terms of a headline means that you're going to focus on the most important thing you want people to know about you. Similarly, when brands pitch the media, they must shape their story and determine what their hook is. That's why headlines are so important. You have to tell your story in the way you want it reported. You must lead the witness.

Pro Tip: If you don't tell people what you want them to know, they will happily make up their own narrative.

This reminds me of the argument I used back in the day when brands who feared social media used to say that they didn't believe in it. Sure, that's a position you can take, but if you're not online and someone is talking about you, you're leaving the opportunity wide open for others to jump in on your behalf. Those who do so might be your direct competitors.

It took a minute for me to figure out my positioning, and I changed my bio countless times. I still change it all the time.

Did I like the word *marketer*? Was *strategist* better? Some combination of the two? It took multiple tries to get it right, and when I say "get it right," I mean for the moment. It's an ever-changing part of who you are. As you evolve, so should your bio.

Creative brand marketing and digital strategist combined all the keywords I wanted to hit upon. Next up was my website. What a mess. I'd created it originally for my book, just to have a place online that people could go. It was OK, not great. But now I needed it to do the talking for me when I wasn't around. If someone was coming to my site, what did I want them to see, think, and feel?

I knew that I needed to position myself as a consultant. I had to make my capabilities clear and easy to understand, but also demonstrate flexibility for all the services I could offer. I didn't want to box myself in. I decided to list my offerings in bullet point format so I could cast a wider net rather than focusing on one specific area. After all, I wasn't aware of what people would look to me for, and I wanted to make sure my services were broad enough but also made sense.

> **Pro Tip:** Take pen to paper and list everything you know how to do and then cross out the things you don't want to do. This will allow you to zero in on what's most important to you and what you need to message.

I intentionally excluded public relations from the list. While some of the functions I was offering were within the scope of a publicist, and I mentioned my background in communications, the words *public relations*, *publicist*, and *pitching* were purposely left out.

DO THE MENTAL GYMNASTICS
Build a Website

When I set up my website, I first drafted a header that directly spoke to what I do and why I do it. I needed to be clear about what my unique selling point was.

Note: Your website is the only place on the internet where you get a 100 percent share of voice, meaning that you have the luxury of positioning yourself in exactly the way that's most effective for you. It's your personal flagship to the world. When you're pitching yourself on your own site, you can't be shy: you have to declare your abilities with confidence. People need to feel your expertise through your words. Zoom in not only on your skills but what you love doing. Your passion will come through! For me, that was storytelling.

Here's how my site read:

Creative Brand Marketing & Digital Strategy for a New Consumer Landscape

Aliza Licht knows how to build brands. With over twenty years of experience as a brand marketing, communications, and digital executive, Aliza's passion is storytelling, seeking unique ways to generate brand awareness and reach the consumer with a multimedia and multifaceted approach. Equally creative as she is a strategist, Aliza focuses on the full picture of a brand's story at every consumer touchpoint. With an emphasis on digital storytelling, Aliza helps brands find their voice and visual identity across channels. Gone are the days when chasing likes drove awareness or revenue. Brands need to think differently, and Aliza has an innovative track record of helping them get there.

*All work is done remotely, and time commitments are flexible and fluid as needed.

New is one of the most powerful words in marketing. By saying "brands need to think differently," I implied that I might know something you don't, and that you need to hire me to find out what it is. The intrigue, ha!

Next, I mapped out my capabilities:

SERVICES CAN INCLUDE:

- TEAM LEADERSHIP AKA "RENT-A-CMO"
- VISUAL IDENTITY & BRAND VOICE IDEATION
- ORGANIC & PAID SOCIAL MEDIA STRATEGY
- LAUNCH OR REPOSITIONING PLANS
- DIGITAL CONTENT CREATIVE DIRECTION
  & PRODUCTION
- INFLUENCER MARKETING & PARTNERSHIPS
- DIGITAL & COMMUNICATIONS
  AGENCY MANAGEMENT
- EDITORIAL STRATEGY, EMAIL MARKETING
  & COPYWRITING
- CONSUMER EXPERIENCE (ECOMMERCE & APP)

I didn't share rates or anything financial on the site, and instead added a contact form. The strategy there was that you needed to contact me to learn more. If you're employed by a company and want your site to function as more of a personal portfolio or visual resume, you wouldn't have rates anyway.

Pro Tip: Don't give away everything on your site. Leave enough intrigue for them to make contact.

I wanted it to be clear I do a roster of different things, and just like an à la carte menu, you can cherry-pick the services you need. My favorite service that I offered was "Rent-a-CMO," where I would immerse into an existing team as the senior layer the company couldn't afford to have as a full-time position. I still selectively do this!

I built my site on Squarespace. I change it often, and I find something new to update every time I see it. The best thing I ever did was teach myself how to make updates. Website maintenance can get very expensive. It's also tedious to change when you're depending on someone else to make a tiny edit. Trust me, learn how to do it. You will thank me.

For my visual identity, I reflected the main colors from *Leave Your Mark*, black and white with hints of mint and red. The website's "about" section mirrored the message I included in my social bios and on LinkedIn. This consistency helped cement the narrative that I was sharing with my network and made my transition from a publicist to a marketer possible.

Once the site was ready, I took off my training wheels and removed DKNY PR GIRL from my shorter social media bios. With such a limited character count, it was essential to focus on the present, not the past. Words matter, and sometimes even though we think we're communicating properly, we wonder why no one knows our story. This fact is true no matter what you do.

3

Analyze the State of Your Personal Brand

E very brand sets out to achieve a certain status and consumer reputation. Bridging the gap between how a brand thinks about itself versus how the public perceives it is the real game.

In marketing, you're always chasing after something—new customers, the cool factor, competition, the list goes on. Your branding is the vessel in which you package your marketing.

Excruciating thought is applied to every aspect of a brand, from its visual identity to its brand voice and, oh yes, sometimes the product too (*that's sort of a joke, but also not really a joke*). If two brands sell basically the same thing, the difference from one brand to the next is oftentimes less about the product and more about how they packaged it, spun their story, and marketed it to you.

Take Last Crumb, a cookie company based in LA, as an example. They consider their cookies to be a luxury product. Why? Let's start with the price. A box of 12 cookies sells for $140. Yes, I just said ONE HUNDRED AND FORTY DOLLARS for 12 cookies. Their business model is in the form of "drops" like they're the next iteration of Supreme x Louis Vuitton. The cookies also come in a luxuriously oversized, heavy box. Each cookie then comes in its own packaging with its flavor name. *Better Than Sex* and *Netflix and Crunch* are two examples of their clever brand voice. But wait for it . . . there's more! If you're not incredibly quick at the draw, you'll miss the opportunity to buy these cookies and must join their waitlist. They are always sold out! Are these cookies that special? They're delicious. But more than that, there's so much pomp and circumstance that goes into the customer experience that the public perception is that they're worth it. Needless to say, they make a fantastic gift!

A brand's core values can also influence where you choose to spend your money (and work!). Mission-driven brands like Warby Parker are founded with the fundamental belief that a company can scale while still doing good in the world. Not only do their prescription glasses start at $95, but their Buy a Pair, Give a Pair program sets them apart from other eyewear brands. When you know that a company has distributed more than 10 million glasses to people in need, that will make you think twice about where to buy your eyewear, no? I've had the good fortune of being a member of Warby Parker's incredible team.

Perception is reality, and brands spend millions upon millions of dollars understanding how they are perceived. From focus groups and surveys to deep-dive data analysis and social listening, a brand's reputation must be analyzed and protected at all costs. Marketing strategies are born from this analysis, and frequently the decision to change direction lies in what is discovered.

As individuals, we can learn from the way brands establish their brand equity. Taking stock of what we stand for, our core values, and how we communicate are how we protect our long-term worth.

Starting this process early allows you to build a strong foundation, fine-tune your efforts, and create a meaningful reputation. What's certain is that every person, no matter what industry they work in, is being judged by many factors. How you show up to those around you is one of the elements that defines your personal brand. If you don't pay close attention to how your brand is consumed, you're likely doing yourself an injustice. On the one hand, you might be coming off exactly how you intend to, which is great! But the more likely scenario is, you aren't. And if you're leaving no impression at all, that's an even bigger problem.

I now had the wonderful opportunity to get back in touch with what made me, me, and that started with how and what I communicate about. When I really thought about it, I had loaned DKNY PR GIRL my personality. Removing her from the equation allowed me to be myself on social media. For years I didn't think I could because I was scared people would figure out that we were one and the same. That was the reason I didn't even make my own social media accounts until years later. Once the secret was revealed, I reclaimed my voice. After leaving the company, that became exponentially easier. I no longer needed to parse my content from DKNY PR GIRL's. Social media managers can relate to this conundrum. You almost have to become a split personality. I would often take a great photo and think about which account I would share it from.

For example, say I'm at an exclusive party and get the money shot of Celeb X & Y. Am I there as myself or as DKNY PR GIRL? Am I sharing this photograph on her feed, or do I get to post it? If you're not on social media, you might not understand why that matters, but here's why: Our social media timelines paint the visual narrative of our personal brands. If I was lucky enough to be at this party and wanted to share that, I should be able to. Since I was anonymous, though, I was paranoid that it would be too obvious if DKNY PR GIRL and I had the same shot or even a different version of the same image. Back then, I would go to the bathroom to post in real time out of fear that someone would look over my shoulder and see that I was logged in to the DKNY PR GIRL account. Remember, the person behind that persona was a fashion industry mystery for TWO YEARS. That's an incredibly long time to keep a secret!

This newfound freedom of being able to post as I pleased felt exhilarating, but I needed to dive deeper into what my content focus would be. My narrative previously was all about my role in PR and what it entailed. Even my career advice was geared toward that.

Albeit, when I tweeted #PR101 content, many followers expressed that the advice applied to any industry. But I didn't want to work in PR anymore, so I certainly wasn't going to post about it.

That's where I turned to my book. I had carte blanche to write whatever book I wanted, and what I hoped to do was support people along their career journey. I didn't think of LEAVE YOUR MARK as my personal brand initially, but I knew that it reflected my belief system, which has been centered around mentorship. I just had to embrace it.

When thinking about your belief system or the things you're passionate about, it's helpful to compartmentalize the different facets of your life to examine your interests and how you convey them more closely. Your messaging can be an eclectic mix, but it also needs to deliver on what your audience expects. To be clear, your audience is everyone who encounters you. It can be your colleagues, customers, friends, or community of followers—which would include all of the above. If there's a disconnect between what you do professionally and how you communicate your personal brand, it can be confusing and also detract from creating a strong message. You can bridge that gap in a strategic way by identifying the common ground.

VISUALIZE YOUR BRAND

Creating a Venn diagram will help you see the sweet middle spot where you can connect the dots between your interests to understand how you are, or should be, showing up publicly.

You can do this in multiple ways depending on what you want to compare. The purpose of creating your own Venn diagram is to visually demonstrate to yourself what areas you focus on and how they overlap with each other—or don't. The circle is the most popular shape to show these ideas, as the similarities between the things you're comparing can easily overlap. If something is unique to one topic, it stays in the area outside of the shared circle slice. Things that are common to both topics go in the overlapped section in the center.

Celebrity Dressing
Fashion Week
Fashion Editorial
PR GIRL Job Role
Pop Culture Live Tweeting
TV: *Gossip Girl,*
Revenge, Scandal

Award Season

Fashion
Social Media
Career Advice
Behind the Scenes

Professional Development
Mentorship
Job Hunting/Interview Tips
Office Culture
My Career Journey
Book

In the Venn diagram example above, I compare my former life as DKNY PR GIRL to *Leave Your Mark* (the book). You can see from the image that the through line between them is fashion, social media, career advice, and sharing the behind-the-scenes viewpoint of my career. The transition from one to the other is virtually seamless when you focus on what connects them. While I am doing this in retrospect for the purpose of this book, it's also a very interesting exercise for me to visualize this! This also proves how telling Venn diagrams can be.

Pro Tip: When you're passionate about something, you tend to talk about it a lot, and sometimes subconsciously.

I couldn't help but dish out career advice as DKNY PR GIRL. No one told me what to post; it was all gut intuitive. I would see a direct message from a stranger asking a question about interview tips, and I felt compelled to help. Seeing someone make a mistake made me not only try to correct it but also share it (anonymously, of course) with my network so everyone else would have an opportunity to learn from it. This was the passion that gave birth to *Leave Your Mark*. That fervor then became even more pronounced in my personal social media channels, where I could support and amplify other women accomplishing impressive things. Aiding others' professional development was my goal. I didn't proactively set out to create a personal brand, but instinctively tried to let my values lead the conversation I was trying to have at scale.

Let's take this visualization a step further. Here's an example where I plot my consulting work with LEAVE YOUR MARK LLC, which at first had grown to include not just a book, but a podcast and private online community. Then I take those two entities and plot them with *On Brand's* area of focus.

The overlapped sections are where my worlds intersect. I would be remiss in not sharing that your personal brand doesn't have to be interconnected with your career in the sense that they need to speak the same exact language. You can message other ideas that don't have anything to do with what you do professionally, but they need to be additive and not diminish the value of your work. For example, my consulting work is in creative brand marketing and digital strategy, but I rarely talk about that. Since 2015, I've gone back and forth between periods of consulting to full-time gigs and back again. Occasionally I'll share projects I'm particularly proud of, but overall, I would rather talk about professional development, mentorship, and how to build your personal brand. I also cover the same themes with guests who join the *Leave Your Mark* podcast.

My background in marketing and communications informs my knowledge on how to do this. It's not lost on me that I would get more clients if I spoke more about digital strategy than what to do or not to do in a job interview, but that's not where my passion lies. Prior to writing this book, I definitely put more communications emphasis on the *LEAVE YOUR MARK* circle than the WORK circle—and that's okay. The *ON BRAND* circle is obviously new. When I think about how I want to message online, I play mostly in the nonwork circles. That said, if I want to increase the visibility of my work, I can strategically decide to amp up that messaging.

All three circles can live harmoniously together, and I can boost or decrease frequency on any of them without causing brand confusion. I could have also made this Venn diagram with two circles and compared my work to everything else I'm doing. You can have multiple versions to analyze your brand from different perspectives.

DO THE MENTAL GYMNASTICS
Your Brand Positioning

Before thinking about how you're going to communicate your personal brand, you need to acknowledge what your personal brand is already associated with. Just like I had to, you must visualize where you are and where you want to go.

I highly recommend trying to make your own Venn diagram. It will help you analyze the different facets of your life and how they converge. From there, you can decide what you want to focus on. We don't often take the opportunity to think about what makes us uniquely us or how our work directs our storytelling, but both of those things contribute to how people view you.

HOW TO MAKE A VENN DIAGRAM*

Step 1: Decide what you want to compare. You could choose areas of interest or analyze how you already communicate by considering the three topics you find yourself talking about the most.

Step 2: Make each topic you want to compare its own circle and place the title of that focus at the top.

Step 3: Add each aspect of that topic to its corresponding circle, making sure that if it's uniquely associated with one circle, you're not putting it in the merged area.

Step 4: Add the elements to the overlapping area that make sense to be reflected in both circles.

*You can find many free tools to create this, but I like smartdraw.com and it's free to try! They have Venn diagram templates, and you can choose to compare two, three, or more categories. I would start with two and then you can make a second version with a third circle.

Step 5: Check your work to make sure what remains outside of the overlapped section is totally unique to that circle's topic.

Venn diagrams can help us see ourselves, where our interests lie, and how those interests influence our communication. **When you're done, ask yourself if what you want to be known for is anywhere in your Venn diagram. If it's not, try again until you figure out the right combination for your brand focus.**

Next, to truly understand the current state of your personal brand, it's not just the topics you focus on that matter. Our demeanor, communication style, and energy affect people's perception of us too.

DO THE MENTAL GYMNASTICS
Your Self-Awareness

This is one of the most underrated skills that is crucial to interpersonal relations. Being self-aware makes it possible for you to recognize your strengths and deficiencies. It's imperative to not only do a self-assessment but to also pulse-check the people in your orbit. Our family, friends, and colleagues might have a different perspective on who we are than we do.

Answer the following questions honestly on how you believe your personal brand currently exists.

1. What are three adjectives that you believe your colleagues would use to describe your **professional** persona?

   a. _____

   b. _____

   c. _____

2. What are three adjectives that you presume your family/friends would use to describe you **personally**?

   a. _____

   b. _____

   c. _____

3. What are your top three professional skills?

   a. _____

   b. _____

   c. _____

4. In one sentence, what would you describe as your one professional superpower?

   My superpower is the ability to

   _____

5. In one sentence, describe your personal brand. (Pretend this is a headline about you. What would it say?)

   _____

   _____

   _____

6. What audience are you trying to influence or reach? (Examples: your boss, potential clients, hiring managers, followers)

_____

_____

_____

7. How would you introduce yourself at a business dinner? Include your elevator pitch.

Hi, my name is _____

and I am _____

8. What is your ultimate career goal?

_____

_____

_____

9. If you had to be known for something, what would that niche be?

_____

_____

_____

10. What parts of yourself do you bring to work?

_____

_____

_____

11. Where do you set your personal versus professional boundaries?

_____

_____

_____

12. What are your professional strengths?

_____

_____

_____

13. What are your professional weaknesses?

_____

_____

_____

DO THE MENTAL GYMNASTICS
Your Message Consistency

If you are currently on any of the following social media accounts, please fill in the below:

1. Your bio on Instagram:

_____

_____

_____

2. Your bio on Twitter:

_____

_____

_____

3. Your headline on LinkedIn:

_____

_____

_____

4. Your full bio on LinkedIn:

_____

_____

_____

_____

_____

_____

_____

5. Your bio on Facebook:

_____

_____

6. Your bio on TikTok:

_____

_____

DO THE MENTAL GYMNASTICS
Your Reflection

Now here's the fun part . . . review what you wrote.

1. Do all your previous answers speak the same narrative and paint a cohesive picture?

2. Do they marry to the items on your Venn diagram?

If your answers are *yes*, you're way ahead of almost everyone. Don't feel bad if they're *no*, though. Since the above items don't live visually together, we forget that they need to add up to the bigger-picture story.

Pro Tip: Consistency and repetition are the secrets to becoming known for something.

Of course, you're allowed to have other social media accounts for passions or side hustles, but the ones that **have your name** on them need to match what you want to be known for and should directly correlate to your goal. If social media handles are not in your full name, you're missing an opportunity to brand yourself. In addition, how you introduce yourself should align with what you're messaging as your bio online. It doesn't need to be verbatim, but it must convey the same persona and double down on your message.

Think about this example: You meet me at a loud cocktail party. You remember my name but didn't really catch what I said I do. You go home that night and do a quick search on Instagram to find me. My bio should reinforce what I want you to know about me in a snapshot. It should reflect how I introduced myself to you at the party. Then, when you go over to LinkedIn to send me a connection request, my headline should reinforce that.

Interestingly, though, people don't connect the dots on this. They don't really understand that these word choices matter and they are telling your brand story—even if you don't intend for them to. If you're strategic in the way that you think about these words, you can proactively shape your message. But what you say and write is only half of the equation. Just because we say that we are *x*, *y*, or *z* doesn't mean that other people know that or believe it.

DO THE MENTAL GYMNASTICS
Their Perception

To understand how your personal brand resonates (or doesn't) right now, you need to ask other people to give you an honest assessment of how they perceive you. To attain real, useful feedback, I recommend that you cast a wide net for respondents (whom you value and trust) from work and life and create a Google Form where they can answer anonymously. You can make your form anonymous by making sure that your respondent's name and email address are not asterisked questions. To make sure you've done it correctly, test this with someone close to you before you send it out. You could also create another version for specific recipients from whom you want direct feedback. This is totally up to you. I've done it both ways, and while it's nice to know who said what, it also limits what people will say to your face.

If you're going the anonymous route, a friendly warning: We live in a culture of "likes" and heart emojis from the people we surround ourselves with. When you're putting yourself out there for critique, you need to brace yourself for the feedback. While it can be uncomfortable to read things about yourself that you don't want to hear, if you go into this exercise with a student mindset, you'll come out of it learning a lot about yourself. The best part is, if you compare these results to the answers you detailed in the mental gymnastics section on self-awareness, your mind might be blown. If I were you, I'd expect a big disconnect there, because how we see ourselves is often not how others see us. Therein lies the magic to personal branding. How can you make these answers blend as one? Keep reading.

Pro Tip: The definition and magic of a strong personal brand is when self-reflection and public perception align.

HOW TO MAKE A GOOGLE FORM

Gathering this information is easy! First, head over to Google and then hit "+ New" in the upper left corner and choose "Google Forms."

In settings, go to "responses" and make sure "collect emails" is toggled to the off position if you want to do it anonymously. The title of your form will be: "My Personal Brand Assessment." Then add the following questions for your recipients to answer (these are some of the same questions you asked yourself earlier):

1. What are three adjectives that you believe describe my professional persona?
   (Choose a short answer for the response type.)

2. What are three adjectives that you believe describe me personally (personality traits)?
   (Choose a short answer for the response type.)

3. What am I most professionally skilled at?
   (Choose paragraph answer for the response type.)

4. What could I improve upon?
   (Choose paragraph answer for the response type.)

5. In one sentence, what is my professional superpower?
   (Choose a short answer for the response type.)

6. In one sentence, how would you describe my personal brand?

(Choose a short answer for the response type.)

Then, craft a group email and put all recipients on Bcc (blind copy).

Example:

From: <your email>

To: <your email>

Cc: <leave empty>

Bcc: <include all the emails of everyone whose opinions you trust, either from work or your personal life>

Subject: My Personal Brand Assessment

Hi everyone! If you're on this email, we have worked together in some capacity, and/or you know me well personally. I would LOVE for you to take this quick survey about me. I'm doing a self-reflection exercise and would appreciate your feedback. Answers will be collected anonymously, so please feel free to give it to me straight. Your opinions are important to me. This will take just a few short minutes.

Thank you so much!

Send this email to trusted colleagues, friends, and family in your network whose feedback matters to you and whom you believe have your best interests at heart. This is an important caveat because you want to ensure the people you listen to want you to succeed. Also, don't share your own previous answers!

The best thing about a Google Form is that the answers populate into a spreadsheet automatically. To generate the spreadsheet, open your Google Form again, and at the top, you'll see "Questions Responses Settings." Click "Responses." Then to the right, you'll see the little green sheets icon. Click it to view your responses in Google Sheets.

Once you've had a chance to review the responses submitted, you should first determine if there's any overlap in the responses. If you want to get fancy, you could even do one form just for your work colleagues and review your personal friends/family separately on another form. It would be interesting to see if there is a difference. Can you identify any patterns across your audiences? Are there words that jump out to you as being an overarching trend?

Next, add yourself as a respondent, and compare how you answered the same questions to the rest of the sheet. Do you see yourself in the same way others view you? If you look at this chart and realize that it's a bit all over the place, that's OK! It's just showing you that you're not consistent across everyone you encounter.

One of the most important lessons, though, is how self-aware you are. If you think of yourself one way and everyone else believes something totally different, there's a magnificent opportunity for you to strategically work to unify those areas.

When you read feedback that stings a little, just take a deep breath and remember that knowing this information will help you grow. But reading positive and informative feedback will also be a treat. You'll be touched when you learn what people believe your superpower is. We often need to be reminded of the impact we make on those who know us best. Absorb their words, take their compliments, and bathe in them for a little. **Own your light**. There are always things we can be better at. Still, if we don't take a moment to feel the admiration and appreciation around us, we're missing an opportunity to reap the rewards of the energy we put into the universe.

4

Tell Your Story and Share Your Wins Strategically

Our public perception is based in part on what we communicate and what we don't. Having a strong point of view on what you want to align with is valuable, and if you completed the exercises in the previous chapter, you're probably feeling clearer about your positioning. But just because you mapped the Venn diagram, reviewed your social bios, and polled your network doesn't mean that you're done. Nope, sorry. You're unfortunately talking to yourself.

"The biggest mistake people make in trying to tell their story is that they don't," says Dorie Clark, bestselling author of *The Long Game: How to Be a Long-Term Thinker in a Short-Term World* and several other books focused on communications, branding, and entrepreneurship. "They assume that it will take care of itself, that they don't have to do it. They don't have to consciously craft a narrative. They think, 'People know me; they'll get it!' The answer is no, they absolutely won't."

While we might think that the people around us are aware of everything we do, the opposite holds true. Dorie teaches these concepts and more to executives as a professor at Duke University's Fuqua School of Business. She is also ranked among the top 50 business thinkers globally by Thinkers50, so listen up as to why people have no idea what your story is.

"It seems like a drum I'm always beating, but people are too busy to care about you. They're too busy to care about me. They don't notice, and they forget. It's not because they're mean; they're not out there to get you. It's that they're just too busy with their own stuff. So, they're not going to pay attention, they're not going to notice, so unless we literally just tee everything up and put it on a platter for them, it's not going to get heard. We have to be willing to do the work, but some people don't want to do the work because they're too shy, and it feels weird. Some people don't want to do the work because even though they wouldn't couch it this way, it's kind of a form of arrogance because they think, '**I shouldn't have to do that. My work should speak for itself because I do good work,**' **and it might feel like purity, but it's actually entitlement.** The answer is, I don't care how good your work is; everyone has to take control of doing this. It's part of the responsibility of being human in the world now," advises Dorie.

For the purposes of this book, I'm going to assume that the efforts you're making here are in service of what you ultimately want to achieve in your career. The narrative that you are crafting should support that goal.

If the biggest mistake people make in communication is not communicating, that might be because telling your story is not always comfortable. The elephant in the room is self-doubt. **You may think you're good at something, but without external validation, you might be intimidated to proclaim it. So instead of owning it, you keep it to yourself, hoping someone will notice.**

Pro Tip: Don't wait for someone to shine a light on you. Make your own spotlight . . . strategically.

What you should be doing is recognizing that you're in control of this narrative. If you don't share your story because you're scared people won't like it or see your worth, you're taking a back-row seat at a fashion show next to a D-list wannabe influencer when you could have been seated in the front row next to *Vogue*'s Anna Wintour (don't try to talk to her, though, ha!).

While you may think that you can't control how people view you, your strategic and consistent communication is a powerful way to try to shape someone else's perception of you. You can't be afraid of the judgment that comes along with sharing. When you put yourself out there, you tell the world that you believe in yourself. You're emanating confidence, and confidence breeds confidence. Today, if you walked up to that front-row seat and took it, people would assume you belong there. (*Of course, back in the day, if it were my brand's fashion show, I would have swiftly removed you because those seats were indelibly marked for a chosen few.*)

Naturally, sharing our gifts with the world is harder in actuality. We've all been there. Something extraordinary happens, and we're bursting with pride. We call our family or best friend and tell them exactly how we feel: Excited! Proud! Grateful! But then, when we share the news with others, we downplay it because we don't want to sound like we're bragging. Inside, a tiny voice in our head acknowledges that we dimmed our light a little. We mentally scold ourselves for doing so. We reason that we didn't want to sound obnoxious.

I've done this so often that it's almost my default setting. I am Queen of the Downplay. If I get a compliment, my first reaction is to say, "Oh, stop!" This is the wrong reaction. The correct response is, "Thank you! I'm really proud of that work."

Don't get me wrong. I'm a big fan of humility, but if you don't talk about what makes you unique and what you're adept at, no one will know. Remember? No one has time to think about you. Hell, you barely have time to think about yourself. So, whatever you want people to associate you with, you need to start building that narrative. Get out of your own way and toss out the fake rules you've established that prohibit you from talking about yourself.

It's vital to recognize and share wins instead of acknowledging them in silence. Doing so motivates you to keep pushing past boundaries. Accolades are the culmination of a job well done. What no one tells you is that by strategically sharing your successes, you're communicating something more compelling to your network: it shows them that you've strived for something and achieved it. This motivates the people around you to pursue their own goals. FOMO (fear of missing out) plays a role here. Seeing someone else succeed makes you take stock of where you are in your own quest. But for you, sharing a win puts a marker in the sand as to where you currently stand.

Life is filled with many conquests but also so many losses and setbacks. Sometimes they happen within minutes of each other. We need to learn from them, and it's important to make sure we take those learnings and apply them to the future. But it's also critical to relish the achievements. It doesn't matter who you are, we all need to be better at this.

I spend my life thinking about a triumph for about 30 seconds. The feeling of satisfaction has the life span of a tweet and then it's gone. I move on to the next goal. You are likely the same. One way to counteract this fleeting moment is to track our wins. When something great happens, take stock of what you did well. Not only will this allow you to pause longer on the success, but you'll end up with a comprehensive list of the tactics that helped you succeed. This is especially useful when you're faced with a repeat challenge. Go into your wins folder and remind yourself how you were able to prevail before.

> **Pro Tip:** Leaving a "how I did this" breadcrumb trail for yourself will help you appreciate your wins but also solidify your learnings for the future.

Our pride is a driving force that keeps us galvanized to strive again, but we can't keep it to ourselves. One of the positives of social media is that it has given us a place to put these wins. Channels like LinkedIn not only prompt you to share them, but they also do the heavy lifting for you by nudging your connections to wish you congratulations. It's actually a beautiful concept. No win should land on deaf ears. But just like anything else, too much of a good thing can become a bad thing. If your constant message is only the sound of you talking about yourself, you're not only boring, but you're also someone who will be viewed as cocky. Once you cross that threshold, people will start to tune you out or, worse, root against you.

> **Pro Tip:** Be your own hero, but not to the extent that you inadvertently become the villain.

We always see social media posts that rub us the wrong way. I bet you can think of someone who shared something today that made you a little ill. This delicate art needs to be executed carefully. These rules apply to any medium through which you're communicating an achievement.

DO THE MENTAL GYMNASTICS
Are You Bragging?

1. You didn't win an Oscar. Express sincere gratitude without making it an acceptance speech. Watch the sugary syrup. Toothaches hurt.

2. Have you ever put a marshmallow in the microwave? Don't puff yourself up. Accurately share your accomplishment, and make sure to also acknowledge anyone else who might have played a role in helping you achieve it.

3. Share the spotlight. If applicable, amplify others who also might have been recognized alongside you.

4. Don't be thirsty. Mention only the people who make sense. Avoid trying to get the attention of important people who are unconnected to what you're talking about or what you've done.

5. Unless you're a doctor and you've just saved someone's life, your tone should match the level of importance of what you're talking about. Go easy on the effusiveness.

6. Be of service to others. Identify a learning that people can benefit from and share it in conjunction.

7. Recognize where you are in your journey. If you're just starting out, don't speak as if you've had 30 years of experience doing this thing.

8. Show empathy. Appreciate that not everyone has the same opportunities or access and be cognizant of that.

Pro Tip: For your personal brand safety, publicly support or amplify five other people for every one of your shares focused on a personal win.

If thinking about sharing a win publicly still makes you physically sick, there's another tactic you can use. Introverts, listen up!

I'm a member of several networking communities that function on Google Groups/Slack. Creating a back-channel advocacy system that runs outside the public eye can help with amplification. It's common in these groups to see private humble asks for support in broadcasting a victory. At first, this might seem odd—like, why is someone asking for congratulations or for someone to share someone else's news? But upon closer review, it opens the door for a mutually beneficial relationship. This method is especially important for the many people who aren't comfortable talking about themselves. Maybe even a group email of support feels wrong to you, but perhaps a one-to-one request for backing wouldn't feel as uncomfortable.

Strategic self-promotion is complex, but there are tasteful ways to do it. If you use your voice to amplify others more than you do yourself, you'll find that essential balance.

I have an always-on strategy supporting other people's wins. I feel genuine happiness when I see my friends succeed. I love inviting people on my podcast to assist in spreading what they've accomplished. I show up in their comments, cheering on their wins. I share their social media posts. When you do that all the time, you generate social capital (more on this later). When people see this, they are more willing to hear about your accomplishments and applaud you when the time comes. Timing is key, though. If you're not going to adopt an always-on strategy, do this before you need the favor returned.

Like any marketing strategy, you should always track your performance (aka your audience's reaction) and apply those learnings.

Pro Tip: Never become tone-deaf to your own words. Pay attention to how your messaging is received, whether positively, negatively, or neutrally.

No response, in some cases, might indeed be negative. If this happens, take a moment to review what you shared (by the way, this can be via social media, email, or any other medium). You should reflect on your wording, and consider how you might phrase it differently in the future. We are all constantly learning.

A LESSON LEARNED LATER & THE IMPORTANCE OF AN OPEN MIND

In 2015, I was asked to speak at the Pennsylvania Conference for Women. One of my fellow panelists, Meredith Fineman, was unknown to me at the time. I'm seasoned at speaking on panels, and it's always a dance between being memorable and not taking over the stage. I aim to make my answers powerful but to the point. There were four of us on the panel, and our topic was *Branding & Perception: How to Maximize How You Are Perceived by Others*. Our moderator, Dorie Clark (yes, that's how we met!), asked excellent questions to derive the most prolific answers from the group. Meredith, a freelance writer at the time, had great tips to share, but in her excitement to convey her knowledge and promote her business, she had inadvertently taken over the panel. I tried to look for openings to share my thoughts, and Dorie certainly tossed questions to each person to answer, but there was little airtime for anyone else to contribute. When the panel was over, I chalked it up as a waste of my time.

Fast-forward to years later, and as luck would have it, Meredith is a member of one of the women's networking groups I'm in. I would see her name pop up occasionally, but we didn't have any direct interaction. In fact, I was sure that she would never realize that I was the same person from that panel in 2015. I knew that it was one of those experiences that was memorable to me but probably had little impact on her. Until one day in May 2020, I saw her name appear in my inbox, privately. I learned that she was about to publish her first book, *Brag Better: Master the Art of Fearless Self-Promotion,* and wanted to know if I would be willing to share the free chapter she had written or possibly do an interview with her (for my *Forbes* column).

Did she not remember our panel?

My gut was to politely pass on the request, but then something made me pause—perhaps I could learn something from her and better understand where she was coming from. I mean, she put her tactics into a book. *Brag Better?* I personally don't like the word *brag.* No one likes people who brag, but I decided that I was going to use this as an experiment, a learning opportunity, because I am an open-minded person (no brag intended, ha!). So, I emailed her back and said, "Let's carve out time to speak about your book and philosophy too." I really wanted to get to the crux of the philosophy part.

We got on Zoom a week or so later. The conversation was friendly, and Meredith was thoroughly enjoyable to talk to. We weren't even ten minutes into our call when she said, "You're probably never going to remember this, but back in 2015, we were on a panel together, and I acted like a damn fool."

Yes, Meredith, I remember, and wow, I am shocked you do!

There was no benefit for either of us in sparing her feelings here. I told her that it was the first thing I thought of when I saw her name in my inbox. She explained that it was a time that she wasn't proud of, and she included it in her book as a personal learning moment. She realized that she shouldn't have opted to center on herself because hearing from all our voices would have been more beneficial for the audience.

We then talked through the concept of her book, and not only did I end up doing a feature on her, we did a LinkedIn Live talk, and I also invited her onto the *Leave Your Mark* podcast. She even came to speak to the members of the LEAVE YOUR MARK Community, my private professional development and networking community where I mentor people who want to leave their mark. How's that for making amends?! See, you just never know.

> **Pro Tip:** Admitting that you learned from a mistake is more impressive than not making the mistake in the first place.

I love this story because Meredith and I both learned something new. One of my favorite concepts in *Brag Better* is really the audience that it is meant for, "The Qualified Quiet," which are the people who've done the work and don't know how to talk about it.

Are you part of The Qualified Quiet? Are you focused on doing the work and hoping people notice how valuable you are?

HOW TO SHARE YOUR ACCOMPLISHMENTS AT WORK

Communicating your achievements can be nerve-racking and overwhelming, especially to introverts, but it's critical to getting ahead in work and life. If you're someone who isn't comfortable speaking about your accomplishments, you need to find a medium in which you are.

For example, perhaps it's easier for you to create a report of your results than it is to talk about them in a one-on-one meeting. You could also work with a trusted colleague to help amplify each other's contributions. Regardless of the way you make your value known, you owe it to yourself to make sure your voice is heard and your success is recognized.

"It's hard to be a woman who brags. It's hard to talk about yourself, but we have this intense inverse relationship with volume and merit, and we reward loud," says Meredith.

If you've done the work and done it well, you need to be able to own that in service of leveraging your career. Meredith suggests that you think about the superpower adjectives that describe how you want to make people feel when they hear or read your words. For example: thoughtful, informative, and funny. Your tonality will, of course, be trial and error. It's essential to see how your messaging lands and to think about your audience and the medium.

Meredith admits, "I know that I am a polarizing person. I might rub people in a certain way, but you have to evaluate resentment. How much of it is a 'you' problem versus a 'them' problem? How much does that person impact your work? If this person is in charge of your raise, it's time to reevaluate. When it comes to feedback, you should always think, 'Does this person have my best interest at heart?'"

While Meredith shares effective tactics in her book, I honestly still struggle with the word *brag*. She admits we don't have a better word.

While that may be true, I'm going to try. Instead of thinking of sharing a win as bragging, I would look at it as strategic positioning. My old PR skills die hard here. Every time you share a success, you're positioning yourself in a way that shows the people around you that you are proud of what you've accomplished and you want others to know that. But it would be best if you did it in a graceful and dignified way. Think of it as education, but make sure that what you're saying doesn't come off like nails on a chalkboard.

Pro Tip: The best way to communicate a win is to pair your positioning statement with a result that serves a larger team goal.

For example: Instead of saying "I am excited to share that I signed client X," say "I'm so happy that my presentation was well received and that we were able to sign client X. Now we can start building that new vertical that we've been wanting to." Here you are taking responsibility for the presentation but using the word *we* to show that your effort resulted in something larger than you.

Of course, no matter what the scenario is, sharing your achievements needs to be a calculated move every time. As I've said before, your audience and the frequency in which you communicate with them need to be considered. These proclamations need to be a rainbow sprinkle topping versus being the whole cookies and cream ice-cream sundae. In fact, a great way to do this is to weave your win into the context of a story. Another good rule is to add them into your messaging mix when you've already had a nutritious diet of other content that doesn't involve talking about yourself. Being a megaphone for yourself isn't something that's enjoyable for anyone else to listen to unless you're a celebrity and having a big ego goes with the territory. For everyone else, ask yourself these two simple questions: "Why am I sharing this?" and "What do I hope to achieve by doing so?"

A common example is when people post on social media that they were honored to speak on a panel. They're sharing this because they want their network to know that they were asked to. However, they're also planting a seed in other people's minds to think of them for future panels.

A better way to say this would be to also amplify other people, saying "I was honored to speak on this panel with amazing women X, Y, and Z."

Another beneficial addition to this win would be to convey what you spoke about and maybe include a takeaway from the discussion. So here you're packaging the win with two other great things: 1) amplifying and supporting other people, and 2) educating your community on something that was shared.

Basically, you've turned what could have been about just you into something more than you.

These shares are rhetorical, meaning that you should not be fishing for a compliment. Your job is to go on the record with the information. That said, you should hope for a warm response. Once you've shared it, though, move on. It's not something that can get repeated. You have one chance to message it, and then it's up to you to strive for another win in the future.

As awkward as it may be in the beginning, you need to own your story. Many people combat the discomfort of talking about themselves by adding disclaimers that are usually self-deprecating. Self-deprecation is a defense mechanism. You figure, hey, if I make fun of myself, I beat them to it—saying things like "I'm not sure why I was asked to moderate this panel, but enjoy!" or "If you're really bored, go ahead and watch this talk I just did." You get the idea—and trust me, it's not an attractive look. **Own your wins. Don't make excuses for them. Don't hedge your bets. Don't diminish what you've done.** By adding these "helping" words, you're watering down your message and conveying insecurity instead of confidence.

If you don't feel like you can do this and this all still feels too difficult, identify people in your network who have similar ambitions. Think of it as a cheerleading squad, but one where you'll work together to magnify each other's wins so you don't have to talk about them on your own. It's much more comfortable to talk about someone else's accomplishments.

Not everything you tell people has to be about a score, though. You also need to communicate other noteworthy moments or goals in your life. Starting a new job? Tell people. Need a job? Tell people. Raising money? Tell people. If we don't know, how can we help? Remaining in the shadows is to your detriment. Be your own publicist, but do it in a way in which people are happy to support you, not mute or unfollow you. Everything you talk about contributes to shaping your personal brand for better or worse.

5

Lay the Framework for
Your Brand

Great brands are founded with a set of core values and a mission. Everything they do stems from a belief system. The same method should apply to individuals. You can't successfully market yourself without being clear about what you believe and how you think. Your beliefs guide your narrative, but a major failure we see in personal branding is when you say you believe one thing, but then you do something that doesn't align with that belief system.

Who could forget when Leonardo DiCaprio flew 8,000 miles on a private jet to accept an environmental award? The comedy! You can't publicly preach one thing and then do another. That, my friends, always comes out in the wash (and in this case, the media).

Your personal brand expands well beyond what you say or how you show up online and in person. It's also exemplified in your actions and, more specifically, where you put your money and support.

So, what is your belief system? Have you ever thought about that before? To understand how to achieve the results you want in life, you first have to become incredibly introspective and uncover what you believe to be true about yourself.

DO THE MENTAL GYMNASTICS
Your Beliefs

1. What is your purpose?

_____

2. What are your core values?

_____

3. What should you align with? (organizations, people, mission, etc.)

_____

4. What adjacencies should you avoid?

_____

5. What do you believe is your ultimate potential?

_____

6. What is getting in your way of achieving that?

_____

Here's where you'll probably come up with a long list of reasons why something can't or won't happen, but then you need to ask yourself:

> *Is this list of obstacles that I just conjured up in my head even true? Or did I think the same thought so many times that my simple thought has now become a belief?*

We all have people that we observe in our lives as positive or negative. Choosing to surround yourself with positivity makes a huge impact on your mindset, but if you're the one draining yourself with negativity, you need to work on that.

How you think about your trajectory becomes how you feel about your trajectory, which in turn becomes a series of actions you take based on those thoughts and feelings, which ultimately lead to results. It's a chain reaction. Let's start by getting judgmental about your thoughts. You need to identify the negative ones and convert them to neutral ones.

DO THE MENTAL GYMNASTICS
Are You Positive or Negative?

Thought: *I will never get promoted. My boss doesn't see my value.*

Feeling: *I'm feeling resentment.*

Action: *I'm going to coast and do as little as possible.*

Result: *My year-end review was negative, and my boss cited my lack of productivity.*

Let's start with how your initial thought set you on a pessimistic path in the first place. Not only was it negative, but it was also finite. You declared it, and then you decided the outcome. You left no wiggle room to think differently. That thought set off the above chain reaction.

How about we rewind and take that same thought and reframe it neutrally:

Thought: *I will never get promoted. My boss doesn't see my value.*

Feeling: *I feel motivated to show my boss how valuable I am, and I have some ideas for projects I can take on.*

Action: *I will create a presentation outlining the areas I see as opportunities and where I think I can add value.*

Result: *I got the green light to start a new project, which will allow me to flex my leadership skills and eventually prove that I'm ready for a promotion.*

What you come to believe can become a self-fulfilling prophecy: People who know they can win, win. People who think they will fail, fail. That doesn't mean that your plans are foolproof. You can believe you will succeed and still fail, but someone with a strong belief system will see that failure as a change in direction and, ultimately, a learning. The universe might be telling you to do something differently or trying to teach you something you'll need to know later. The path might not be obvious in the beginning, but if you put faith in the journey, you might find that you're on the right one.

YOUR BRAND FUNDAMENTALS

As we work on this together, you must keep an open mind. I want you to think of yourself as your own client. These are my tried-and-true tactics for creating your brand foundation. Your belief system will help guide everything you do, including starting here, with the foundational elements of your brand.

The following items are non-negotiable and where you begin to shape your narrative.

1. A strong bio

2. An all-star LinkedIn presence

3. Ownership of your name

4. A personal website or online portfolio

5. Being searchable

6. Professional profile photo

7. A strategic email signature

Extra credit:
8. A newsletter

9. A podcast

YOUR BIO IS YOUR MOST IMPORTANT BRANDING TOOL

Back in the day, I really thought that having a bio was only for celebrities. It requires a bit of bravado to even think about having a bio. Some of you might be thinking, *But I don't have enough to write.* OK, to be fair, if you're starting out, your bio will be shorter, but that doesn't mean you don't have anything to say. Each of us has experienced something, but more than that, we all aspire to do something. Depending on your career or life stage, your bio can be a mixture of experience, passions, and aspirations.

There are two voices that you can write your bio in. The first one is third person, using your pronouns and pretending like you're not the one typing it. A bio written in the third person is more formal and, if I'm honest, a bit drier. If you were asked to speak on a panel, this is the type of bio you'd need to give them. You can use this bio on LinkedIn in your About section or on your website. The other kind of bio is written more like a story in the first person.

My friend Corey duBrowa has one of the best LinkedIn bios I've ever seen. With more than 20 years as a communicator of ideas, Corey is an executive who has long been considered one of the top corporate communicators in the US, working for some of the best brands in the world. I'm talking about Google, Salesforce, Nike, and Starbucks, to name just a few. He's always listed in the top 10 in *PRWeek's* U.S. Power List of communications executives. As far as I'm concerned, his resume is the gold standard, and looking at his history of impeccable experience working directly for luminary founders like Phil Knight and Howard Schultz, one would think that his bio would a) be in the third person and b) be really formal. But it's not. It's written in the first person with humility and a powerful narrative. Corey tells the reader a story about his career, interests, and key wins. When you read the bio below, you'll see what I mean about humility. Nothing about Corey's bio screams "look at me"; nothing about it feels like boasting. He's painting a picture for the reader. He's also sprinkling in what's important to him and why he chose to work where he's worked. He very purposefully says that he contributes to talented teams, making it known to the reader that his success is not achieved alone.

Corey's LinkedIn bio:

Introducing the world's biggest sports brand to new customers in a growing region (in a different language). Counseling the founder of the world's largest software company as he transitioned to his next act as one of the globe's most important philanthropists. And helping the world's biggest coffee company return to global prominence (indeed, record revenue, profits, and market valuation) while championing its people and values as core to that success.

These are the moments that have defined my more than twenty years as a communicator of ideas, an advocate for employees and customers, and a change agent for some of the highest-impact brands on the planet.

I have always been about reducing the distance between "work" me and "off-duty" me—the jobs and companies I've loved best have found a way to bridge the skills and interests I possess and bring all of me to the table in service of fresh energy, change, and innovation.

From Nike to Google, and Saks Fifth Avenue to Starbucks, I have been able to shift between radically different industries (footwear, apparel, and sports equipment manufacturing; enterprise and consumer technology; various flavors of retail) while contributing to diverse teams with a sense of purpose, pride, and passion.

Life is too short to do something you don't love. I love what I get to do and come bounding up the steps every day, eager to do it again.

And there are people like my friend Alfredo Hurtado. Alfredo is what I call an unapologetic, fearless marketer. He's authentic to his brand, which is, to its core, extremely polarizing, but most endearingly. He says it like it is. Alfredo's bio on LinkedIn is currently "The most dangerous man in the world." He's not—he owns a streetwear brand—but he'll undoubtedly get your attention.

I love Alfredo's bio for its commitment to showing the real journey of someone who has worn many hats and is making his way in this world. Alfredo brings his authentic self to LinkedIn in a way that adds value to his business. Impressively, he didn't get to go to college until age 25.

Alfredo Hurtado (accidentally) read his first marketing book at six years old and was the host of a children's radio show by the time he was eight. When he was nine, he designed the logo for his mother's patio furniture shop, for which he never received payment; he holds a grudge against her to this day. At seventeen, he was an associate editor at Mexico City's El Economista *newspaper.*

Since then, he has worked with brands such as Bacardí, Calvin Klein, Cerveza Sol, Gatorade, Hennessy, Jarritos, Marlboro, Moët Chandon, Nike, Sidral Mundet, XBOX, 7UP, and even U2, helping them with online and offline marketing strategies as well as apparel merchandising and licensing consulting. In 2013, he turned Cerveza Carta Blanca into the most popular Mexican beer brand on social media, ahead of juggernauts like Corona and Indio, and despite the fact that Carta Blanca was only sold in four states and that it (probably) had the lowest budget in the history of marketing.

In addition, Mr. Hurtado has been an English teacher, an errand boy at a Mrs. Fields location, an extra on TV commercials, a painter (of walls, not pictures), a magician at a children's party (once), a medical interpreter, a restaurant greeter, a receptionist at a Hollywood management firm, and a production assistant on a telenovela. He used to run the greatest Twitter account of all time but closed it once he realized that nobody uses Twitter anymore. (Martha Stewart was a fan.)

In 2011 he co-founded CoNeCT, a digital advertising agency. He left the business in 2014 but still serves as a creative consultant for them.

In 2015, Mr. Hurtado co-founded SWORDMAKER STUDIOS, a turnkey apparel solutions company based in Los Angeles and Mexico City, although the company's main US office is in Houston, Texas, for reasons that absolutely no one can remember. (It probably has to do with taxes.) They create white-label clothing and accessories and provide retail and marketing consulting for clients on both sides of the Río Grande. The company also owns HOLY JOE, which was the only apparel brand in the world accepted into Licensing International's inaugural Diversity and

Inclusion Accelerator Program in 2021 and is now the fastest-growing Hispanic-owned clothing label on Earth.

Mr. Hurtado spends his time between Los Angeles and Mexico City. He has a degree in Electronic Media Management from California State University, with a minor in Apparel Merchandising. He enjoys long, romantic walks to the bank, and firmly believes that writing about oneself in the third person is slightly idiotic.

I hope you enjoyed reading that as much as I did the first time. No two bios are the same, and how much personality you show is up to you, but you must be strategic. Everything you share needs to be in service of the reputation you want to have. People won't remember a lengthy list of bullet points, but they will remember a great story. Many people do the same thing and, at least on paper, have similar experiences. The one thing that sets you apart is you. **No one has your story.** When you write your bio, remember that.

Your bio is a way for someone to get to know you without meeting you. It should be an overview of your experiences, your wins, moments you're proud of, and things you're passionate about. The other thing that's important to consider is what industry you're in. Alfredo is a marketer and founder of a streetwear brand. It is entirely fair game and on brand for his role to push the boundaries of professionalism. For example, if Alfredo were a lawyer, I would tell you that his LinkedIn bio isn't fitting.

Pro Tip: When writing your bio, consider the audience whose respect you need to succeed in your industry.

The order in which you list information depends on the format. It's most useful for the reader to first learn what you're doing currently and then go backward in time to learn your prior experience. Awards, press, board positions, and volunteer work should go last. List the information in order of importance. Remember, people have short attention spans. If you're opting for more of a story, you can take the reader down a chronological path, too, but it better be a good story if you want people to stick around until the end. I change my bio all the time. I've written in the third person, but I've had longer narratives that tell my story in the first person too. Choose your most important and impactful experiences to share. This should be a strategic snapshot of your career, not every single thing you've done. You have your resume for that (and even that should be somewhat abridged to one page).

Part of building a great personal brand is making sure that your name is synonymous with trust. It's not acceptable to exaggerate your accomplishments or stretch the truth. I say this because I've seen way too many resumes and bios on LinkedIn where I know the people and the roles they've held, and yet they've managed to promote themselves to a more senior level. I've also seen mid-level people take full ownership of significant projects. We know that if you're a mid-level employee, you're probably not the person who spearheaded a major initiative. You may have contributed in a great way to the project's success, but you didn't own it. So make sure that the accomplishments you list, whether on your bio or resume, align with your experience. It's undeniable when those accomplishments are being exaggerated. Be true to who you are and where you are on your journey.

ONE SIZE DOES NOT FIT ALL

You'll have many versions of your bio depending on where you're putting it, which means different lengths of the same thing. You first need to start with the Papa Bear–size version (long-form bio), then take that and make your Mama Bear (short-form bio), and then finally, the Baby Bear version (the one-sentence bio) for your social media platforms. Imagine putting your bio through a funnel and distilling it to its purest form. That's where you need to land for your social media channels. Your bio is never final. The words with which you describe yourself should be rolled out in priority order. For example, if you're an aspiring marketer, the word *marketer* should not be the last word at the end of your bio. Give it star billing at the beginning.

> **Pro Tip:** Set a quarterly reminder in your calendar to review your bios across channels.

As your experience evolves, so will your bio and what you choose to emphasize. Just remember that if you change one bio, you need to paintbrush that change across them all. Remember, **repetition is reputation!**

YOUR NAME IS WORTH A LOT

Well, it's the only thing you truly own, right? We are not the companies we work for or even the companies we might be building. We've seen too many founders get ousted from their eponymous companies to make that mistake, right?

Your name deserves to be in lights, and that means investing and buying yourname.com and the email address that goes with it. This can be done on a site like GoDaddy for a small but worthy investment. When my kids were born, I bought them their website domains and emails. You might think that's excessive, but it's not. You're investing in optics, and the perception of having your own domain and email is more luxurious than having a random email or even a Gmail with your name. When you're building your personal brand, these are the little details that show the outside world that your efforts are intentional. You care about how you show up. This is paramount if you're a founder and trying to build a company. Give yourself the gift of a good first impression. It's priceless.

For those of you who are shuddering at the thought of creating a website because you have nothing to put on it or have no idea where to begin, relax; this won't hurt. For starters, I'm referring to a straightforward website that you can easily make yourself. This directive goes for everyone. I don't care if you're a college student, a corporate employee, or a CEO. You need to create a brand presence for yourself that you own, and you do not own your social presence. You are renting that. Remember that if Instagram was deleted tomorrow and that's the only platform you're on, your brand is literally gone.

Think of your website as a visual resume. What are the highlights that would be impactful if they were shared via images? Some examples of tabs you could have are: Home, About, Press (if applicable), Projects or Work, Clients (if applicable), Contact, etc. As I mentioned previously, I recommend doing this yourself. Squarespace has ready-made, beautiful templates that will give you the visual cues as to what type of content should be plugged in. Once you get the hang of the way the site works, you'll have no problem updating it. For the areas of your site that require images, pay attention to the sizing specs they suggest. Then you can hop over to Canva.com and make a custom asset with those exact specs. It's really easy, I promise.

When you buy your site URL originally, make sure you choose "auto-renew." It's one of those things where you can easily miss an email and then suddenly you've lost your name. A reminder here that you can go back to Chapter 2 to revisit how I set up my website.

BE EASILY UNDERSTANDABLE
AND SEARCHABLE

Even though we have different versions of our bios to accommodate the maximum character count, we're still talking about one singular narrative. No matter where you build your social presence, remember that most people will head to the platform that *they* use most when they're looking to find you. So, for example, just because you're applying for a role doesn't mean the hiring manager is going to only look you up on LinkedIn. If that person is active on Instagram, you better believe that's the second place they'll search for you. Whenever possible, make sure your full name is being used as your social media handle as well as the "name." For the link you include in your bio, you can either link back to your website or use a hosting platform like Norby that allows you to create unique landing pages that showcase your work. People are lazy. Make it easy for them to find you, and when they do, make sure that the image you're portraying across your channels is consistent and one you're proud of!

If you have a social account that's not in your name, don't let that give you a false sense of security that you can post whatever you want to. It's often easy to connect the dots and figure out who the owner is even when you're trying to remain incognito.

Having an online presence of any kind has become an important factor in the job search. Depending on your industry, not having an online presence could be viewed as a negative. I'm not referring to being an influencer. I'm simply saying that at the very least, you need to be on LinkedIn. For those of you who have opted to include only your first name and last name's first letter, like Aliza L., why? What are you trying to say here? Be proud of your full name. Make it mean something. If you work in marketing, communications, or social media, you absolutely need to have a social presence for no other reason than to know (and show you know) how the platforms work.

YOUR PROFILE PHOTO

No, you don't have to have this professionally shot—a cell phone photo is fine—but it's smart to have a friend take this picture of you (or get a tripod and use the camera's timer) with the intention that it will be used as your profile picture. So many people seem to struggle with this. You should be alone in this shot and facing mostly forward. You should not have someone's arm around your shoulder. Make sure the light is in front of you, not behind you. You are not in witness protection! A clean, solid background is always best, and in truth, patterns, in general, can be distracting whether behind you or in your clothing. I've seen some people not include a profile picture because they don't want to be judged for how they look. While I understand that people make assumptions based on appearance, not including a photo gives the impression of an incomplete profile. So instead of looking strategic, you appear as if you didn't finish the thing. The repeated association between your name and what you look like is essential in branding.

> **Pro Tip:** Using the same photo across all your channels helps with recognition, but if you're not going to do that, make sure that your other photos don't detract from your most professional one (LinkedIn).

YOUR EMAIL SIGNATURE IS A LUXURY PROPERTY

Let's start with the low-hanging fruit—your email signature and, no, not the one you use for work. Look at your personal email account; what's the signature there? Please don't tell me it's "Sent from my iPhone." This is free real estate for branding what you want people to know. I don't believe you work for Apple, so stop doing their marketing for them.

Think about how many people you encounter daily, how many new people you're introduced to, and how many points of connection are made. Too many to count, I'm sure. If your signature is blank, you're missing an opportunity to shine a spotlight on a few key things that are important to you. Going back to the golden rule that no one is thinking about you, remember that the harder it is for people to know who you are, the less likely they are to try to find out. If you're introducing me to a person in your network, that person should be able to easily see not only my contact information but a quick snapshot of pertinent information. If we were emailing, you would see that I provide my company, title, cell, website, link to my books, podcast, newsletter, community, and social channels.

Pro Tip: Your email signature can be used as lead generation for anything you are trying to drive traffic to.

This is also an area that should be updated regularly (put it on your calendar for a quarterly update with your bio), but don't include links to sites that will be outdated quickly. Make sure any links included are evergreen. Instead of saying something like "Listen to the latest episode of my podcast" and linking to that episode, say "Listen to my podcast" and link to the main show link. You'll quickly forget what you linked to and want to be sure the person is getting the macro view of anything you're promoting. That new episode could easily be an old episode as weeks go by. You also don't want to accidentally send people to a dead (404) page. These are just examples, but you get the idea.

EXTRA CREDIT: OWN YOUR AUDIENCE WITH A NEWSLETTER

Newsletters are a great way to share your expertise and point of view. They are also essential in building your database. Why would you want a database? Because collecting emails means you can own your audience without the interference of an algorithm. The social media platforms decide how far-reaching your content will be. If you have a newsletter, you have direct access to your audience whenever you want it. Yes, of course, there are still obstacles like promotions folders that might keep your content from reaching your desired audience, but it's still way more in your control. Creating a newsletter and providing free content that people are happy to subscribe to can help you build your audience and your brand voice.

> **Pro Tip:** Even if you ultimately want to sell something, you should give pieces of content away for free just to create a funnel for email address acquisition.

Social media platforms could one day disappear, but your brand presence will be safe if you build a database with thousands of emails (and cell numbers).

If you're going to start a newsletter, consistency is key, so start as you mean to go. Decide what a realistic schedule looks like. Tell your audience the value they'll get by subscribing and the frequency with which they can expect to receive it. Set the expectation and meet it.

I have two newsletters. The first is one that I own, and you can subscribe to it at alizalicht.com/newsletter. It's hosted on Squarespace, but another popular vendor is Mailchimp. Both platforms have a monthly subscription based on how many people you're emailing per month. I learned this the hard way because it's not how big your database is, it's that number multiplied by how many times you email them that counts! Mailchimp also has a great tool where you can resend to the "un-openers."

My second newsletter leverages LinkedIn's newsletter platform. I double-expose the same content there that I send out in my personal newsletter, allowing LinkedIn to do the work for me to build exposure on it. My goal is to grow my personal database, but I'm not mad at having that same content further amplified within LinkedIn to an audience that I probably wouldn't reach otherwise.

EXTRA CREDIT: AMPLIFY YOUR VOICE WITH A PODCAST

Podcasts are an incredible way to expand and cement your personal brand. To be clear, you don't have to produce one yourself. Instead, you could be a guest and use other people's podcasts to build your notoriety. There are countless sites you can sign up on to pitch yourself as a guest. Either way, podcasting is a fantastic networking tool. In fact, an underrated fact about hosting a podcast that no one ever tells you is that it's probably the most effective method for you to meet people who might never take a meeting with you otherwise. I say that not because you're unworthy of a meeting, but because no one has time for meetings with people unless you're doing business together, want to do business together, or have a personal relationship. But with a podcast, your invitation to that CEO you're trying to connect with will be so much better received.

Imagine you're a consultant and you cold email a CEO to see if they would like to meet and learn about your services. You're likely to get no reply unless that CEO is currently in the market for exactly what you're offering. But as a consultant who has a podcast with previous stellar guests, when you reach out to this CEO and invite them to come on to share their business acumen with your audience, they might actually take you up on it.

Who knew? I didn't.

I didn't do it for the networking aspect, but it's proven to be a surprising result. People love talking about themselves, and why not give them the platform to do so while at the same time getting to spend an hour with someone you probably wouldn't be able to get into a room with otherwise. Another fascinating thing about this hour spent is that it's without distraction, and you are both completely focused on the conversation. I mean, when does that ever happen without someone picking up their phone?

There are a couple of things to note before you embark on this podcast route, though. First, starting a podcast is like getting on a treadmill with no off button. I'll never forget when I banked my first eight episodes, thinking how great I was to be ahead. No stress for me! I was going to front-load this content and glide through my first and only season with ease. That was a lie I told myself. I committed to a weekly show, and before I knew it, I'd flown through that content and lost my lead. In addition, I didn't count on the fact that people would like it, which meant that I was fooling myself that I was only doing one season. As I write this, I've done more than 150 episodes. I spend no fewer than five hours a week working on the show, and I have an audio editor and someone who helps me with my show prep and marketing assets. It's an incredible amount of work that also requires investment, because editing audio is not a good use of my time, and I bet it wouldn't be for you, either. That said, I enjoy producing it, and I think it's worthwhile as an additional facet of my brand. I just didn't want to fool you into thinking it was easy!

Here are the basics of how to start a podcast. You can easily Google all of this, but I wanted to include the high-level steps to give you a sense of the commitment you need.

How to start a podcast:

1. Decide your niche/concept and name, but do a competitive analysis to see what's already out there.

2. Commit to how often you want to release episodes. Consistency is imperative to keep an audience engaged and for growth.

3. Buy a microphone (and background noise/echo reducing accessories) and full-coverage headphones that you can plug into your computer. The Blue Yeti mic is popular, and there are many types of full-coverage headphones.

4. Choose your hosting platform. There are many you can go with here: Anchor, Libsyn, BuzzSprout, Podbean, Simplecast, Soundcloud, the list goes on. I use Anchor as it's simple and I can easily do the backend production myself. I started on Libsyn, though, which is more complicated. That said, Libsyn has great analytics.

5. Map out who your potential guests could be. Have at least 10 at your fingertips.

6. Download a free podcast release form for your guests to sign. Make sure to also include what your expectations are, e.g., social sharing.

7. Record your first (and at least six) episodes. Sites you can record on include Zoom, Zencaster, Riverside.fm, and many more. I usually do Zoom because it's reliable, but the others are great too. It's best for audio editing to record two separate audio tracks.

8. Invest in an audio editor if you can afford it. These experts range in price. Do your research and get peer recommendations. Or if you have the time and patience,

try doing it yourself! I attempted to do this early on, but it was too tedious for me.

9. Once you have one live episode on your hosting platform, you can share your RSS feed to many other platforms. It's one link that pushes your show across anywhere podcasts are heard.

10. Set up your corresponding podcast social media platforms to amplify your episodes using video from your recording.

11. Subscribe to Headliner to make your episode audiograms. These are the promo clips that include pieces of your audio. Headliner is great because they have some automatic tools that make this process seamless.

To summarize how I see every medium I've shared in this chapter, I'd like you to think about Barbie. I was a huge Barbie fan growing up and owned many versions of the doll and her brand extensions. I needed to have them all, whether it was Barbie Dreamhouse, Barbie Corvette, Barbie's Hair Salon, Barbie's Condo, Barbie's Pool, or Barbie's Trailer Home. All these elements helped crystallize Barbie's world and, in turn, my perception of her life. In the same way, all these different tactics, from bio to social to newsletter to podcast, help amalgamate your brand across mediums. There are also so many more you can explore.

Remember, when I first wrote *Leave Your Mark*, I didn't immediately think of it as a brand. It was just a book. But when I got the LLC, I started to ideate beyond that one medium and slowly began expanding my brand-building elements. You can rip a page from my playbook and do the same. Build one platform at a time, and keep adding to your world.

6

Establish Your Personal Brand at Work

All the previously discussed fundamentals are effective in building a strong brand foundation, but we can't discount the importance of how we are in real life, especially in the way we interact with the people we work with. If you're an executive or want to be one day, pay attention.

First, you should know that a great deal of work goes on behind the curtain. This is Wizard of Oz–level stuff where people are privately pulling many strings. When I started writing this book and reached out to Ross Martin again, I intended to gather his insights on how he markets his clients at Known. What I didn't realize was the secret Ross would share.

Much like his MTV Scratch days, Ross spearheads yet another black ops department within his company called Known Leaders. Known Leaders works with some of the most successful CEOs and CMOs in the world to help them define their personal brands. Their client list is top-secret because while these people are incredibly successful in shaping the brands (Apple, Hasbro, Citi, and IMAX among them) they work for or founded, they haven't invested in the thought process needed to think about their personal brands in the same way. (*You know what they say, the shoemaker's kids never have shoes.*) It's a confidential list because even though there's no reason to feel shame, these executives would rather not let the world know that they're working on themselves. It's way easier to market something other than yourself, even if you're one of the greatest minds in marketing.

In speaking with Ross, I validated my belief that we all spend too much time marketing the companies we work for and, as a result, forget to market ourselves. We make our company's name matter and not our own. I affirm that every person, no matter what they do, needs to work on their personal brand. Ross agrees.

"It starts with an understanding of why you even need to have a personal brand, right? Ironically, so many CMOs, many of whom are clients and friends, have never spent any time on their own personal brand strategy. They have massive careers, and they're some of the best in the world at doing it for their brands, they just never got around to themselves. Through our work together, they realize that—as awkward as it may be, or as self-indulgent as it may seem—**if you're not intentional about your own personal brand, you have lost control over what people think or what they feel when they experience you.** You might be freaking amazing at leading the brand of a bank, a consumer product, or a healthcare company, but you never even thought to answer, 'Who am I, and what do I want to make people feel?' That's the first step. If you're a business leader, everyone assumes that you understand how your personal brand is living in the world. It's comforting to know that if you *do* work on your brand, you can see tremendous results in your life and your career," advises Ross.

Pro Tip: At the beginning of a new role, you have the exciting chance to decide how you want to make people feel when they engage with you.

Every time you start a new position, you have an opportunity to rebrand yourself or double down on what you have established as your personal brand prior. While your brand attributes can evolve over time, your personal brand is singular. In the workplace, you can't be one way to one audience and a different way to another. Industries are small and people talk.

These are the dos and don'ts of your brand in the workplace. But for fun, we're going to start with the don'ts!

DON'T BRING YOUR WHOLE SELF TO WORK

First of all, I loathe this phrase. While "bringing your whole self to work" is a trendy recommendation by workplace experts (who usually don't actually work in offices, by the way), the truth is that not everyone should bring their whole self to work. Of course, there are personal parts of you that should be integrated, but others might not resonate at work or be appropriate for work. If that's the case, bringing them to work will not be beneficial to your career.

Ross explains, "Bringing your whole self to work is a wonderful aphorism. It works really well in a social post on LinkedIn, but in practice, especially for more senior leaders, it's increasingly uncomfortable to bring your full self to work. You're a target, vulnerable, and have a lot to lose. Most of the time, you're playing defense, and there's not much room for self-expression because there are landmines all around you, and if you step on one you might blow up your company, your career, your family, by saying or doing the wrong thing. So, it inhibits personal brand expression, and frankly, it makes for less interesting, less dynamic, and less inspiring leaders. We try to fit ourselves into popular conventions of what leadership looks like and how leaders speak, which creates more generic corporate suits and that's a shame because not only do you lose, but everyone around you loses too."

Ross isn't wrong, and while it may seem like a shame that we can't just all be exactly how we want to be, making a name for ourselves needs to be added value, especially to the company we're aligned with.

Pro Tip: Building an effective personal brand means that you're strategically sharing parts of yourself that support your goals. You're not putting everything on display.

Adam Neumann, the founder of WeWork, is probably the best example of a leader who at first was very intentional about his personal brand and his company's culture. He cared about how his employees felt. He brought his whole self to work and created a cult-like environment at WeWork. In the beginning, his messianic ways seemed to be laying the blueprint for the CEO of the future. I'm sure at the time things were going well, other "normal" company CEOs were watching him, wondering how they could be more like him to create a dynamic environment of loyalty, energy, and passion, while their employees looked on longingly at the "fun company." But then, employees were nearly forced to go to raucous parties, drink endless amounts of alcohol, and attend WeWork's summer camp for more of the same. Neumann's bizarre antics included everything from walking around barefoot everywhere (hello, even New York City streets) to jumping on tables to scream at people when things didn't go his way.

Neumann is the poster child for what can happen when you mix a dangerous cocktail of ego and personality. As his company grew, his personal brand became synonymous with excess and hardcore partying. He ultimately made poor business decisions, which resulted in him being removed from the board, taking a $47 billion company down, and leaving thousands of employees in the dust. But don't count him out just yet . . . the super-connected phoenix always rises from the ashes, and Neumann just secured an investment of $350 million for his next venture. People really do have selective memory.

DON'T MAKE YOUR PERSONAL BRAND A COMPANY LIABILITY

Let's talk about Elon Musk. Put aside for the moment that he owns Twitter, because the examples I'm about to share are previous to that.

Elon's personal brand on social media has always dwarfed the social footprint of his companies. Musk's Twitter following of 125 million (at the moment I'm writing this) makes one of his companies, SpaceX, at a mere 27 million followers, look like child's play. Of course, there's no way to separate the two. As long as he is CEO, Musk's personal brand will affect his business. To note, it's so mighty that he has the power to influence the success or tanking of a company's stock with a single tweet or an SNL performance (sorry, Dogecoin).

Musk plows through the boundaries of what's considered safe for a CEO to say. At SpaceX, several staffers wrote an open letter criticizing Musk and making several demands, including: "SpaceX must swiftly and explicitly separate itself from Elon's personal brand." Those employees were investigated and fired. *Way harsh, Tai.* To say that Musk plays by his own rules is an understatement.

> **Pro Tip:** No matter your level, everything you do can affect your company standing.

Neumann and Musk are two extremes, and there's a robust spectrum. No matter where someone might fall on it, contemplating how one's personal brand affects their company standing is a must. For us regular humans, pushing the boundaries is riskier. The stakes are higher because most people can't afford to be fired for cause. For those vying for Internet fame, just a reminder that social content is never worth risking your job for, tempted as we might be to share it.

DON'T PREACH EMPOWERMENT AND THEN CUT PEOPLE DOWN

People can't follow those they don't trust or like. When you work for someone who preaches empowerment but is abusive to their team, those two scenarios cannot coexist. The best leaders inspire greatness by being sincere not only to the mission of the company but also to their people.

Insecurity is a disease that can run rampant, but it can make some people do senseless things no matter what level they are in the hierarchy. I've witnessed this from CEOs down to interns. I'm not kidding. I once had an intern who was caught sabotaging another intern. He would secretly delete her work, throw out her lunch from the fridge, and hide her personal items, making this poor other intern feel like she was going mad. Thankfully, the cameras in the office worked, and we were able to prove this and fire him. Fun fact: it didn't stop this person from listing me as a reference years later. MIND BLOWN.

If you go to this dark side, people start paying attention to the patterns. People notice when you're nice to some people, horrible to some, and indifferent to others. When your moods swing from east to west, people don't know what they will get, creating a volatile, uncomfortable environment. One executive I know had such drastic mood swings that the different teams would report back to each other when they knew that her frame of mind was precarious. "Cancel your meeting, go home sick, do whatever you have to do, but don't present anything to her today" was a standard recommendation in the office. The moment you start to build this reputation, it swells from one meeting to another, and soon enough, it leaks outside the walls of your office. One employee tells the next, the other vents to her friend, that friend tells another, and suddenly, the company is battling Glassdoor reviews that state what a treacherous culture the company has.

One would think that people who act like this would be self-aware, but the truth is they're a toxic mix of egomaniac and deeply insecure. Sometimes there's more to the story. The saddest part, though, is how this behavior can affect the mental health of everyone this person encounters. It makes the recipient of this conduct start to doubt their self-worth.

I spent almost my entire early career never interacting with people like this, but later on, I had my first taste of a toxic work environment, and wow, was I naive. When I entered this foreign environment of mind games and fear-based tactics, even my rock-solid mentality was shaken.

Waking up every day to emails that were sent starting at 4 a.m. in ALL CAPS shouting about what needed to be done (or wasn't done correctly) didn't go well with my morning Dunkin'. When you start to distrust your abilities, even though you never have in your entire life, you need to seriously cut the cord. On top of that, if you have an admirable reputation but are aligned with someone who doesn't, what does that say about you? As my grandmother Hilda always said, "Show me your friends, and I'll tell you who you are."

Pro Tip: Your personal brand can be tarnished by the people you work for and surround yourself with.

Celebrities are not immune to this either. How often have you seen an A-lister who is charming and wonderful on camera and then is known as evil to work with? Media headlines love exposing these people. As of late, it seems that internal employees are the ones fueling this PR. But the reality is that if your public personal brand is marketed on kindness, but you're abusive to your staff, sooner or later it's going to become widely known. A tiny crack in your personal brand starts to form with each person you do this to. Whenever one victim of misconduct figures out there are others, it gets deeper and deeper until one day, there are so many people who've experienced this that your personal brand just shatters. When it does, it can take down your career. Job firings. Deals scrapped. It's a domino effect. Once one sponsor or investor pulls out, the rest will quickly follow. It's hard to come back from that, and some people never do.

Everyone from time to time loses their cool (although I'll admit, I have never in my life yelled or even raised my voice to a team member). But for argument's sake, let's assume that's true. Work stress is legitimate, and you don't have to be a senior member of the team to feel it. Pressure permeates across all levels. For the benefit of your reputation, though, remember that if you want people to work hard for you, give you 200 percent, and put the directives of the company first, then you have to lead by example.

Conversely, if you have a mentor mentality and your middle name is collaboration, the goodwill you spread can truly lift others up. The people around you will notice your kindness and your ability to find the positive even in a crappy situation. They'll follow your lead and style of management, and the behaviors will start to stick.

Pro Tip: If people respect you, you become the best kind of influencer among your peers because your character traits will also inform theirs.

That's the irony, really. The people who criticize and shame others inspire the people around them to purposely underperform. Sentiments like "He's never happy with anything anyway, so what's the point of trying?" or "She doesn't want to hear a contrarian opinion, so I'll just yes her to death." These are the ways employees can destroy a company when they're really just trying to protect themselves.

> **Pro Tip:** If your team knows that you're not going to get angry when you hear bad news, they won't try to cover up their mistakes.

If you're a doctor and you're in the middle of saving someone's life, you get a pass. But for everyone else, there's nothing we're doing that is so critical that we need to treat other people as less than. When you consider how you show up to your team, your family, your friends, the waitress at a restaurant, your cab driver, the person who cuts your hair, etc., think about how your personal brand comes off. A company CEO who yells at a waitress because their order is wrong is speaking volumes about who they really are. True colors, my friends, always shine through. Keeping your personal brand all glossy to the groups you choose to while exposing who you really are to those you deem inferior is a recipe for disaster.

If you're unaware of how you communicate or how others perceive your communication, ask for feedback. If you want a well-rounded view, ask people at multiple levels of seniority: your boss, your peers, and your direct reports. Understanding if you are an effective and respected communicator is an essential factor in growth and promotion. People might be intimidated to tell you the truth, so utilizing an online tool where you can gather this information from participants anonymously is even better.

DON'T GET NEGATIVELY LABELED

It's instinctive to mentally categorize the people you work with into different groups. We engage with so many people in our professional worlds that, in a way, it's how we organize them.

From the perspective of brand-building, though, we need to be aware of the labels that could be assigned to us if we aren't careful. *Am I collaborative or competitive?* is probably the most important question to ask yourself. Are you someone who looks out for number one, YOU, or someone who truly believes there's no "I" in "team"? The answer you choose becomes your reputation, and even if you have an unrealistic view of yourself, the people around you know the real score.

The same goes for work ethic. People who coast through their work doing the bare minimum or consistently miss deadlines become known for that. It all comes out at year-end review time. If you're in charge of other people, though, this labeling will hurt your personal brand and your ability to motivate your team. Team members are constantly clocking their bosses to understand where the weight of the work is being distributed. Your personal brand needs to stand for excellence if you expect excellence.

Being a successful person isn't just about work ethic, though. As a leader, your ability to make decisions also contributes to your public perception. Someone who can make decisions quickly and strategically comes off as confident. Someone who needs a lot of other opinions to make a decision may be viewed as weak. That's not to say that you shouldn't be thoroughly informed by others to make your decision, but if you're being paid the big bucks, you better have the confidence to decide the best course of action. People want (and need) to have faith that they're being steered in the right direction. If a boss can't decide, it's not a confidence builder for the team.

Then there are always those who decide and then change their decision to align with someone they deem more prestigious who has now shared a different view. This has to be my personal biggest pet peeve. There's also the unfortunate scenario of someone so intimidating that the people around them don't feel comfortable sharing their true opinions.

Pro Tip: If you want to bring out the best in people and get their greatest contributions, you must create a safe environment so people feel comfortable sharing their thoughts.

———

DO COMMUNICATE EFFECTIVELY (ESPECIALLY WHEN WORKING FROM HOME)

Your writing ability is one of your most important assets. It demonstrates how professional you are and can highlight your effectiveness. If you're a "camera-off" type of person or someone on the quieter side, all you have is email to communicate who you are.

Working remotely has demonstrated how tonality and the way an email is crafted can affect the receptiveness of people you work with. On top of that, emails are always so tricky. Personally, I think the period needs a new PR person because somehow using one sends a message to the reader that you're a really serious person and possibly—*gasp*—cold.

Consider this:
Thank you.
versus
Thank you!

Hi.
versus
Hi!

OK.
versus
OK!

We all overuse exclamation points now out of fear that our emails will be taken the wrong way and we will offend! In the world today, with remote/hybrid work becoming the standard, most of us don't have an opportunity to make connections in person. G-d forbid your email comes off as rude or dictatorial. When in doubt, we soften our words with exclamation points and emojis. Maybe it's just me, but the people who don't err on the side of caution tend to come off harsher, especially when you don't have the benefit of in-person to soften the delivery or build the foundation of communication.

But the other factor to consider is, do you communicate at all? There's always that person on the team who doesn't respond to emails. She needs to be chased down to do her job and, frankly, is annoying to work with because of her lack of responsiveness. Being challenging to communicate with becomes something you're branded as, whether you know it or not. Can the people you work with depend on you? When you're asked questions that you don't want to answer, do you ghost? These factors contribute to your work reputation.

If the biggest question we can answer in building our personal brand is "What do we want to be known for?" the opposite holds true as well. That is, "What don't you want to be known for?" I comb through all my emails at the end of the day to ensure that I'm being responsive and that the people who depend on me for answers get them. If you're managing people and they can't move forward without your go-ahead, it becomes very challenging to work with you. The chain reaction of being on deadline, needing your supervisor's answers, not getting them until a day or two later, and then your supervisor turning around and asking you why the project is late is real.

Then there are always the people who don't know that they're condescending on email. This can happen irrespective of seniority. You could be a coordinator speaking down to an intern or a CEO speaking to a VP. You could be speaking down to someone on *your* level. It doesn't matter. You need to make sure that you're aware of how you communicate. Ask a trusted colleague what they think of your written communication style.

I'm cognizant that my communication style might come off as very direct to people who are new to working with me. I tend to prioritize speed and efficiency over pleasantry. I'm not someone who starts every sentence with "Hi! How are you?" This is especially true if we go back and forth multiple times in a day. I don't have the warmest communication style, and sometimes, if you don't know me well, that can be off-putting or intimidating. Over the years, the people I work with know this about me, so they don't read it the wrong way. But regardless, being aware of this is helpful when working with new people.

Being transparent about how you communicate or prefer to connect is helpful at the onset of a new working relationship. This is especially crucial if you're managing people. Years ago, a direct report asked me, "I know you're in meetings all day, and I don't want to bombard you with emails, so would it be helpful to gather all my questions for you throughout the day and compile them into one email?" I was never so happy with a question! Yes, absolutely yes was my answer. That way, I knew that her one email would require my undivided attention, and she also knew when to expect my feedback. Perfection!

Aside from manager to direct report communication, there is so much that our written words need to convey. In many cases, what used to be as simple as walking over to someone else's desk now might require an email or a Slack because the person who used to work five feet away lives in another city and works remotely. Communication has never had to be more buttoned-up than it does today, but on top of clear writing, we also need it to be persuasive.

DO THE MENTAL GYMNASTICS
Persuasive Writing

Being a persuasive writer isn't something we actively think about. Of course, if you're pitching someone, you'll always think about how likely the person is to do the thing you're asking for. But outside of a classic pitch, we don't often consider the effectiveness of our emails. One of the best ways to confirm that your communication is persuasive is to make sure that you're being complete in your thoughts. Here are some cues to ask yourself when you're drafting an email where you need someone to take real action.

1. What is the goal of the email?

2. Is there a CTA (call to action) for the person receiving it?

3. Are you presenting all the information needed clearly and compellingly?

4. Are you too wordy, and are there sentences that can be omitted to tighten up this communication?

5. Is your writing too dense? Would bullet points be useful?

6. Will your tone of voice leave the person wanting to take the necessary next steps?

7. Did you acknowledge your appreciation for this person's attention to this matter?

8. Did you proofread your email and make sure that everything that needs to be in there is?

9. Were you clear on the deadline and your expectations?

Pro Tip: Never fill in the "to" or "cc" section until after you've proofed the email, just in case you hit send by accident!

Everyone, and I don't care what you do, is overloaded with emails. "Zero inbox" is a life goal of mine (it will never happen). Because of this, brevity and clarity are crucial. When you're getting hundreds of emails a day, no one has the time or patience to read a novel. Make sure your emails count, and the phrase "less is more" has never been more apropos than in this form of communication.

DO LEAVE YOUR JOB PROFESSIONALLY

No one ever takes a job thinking about their exit, so the moment you start contemplating your departure is always at the crossroads of a few possibilities. On the one hand, you're happy but leaving for a better opportunity. On the other hand, you're parting ways because you're not happy, and you're presumably headed for greener pastures. You could also be leaving for neither reason in this scenario, but you've reached your endpoint, and you're out. It doesn't matter what the situation is, though. Regardless of your direction, you're closing one door to open another. But more than that, the choice to leave your relationships behind or not is yours.

If you're smart, you know that every single person you meet along the way can play a role in your future. If you're not, you might believe that only the people ahead of you matter. That's not the case. Every relationship you make, or break, puts another stake in the ground for what your personal brand stands for. You may think that you leave the "bad" people behind, but you don't. There's an indelible imprint in their minds of who you were during that time. That, my friends, carries on whether you're there or not. **If you take one thing away from this book, and I mean this, please remember that your reputation is built on your past.**

Pro Tip: When you're leaving a company, a business deal, or a relationship of any kind, the taste you leave in someone's mouth becomes your defining flavor.

I implore you to leave with your head held high and depart as graciously as you arrived. Industries are like high schools. You know who everyone is, and you also know their superlatives. "Most Likely to Be an Asshole" should not be yours. Blind item posters beware, we always see you.

There's a false sense of palate-cleansing when one role ends and a new one begins. Of course, it's always an opportunity to rebrand and strive for the best version of yourself, but conversely, the people you left behind already have a final opinion. The jury comes back with their decision the minute you decide to burn down the place in the wake of your exit. And when I say burn down, I mean trash talk the company and your former coworkers.

This is easier said than done. So much emotion goes into leaving a role or a relationship. It's endless hours of mental anguish. Regardless of why something is ending, always try to tie your experience up with a bow. Every pivotal moment in your career is an opportunity to reinforce your personal brand and what you want to be known for. No matter how tumultuous an experience is, you'll always make the right decision if you check your mental filter and ask yourself how you want to leave your mark at that company.

PART TWO

Amplify Your Brand (and What to Do if You Mess It Up)

7

Become a Captivating Speaker and Own the Room

I was nine years old when I first realized something was wrong with my speech. I came home from school crying to my mother that I was called on to read in class, but the words wouldn't come out. My mother was swift to find an answer. It turns out that I had a stuttering problem. Not really the type where you repeat sounds, but more that I would hold my breath and get stuck on certain letters. Vowels were my enemy, and it sort of sucks when your name begins with one. My mother wasn't going to let this issue become my defining character. Cut to years of speech therapy throughout all my years of school and into college, and somehow, with great doctors, I overcame this. But while I was going through it, I shied away from any situation that would put me in a position to publicly speak. If you told me back in third grade that I would one day go on TV and speak onstage with audiences of hundreds of people, and enjoy it, I never would have believed you.

Pro Tip: Anyone can learn to be a dynamic speaker if you embrace the process, get great coaches, and practice!

I'll never forget the first time I ever had to do a TV segment. It was 2010, and I was working at DKNY. We were launching a new fragrance called DKNY Pure. There was a sustainability aspect to this fragrance. We had a partnership with actor Adrian Grenier's company, SHFT, which focused on sustainable products and living. Estée Lauder was our licensee and was producing the fragrance. I got a call one day from the PR person at Lauder, who told me they needed someone to go on *The Today Show* with Adrian in two days. They then asked me if I would be willing to do the segment with him. *Mic drop. The Today Show* is not where you start on television, let alone with a celebrity. I had a slight panic attack and then talked myself down by recognizing what an incredible opportunity this was for me. I had to rise to the occasion, but I was completely unprepared. Estée Lauder was working with a strategic communications expert at the time named Jillian Straus, of Straus Strategic Communications, who would media train me for the appearance (and many more speaking engagements later on). Jillian has a diverse client base with a mix of CEOs of Fortune 500 companies, executives, start-up founders, professional athletes, supermodels, A-list celebrities, and authors. Her clients include American Express, Booking .com, and IMG, among others, and she preps them for interviews with everyone from *Bloomberg TV* to the *New York Times*. She advises clients around the world on all aspects of public speaking, including message development for on-camera and print interviews and writes speeches for off-air presentations such as TED talks and keynote addresses.

To prepare me for this segment, she wanted four hours with me, but I only had time for two because I was so busy with work.

Little did I know what a valuable time investment it would be. I'll never forget when Jillian came over to teach me how to hold my own in a segment. For starters, I was a supporting actor. Adrian was going to get the bulk of the time and questions, so when and if Hoda and Kathie Lee turned their attention to me, the other human sitting there, I had to be absolutely sure that I could deliver our marketing message in the 15 or so seconds that were left, before they called for a commercial break. Jillian worked with me to nail down my sound bite. She helped me define my key message and how to deliver it, also making sure to include the brand name. You would think learning one line would be easy, but under pressure like that (and extremely bright and hot lights), it's easy to forget everything. Practicing the delivery of that crucial statement within seconds is the most important thing you can do. Speaking directly to the point ensures that your message will be conveyed in the way you intended.

This segment played out exactly as I'd imagined, with me sitting there in silence while Adrian got all the airtime. As I watched him have his lovely interview, I kept thinking about when and if my turn would come. Listening intently for my cue, I sprung to action the minute Hoda turned toward me and asked me if I thought that everyday people would support a sustainable lifestyle. Remember, this was 2010! While her question was interesting, it didn't give me the lead-in that I needed to deliver my practiced sound bite. Naturally, why would anything I prepared for happen the way I planned? Nevertheless, I had to make sure that I answered her question and then somehow also delivered my brand-focused line. Jillian taught me how to answer a question and then bridge that answer to deliver the message my company expected. It shockingly went off without a hitch!

Jillian has worked on both sides of the camera because she is also an author. She spent over a decade working on *The Oprah Winfrey Show*, ABC News, and CNN. Back in her early days as a production assistant at *Oprah*, she did anything that needed to be done, from making copies to helping celebrities in the green room. She was lucky enough to interface with everyone from Madonna to John Travolta to John F. Kennedy Jr., and obviously Oprah herself. But she would also go out into the field and interview people, one-on-one.

"So here I was, this young 20-something woman from Los Angeles, and my job was to interview a group of male coal miners in their 50s in a coal mine in Somerset, Pennsylvania. I had to learn the ability to connect with people with all kinds of jobs, whether they were from the celebrity world or just regular people. And that was such a great education for me because it really taught me and laid the groundwork for what I do today," recounts Jillian.

If you want to be a strong, strategic communicator whether you're presenting on Zoom, in a conference room, going onstage, on television, or even prepping for an interview, Jillian has easy-to-employ tactics:

THE ESSENTIAL ELEMENTS OF BEING A GREAT SPEAKER

Be Human

Showing your human side allows people to really connect with you. It doesn't matter if you're making a toast at a wedding or presenting at a meeting because **when people like the messenger, they listen to the message.** This is something that we can easily forget.

Showing your human side comes with a caveat. We saw everyone from world leaders to CEOs during the pandemic showing us a glimpse into their personal lives. You might think, *Aww, high-profile people are just like us!* And yes, an insider's view into that person's life will make you more likely to connect with their message and be persuaded by them. It's why people love

TikTok and seeing their favorite celebrities let their guards down in an authentic way.

However, both Jillian and I agree that it doesn't work the same for regular people or people who are still working to establish what their personal brand stands for. (Yes, this is a double standard.) Your boss, investors, and customers want to know that you have your act together. If you share a view into your world that doesn't support that idea, you create a tiny fault line in your personal brand. That's not to say that you can't be human; you can, but when you're sharing a glimpse into your personal world, just make sure that what you're showing enhances your overall persona and aligns with the message you want to convey.

Jillian takes it a step further with this clarification: "I think what people assume when I say show your human side is, 'Oh, I can just let it all hang out.' That is not what I mean. And I think in the Zoom era, some people are doing that, right? They have too many things going on in the background. But I think a good example of showing your human side is if you're on a Zoom presentation and trying to talk about the challenge of being a working mother. If you've got a laundry basket behind you that still needs to be folded, it perfectly demonstrates you are using your human side to make a larger point. But if you're talking about the company's earnings on a Zoom call, I don't think the laundry basket behind you helps your message. So, show your human side in a way that supports the larger story that you're trying to convey."

Tell a Great Story

People won't remember a PowerPoint presentation or the statistics you've rattled off, but they will remember an engaging story. Communicating in the form of a narrative captures your audience's attention because if you open with a hook, they will stay with you, wondering what happens next.

Let the Facts Speak for Themselves

"You don't want to tell people what to think or how they should think. You don't want to twist or sugarcoat the facts. I think we see much of the news today as a manipulation of the facts. Facts do speak for themselves. Of course, there are always situations where the facts enhance our message, but other times, especially if you're a boss having to convey layoffs at your company, the facts are less desirable to share," says Jillian. She advises being straightforward about them anyway. "You can express your regret and emotion about it and even show your human side when having to relay those negative facts. But you must let the facts speak for themselves."

Send a Clear, Concise, and Consistent Message

Say things succinctly in more than one way to get your point across. People don't act on something you tell them until they hear it in at least three different ways. We must have clear, concise, and consistent messages that we repeat. We need to be clever in the way that we repeat messaging so as not to be boring, but there's a way to reinforce what you intend to say without being redundant.

It's Not About You, It's About the Audience

It doesn't matter if it's a speech, an investor pitch, an interview, you name it: understanding and delivering your message tailored to that audience is the goal. "If you're a female founder pitching a male venture capitalist, you might need to make them understand a product for women," says Jillian. "Tailor the speech so that the audience will hear it."

But there's another ingredient essential for success in delivering your message. Passion! Passion is contagious. In a world where virtual interactions are more common than in-person, passion is expressed through your delivery of words, your facial expressions, and your hands. Says Jillian, "If you're presenting to me on Zoom, you can't walk toward me, and you can't stand up and give me a power pose, but I can feel your passion through the use of your hands in the way that they help convey your words and the tone and energy of your voice. That's, of course, in addition to the expression on your face."

Jillian's rule of 3 C's is easy to remember. Every time you speak publicly you must:

CAPTIVATE

BE CONCISE

CONNECT

WAYS TO CAPTURE YOUR AUDIENCE'S ATTENTION

Not to stress you out, but you need to captivate your audience within the first 10 to 15 seconds! If you fail to do so, they'll start to tune out, check their phones, and it will be hard to regain their attention. What's worse is that you'll sense this happening, and therein lies the pressure of public speaking.

There are various ways to grab your audience's attention. For example, start by asking a question or begin by telling a story. Perhaps you even have something in common that you could open with. Next, you must always be concise. Have your elevator pitch ready. People have a limited attention span and often tend to go on and on about themselves. When someone asks you a question about yourself, they're interested to a point—meaning they want to hear the answer, but in a statement short enough to allow them to absorb it. If you run on too long, you risk the audience glazing over and tuning out. And finally, you have to connect. "You must find a way to connect with the audience, and that goes back to showing your human side or telling stories to make them empathic to you and interested in what you want to say," advises Jillian.

One way to ensure that you don't make a connection with your audience is to read from your deck or notecards. "I always say to my clients, you are not reading your deck to me. I can read a deck myself. There's nothing more boring. So, when I say captivate someone, I don't care how good that first slide is; that is not going to captivate them. That deck is a supporting actor in a play or a prop in a play. It is not the star," advises Jillian.

Personally, when I'm putting a presentation together, I build my deck like a sandwich. The title slides are the bread, and the slides in between are the turkey, lettuce, tomato, etc. Using the bread, aka title slides, helps your brain understand where it needs to go, but the story you're telling from your memory, not the deck, is what's in between the bread. I use the title pages to guide me, so the progression of the information I'm delivering makes sense. It also helps me know what points I must hit. I might keep other key pieces of information in my presenter's view in the early stages of practice, but the truth is by the end I know it so well that I don't even need to look at it. Once I see the title, it prompts me, and I know exactly what I'm going to say.

That's not to say that I memorize a script. Do not do that. You need to sound authentic. The other problem with memorization is that should you lose your spot mentally, it will be a) obvious that you memorized it and b) hard to get back on that content train. "If connection is the goal (and it should be your number one goal), you're not going to get it by looking down at an index card or staring at your slide; you're going to get it through eye contact and smiling, and you can't read a piece of paper while you're doing that. So, the point is, that you must do your homework, make your notes, and be familiar with them. A good speech or presentation doesn't get delivered the same way every time," says Jillian.

As Jillian notes, your deck is a supporting actor, and no experience proved her words truer than when I had to practice for my TEDx Talk. I had exactly 12 minutes to deliver "The Power of Being Real," my story on how authentic storytelling helped build the DKNY PR GIRL community. I wasn't allowed notes or a teleprompter. There was no presenter's view. All I had was myself and the audience seated in the *New York Times* theater. Good-bye, deck. I trained for this presentation by really understanding that my title cards were the threads that would allow me to get from point A to point B to point C. In this case, they were title cards I had to memorize in sequence and then know the story well enough to share it without needing the support of anything else. It was some of the toughest prep I've ever done, mainly because it was timed so exactly. Knowing the story inside and out allows you to deliver it like you're telling a friend personally versus making a speech.

Standing up on that stage was exhilarating. Moments before any talk, though, I have a temporary worry that I'll stumble over my words. If you watch this video, you can see me take a deep breath right before I start speaking. My old speech issues always pop into my brain before any big talk. I almost tripped on my words, but I caught myself. Once I started, I was on a roll. When the talk was over, I knew I had nailed it. It was an adrenaline rush!

Throughout my talk, I made sure to make eye contact around the room. Since your audience is your most important constituent, you must continuously read the room. If you're presenting virtually, have someone else be the presenter of your presentation. Your most important role is keeping eye contact with the people watching. If you lose sight of the audience because your deck is getting in the way, it can be easy to lose that connection. If possible, have an ally in the audience who you know will be camera on to help you focus your energy. When you're presenting in person, you can identify one or two people around the room to whom you'll direct your words. Remembering to smile is critical. Even more crucial is ensuring your words have a moment to land. Sometimes being nervous can make us rush through the content, and it's imperative to remember that you know what you're going to say, but your audience doesn't. You need to give them time to listen and consume your words. Pausing for a second or two allows them to do that and also grants you the ability to regroup and take quick stock over the audience and whether they're paying attention. Of course, if this is virtual and everyone's camera is off, that's impossible to know, but make sure that they're paying attention wherever you can. You can always stop to ask if anyone has questions.

Now onto your outfit. If you want to be relatable and relaxed, a suit is probably not the right look. Your clothing should reflect your goals but also who you're addressing. The wrong outfit can also be distracting. Busy prints, big sleeves, and mixes of bold colors might take attention away from your words. It's also always a good idea to sit down in your outfit and take a quick picture of how you look. Your clothing will appear differently on camera than it looks in your mirror at home. I learned this the hard way with a horrible peplum top that fanned out and made me take up half the TV screen.

Next, you need to think about what your clothing looks like in the environment you'll be speaking in. What's behind you? Will we be distracted by that? Is the view you're giving people supporting the image you want to project? Where is the light coming from? It needs to be in front of you, not behind you. What chair are you sitting on? Are you behind a desk or in a director's chair with your legs out there for everyone to see? That's going to make you think long and hard about your choice of shoes as well.

Jillian advises to ask yourself, "Am I forwarding my agenda with my Zoom background and the way I'm dressed? If I coach someone going on TV as an expert or an executive, I might tell them to dress very professionally. For example, wear a suit. But if they're going on as a child psychologist, I would say, be more human, more friendly, wear a dress or a sweater and pants. So, it really must be consistent with whom you're showing up as that day." While it may seem calculated to plot your look like this, it's part of the overall package. Just remember that your audience is consuming more than your words.

HOW TO BECOME A PUBLIC SPEAKER

Becoming someone who is asked to speak publicly starts with two things: demonstrating thought leadership or expertise on a subject in combination with executive presence. So, if you want to be someone who people recognize as a speaker, show them that you're worthy of that role. You might be thinking, *Well, how do I do that?* Start sharing your knowledge on a particular subject on your social platforms and/or in written form. Become synonymous with your field or craft. Share articles of what's already out there and add commentary and get on video to discuss the topics. Do this consistently so people begin to notice that this is the subject you talk about and that you're experienced at delivering this information.

> **Pro Tip:** If you work at a company and public speaking is your goal, you must understand your company's media policy first.

Every company has rules for who can speak on behalf of that company. Even though you might think that you're not speaking on behalf of the company and that you can just speak about your work "in general," the reality is that any media entity, whether a show, website, conference, etc., always leverages the status of the company name to add credibility to the speaker. Therefore, anything you say represents your company.

If your company is open to employees speaking at conferences, start by researching opportunities in your industry. Look at the events from the year prior to understand the topics and previous attendees. Figure out who ran the event and if there is a contact to get in touch with to understand when the next conference might be held. If you happen to know a past speaker, reach out and ask if they have someone they could introduce you to.

If you're not yet a person who is invited to speak on a panel, another strategy is to offer yourself as a moderator. Finding moderators is often a tedious task for conference organizers, and being one is a great way to start flexing your public speaking muscles. But before you do that, make sure you have video footage of yourself speaking. This could be as simple as social media posts with you speaking to the camera, but people need to see you in action before they would be willing to sign you on as a moderator. I actually prefer moderating conversations—it allows me to live out my fantasy of being a talk show host, ha! Which is also the reason I have a podcast.

Remember that one speaking gig leads to the next. Stay on top of your industry trade news to know which events are being announced. Add these experiences to your bios and your website (if there are enough, it could be its own tab), and share clips of your speaking engagements on your social media. Promoting your abilities as a speaker will not only make it easier for people to think of you when opportunities arise, but it will solidify you as a person with expertise on a certain subject. That said, always think about your role and how going on the speaking circuit will make your boss or other stakeholders feel. While we never want anyone or anything to get in the way of our progress, when you have a corporate job, there are many factors to consider.

Pro Tip: Don't complicate your day job for 15 minutes of conference fame. It's not worth it.

If you're an executive, choose your speaking engagements carefully. It's imperative that the company you keep be at your level and of the same caliber—not just title-wise, but brand-wise. If you're very, very senior, consider limiting your speaking to keynote speeches or fireside chats only. For you, it's about quality, not quantity. Every speaking gig should work to enhance your personal brand. Being the poster child for industry conferences isn't an elevated look. More is not better. More is just more.

If you expect to make tons of money from speaking, think again. Payment for speaking comes when you're at a certain level in your career, and even then, it's a rarefied group of people who make their entire incomes from public speaking. Think of your payment at first as street credibility and personal brand-building. While you might say that your time is money, when you're creating your reputation as a speaker, they are really doing you more of a favor than the reverse. Take the free engagement to eventually get the paid one. It's beneficial experience no matter what, and the only way to become adept at public speaking is to practice often and with a real audience. Don't let your ego get in the way of this. Your time will come if you keep at it. Promise!

EMBRACING YOUR VOICE AND MANAGING UP AT WORK

Of course, many people shy away from speaking, even in front of small groups like team meetings, without the stuttering issue I had. For me, avoiding a school play growing up and opting out of presenting to my class were choices I made to protect myself. It hurt to make those decisions because I'm not a quiet person— quite the opposite. There's nothing wrong with being quiet, but sometimes the downside of quiet can be invisibility, especially at work.

Though researchers have estimated that 30 to 50 percent of the population are introverts, we live in a world where extroverts are rewarded. That's not to say that introverts don't win, they absolutely do, but when you're aiming to establish your persona, you need to consider that if you're an introvert and not someone who readily socializes with colleagues or speaks up in meetings, you're going to have to work a lot harder to create an impactful personal brand.

I'm not suggesting that you constantly need to grab attention to build your brand. Nor am I saying that you change your personality. Instead, I recommend making sure that people understand who you are and the value you add in whatever way that feels comfortable to you. This doesn't always have to come from your voice. It can be in written form or communicated by someone else, but it needs to be shared. Nothing, however, beats the impression you leave in person.

EXUDE EXECUTIVE PRESENCE

"Owning the room" means that when you show up, you have the ability to shift the energy and attention of the room in your direction. While it shouldn't mean that you bulldoze a meeting, it should result in your presence having impact. This is likely a natural skill for those who have it, but there are coaches who can help you get there too.

Alisa Cohn is one such person. She's an executive coach in New York who helps start-up founders mature into world-class CEOs. She was named the Top Startup Coach in the World at the Thinkers50/Marshall Goldsmith Global Coaches Awards in London, and her book *From Start-up to Grown-up: Grow Your Leadership to Grow Your Business* delivers the reader her two decades of coaching experience in easy-to-follow steps. She's worked with start-up companies such as Venmo, Etsy, Draft-Kings, The Wirecutter, Mack Weldon, and Tory Burch. She's also coached CEOs and C-suite executives at enterprise clients such as Dell, Hitachi, Sony, IBM, Google, Microsoft, Bloomberg, the *New York Times*, and Calvin Klein. *Inc.* named her one of the top 100 leadership speakers. *Need I say more?*

Alisa's book explains that the success of a leader isn't just about having a voice; it's about having an executive presence. She advises that when you think about executive presence, you first need to understand what is necessary to be successful.

The eight elements of executive presence are words that all begin with C:

Composure

Connection

Confidence

Credibility

Character

Command

Charisma

Conciseness

Says Alisa, "The CEO needs a certain kind of executive presence to be effective, and a middle manager needs a different kind of executive presence to be effective. When I help leaders think about executive presence, I use the model of gravitas, communication, and appearance. Gravitas has to do with your ability to show up as an owner in a way that means having weight inside of the meeting. That could be because of the way you're speaking, the way you're using hand motions, your height, or the weight of how you own the room. The second is communication, making sure that you are addressing the audience's needs. If you're speaking to a group of executives, you're going to be speaking very differently than if you're speaking to a group of junior employees or vendors, for example. Are you able to also listen and engage at an authentic level, so people really feel like they're connected to you? And the third has to do with appearance. Are you showing up and looking the part?"

The idea of looking the part is well debated, but we tend to have ideas in mind for how people are supposed to look in specific roles. "Certain founders don't need to wear jackets and ties or be formally dressed, but they need to distinguish themselves in some way that says that this presentation matters to me," says Alisa.

Having an executive presence means that when you enter a room, the atmosphere changes. It means you give off an air of expertise. It could be because of your seniority, the way you carry yourself, or even how you're dressed. When a doctor enters the room in her white coat, there's an immediate level of respect that you have for that person without even hearing her say a word. *Am I right?*

While Alisa isn't a communications coach, she advises her clients to consider the goal of the meeting. "Are you trying to close the deal right now? Are you trying to advance the game? Are you trying to communicate a specific message? What do you want that message to be? How do you want to make sure that you are articulating that message? What is the story you are telling, and once people think about it from the point of view of "my goal is to do X," they need to think about what that story arc will be. Once you know that, it changes how you show up in the room," she says.

There is a direct connection between executive presence and influence. When you exhibit executive presence, people assume that you know what you're talking about. Whether that's true or not is another story. However, what is clear is that effective leadership isn't possible without executive presence and that influence is the result of them both.

The Wharton School of the University of Pennsylvania has a course called Executive Presence and Influence: Persuasive Leadership Development. This course promises to help you master the leadership skills needed to inspire, empower, and influence outcomes. According to the Center for Talent Innovation, leadership presence accounts for 26 percent of what it takes to get a promotion at work. According to research from Gartner, executive presence skills are ranked second in the top 20 leadership traits that make a difference. When you read statistics like this, they feel in contrast to the previously discussed introverts. If your goal is the C-suite, then your ability to influence others and motivate teams is essential to executive readiness. All these traits contribute to your personal brand.

Can you have too much presence? Absolutely. If someone has too much gravitas, they start to absorb all the oxygen in the room. People who exert too much executive presence might also believe that their opinions matter more than others. No matter how senior or important you get, it's essential to remember that being open to other viewpoints and being willing to listen to others are also significant signs of leadership. If you're a very self-aware person, you might be in tune with your presence and how others perceive it, but sometimes we're not aware that people are watching.

AN INTERVIEW IS AN AUDITION

My friend Barbara Barna Abel is a dynamic personality, and it's also her job to spot talent for a living. Since launching her casting, talent development, and communications coaching company, Abel Intermedia, in 2001, Barbara has worked on more than 100 unscripted alternative projects and jump-started the careers of prominent figures in the industry. Her clients include television networks, PR firms, athletes, models, celebrity chefs, business executives, and young creatives. Her long list of credits includes the groundbreaking RuPaul show on VH1, *Queer Eye for the Straight Guy*, and *What Not to Wear*.

While you might hear the word *casting* and think, *I'm not an actor, nor am I going on an audition*, how wrong you would be. **A job interview is an audition. A client or investor pitch is an audition. Presenting to your company is an audition.** If you go into any presentation thinking of it as if it's an audition, you will change how you present. But Barbara has even better, more surprising advice: "No matter what your level is, one of the tricks to presenting is not focusing on the pitch at hand, but rather making friends." Hmm, that's not what most people would think about when going into a situation where they need to present.

Making new friends? You might think, *I have enough friends, and I'm probably never going to see these people again.* But what you don't know are the factors working clandestinely. For example, in many cases, you might believe you're interviewing for a role, but that role has actually already been decided. You might assume you're just presenting in an internal team meeting, but someone senior in that room is looking for the next star employee to move up in the ranks. While you can't control the outcome, you can focus on how you appear. Barbara advises, "Come in and focus on that thing you can control, which is be delightful, be present, understand that you're here to make my life easier, and what would make my life easier is you being fabulous so that I can hire you. So, that's all about an energetic perception. Leave the room better, more upbeat, and [more] wonderful than you found it. If you're delightful, I'm going to remember you, and I might go tell somebody else. Everything we do is a transference of energy. That is what people pick up on. How present are you, how open are you, and are you connecting?"

There's a lot we can learn from the casting process. First, the idea that you're displaying your personal brand long before your interview, meeting, or audition starts is undoubtedly something to consider. "Don't make the mistake of thinking that it only begins when the red (record) light goes on. Don't miss the idea that if you're going for a job interview or an investor pitch, it started the moment you walked in the door and spoke to the security guard downstairs. Every single person you come in contact with or walk by is all part of this process," warns Barbara.

In the casting space, it's not uncommon to send someone into the bathroom to see how the person is behaving when nobody's watching. The intent is to get a glimpse into this person's true demeanor. What might they be like to work with? Did they make a call in the bathroom and rant about something? Were they rude to the bathroom attendant? At a certain point, many contenders have stellar credentials. Whether it's acting chops or a start-up, it's less about ability and more about who that person is when you get down to the final round.

"When you narrow down the choices, anyone we're choosing should be able to do the job, so the deciding factor could often be, do I want to be in a van with you for 13 weeks over bumpy roads in the middle of nowhere shooting that incredible travel show that everyone wants to do? If the answer is no because I think they're going to be a pain in the butt or that they're not very nice, and I remember seeing how rude they were to the security guard, you're not going to get the job," advises Barbara.

See, that's the funny thing about presenting. It's not just about when you're prepared and ready to be on. A really easy way to see a person's bona fide traits is to pay attention to how they behave in moments when they don't realize that they're being judged. Like when you're dealing with customer service, for example. It's so easy to lose yourself in frustration, but if you get angry and you're someone notable in any arena, you might just find the results of that exchange on social media after. These are easy traps to fall into if you're not careful. Not to mention the fact that people take a video of everything they see. The phone is always ready to capture a moment you least want to share.

8

Understand the Digital Playground

Social media has given us the ability to share our voice, build our image, and amplify others. It might feel like enormous autonomy, but it's also restrictive in unsuspecting ways. There's this misconception that we have freedom of speech, but the countless people who have been fired or lost contracts because of their public comments tell a contrasting story. A misguided post doesn't even need to be current to count. A screenshot from years ago can resurface and turn your world upside down. There are too many examples to list, but let's take two very different scenarios.

1. Tweets That Came Out from Under the Rug with TikTok Star Tinx

TikTok's favorite big sister, Christina Najjar, aka Tinx, got a taste of her past coming back to haunt her when tweets of her calling Kim Kardashian and Lindsay Lohan "fat" and Tori Spelling "pathetic" resurfaced. Her mean-spirited past statements were a shock to her millions of beloved fans, and they surely let her know. Building a brand of big-sisterly love, female empowerment, and body positivity is the opposite of these tweets, which were posted in 2012 and again in 2014. There were many more that were reported as well, including calling a journalist's wife "ugly." Later in the book, I'll dive into a whole section on cancel culture and crisis communications, but for now just know that she apologized on Instagram and chalked it up to her insecurity. Hey, she was young and everyone makes mistakes.

2. Tweets Aging Badly with Actress Felicity Huffman

Felicity Huffman went from having an admirable Hollywood career to being caught in a college admissions scandal. When the sh*t hit the fan, the lovely people of the internet went on a scavenger hunt to see what Felicity's past social presence looked like. Of course, they found the perfect 2016 tweet where she asked for school "hacks" for back-to-school season. You can't make this up.

That's the ugly side of the internet, and it can be hideous. Some people take comfort in saying that their social profiles are personal, but the smart ones know that there's no such thing. Don't mistake thinking that you can compartmentalize the internet. Don't pretend like you can remember and vet every person who follows your private account. You can't.

I can write a whole other book on all the bad things that can come from putting yourself out there on social media, but let's assume that you're going to really study this book and you're not going to blow up your reputation on the internet. Instead, you're going to wield the power of digital to build your personal brand and use it for good. If leveraged strategically, it can be one of the most effective ways to build authority and influence in your career or business.

Aside from deciding what platforms make sense for you (we'll dive into that soon), you need to determine what your intention is for being on social media in the first place. If you plan to use it for your professional gain, the first place that intention gets summarized is in your bio.

THE IMPORTANCE OF A CONSISTENT BIO

I feel like I'm always preaching this, but your bio is worth its weight in gold. If we think back to the longer-form bio discussed in Chapter 5, what is the sound bite of that story? What's the editorial version of your LinkedIn headline? I say "editorial" because your social media bio doesn't have to take itself as seriously as your LinkedIn profile bio does, but still, they both need to have synergy with each other.

To put it simply, you need to think of the social media landscape as one big cocktail party—and there are many bars at this party, with the same drink selection available at each. Similarly, that's how your social media bios should be presented across channels. Connect the dots for people. Leave them a path to discover and follow you wherever they spend time online.

If your intention is to use social media to support your professional goals, then you need to make your bios do some work. Honestly, these platforms should charge rent for these bios because that's how important they are. So, rule number one is bio consistency, and then rule number two is making sure that what you write in your bio supports the message you want to drive home.

Pro Tip: Use your social media bio to promote what you want to be known for. It should speak to what you do or aspire to. Highlight what is most important for someone to know about you in a snapshot.

For example, if your goal is to be a journalist, but you use your social media bio to tell me that you're obsessed with Netflix and Taylor Swift, that's not serving your professional goals. I love both Netflix and Taylor, but that bio isn't doing the work it needs to, and it won't get you where you need to go. Instead, I want to see the word *journalist*, *reporter*, or *writer* front and center to know what you do. If you haven't achieved this yet, you can add the word *aspiring* to whatever role you hope to have one day. Why? Because these keywords are searchable! You might be thinking, *Oh, my account is private.* Guess what? Not only can I still see your bio, but being private doesn't stop people from requesting to follow you. They don't think you're private because this is your "personal" account; they think you just don't want people you don't know seeing your posts. To be safe, you need to assume that whatever you share should be rated P for Professional, just in case.

"OPINIONS ARE MY OWN AND DO NOT REFLECT THOSE OF MY EMPLOYER"

This is one of my favorite lines because it means nothing. A little disclaimer for those of you adding where you work to your social media bios: you are now representing the company you work for on social media, whether you intend to or not. Even if you don't add the company name to your social account, I would bet my life it's on your LinkedIn. Therefore, any way you slice it, your words can get you into trouble and could possibly get you fired.

> **Pro Tip:** Everything you do on social media reflects on your employer and can be used against you.

The question of whether to add your company to your social media bios can be answered differently at various times.

Knowing whether it makes sense to include it or not is simple. Answer this question for yourself:

Why do I want to include where I work in my social media bios?

Some possible answers are:

1. My company is prestigious and adds credibility to my name.

2. Adding my company will attract its competitors, which will benefit me when I'm eventually job hunting.

Both of the reasons above are valid; however, the caveat is that your posts no longer reflect just you. You are bringing along your company for the ride, and that can be good or bad for both you and your employer. You can also decide at different times to include your company affiliation and when to take it off. For example, let's say you know you're quitting to launch your own business. Taking off your company name early will help you and your community get acclimated to the fact that you are representing only yourself. I removed my company affiliation when I knew I would be leaving soon to consult again. That said, assess if removing your company affiliation will sound an alarm with your boss. Be careful that you don't show your hand too early.

Today, cancel culture is so fast and furious that you don't even have to list your company in your social media bio to get fired from said company—but if you include it, it will be far worse if you mess up. Even if your social media account isn't associated with your name and you use it to vent all your thoughts on what is going on in the world, in politics, pop culture, etc., you just never know when a post might catch fire. When that happens, the internet trolls will come after you. If they do, trust me, they'll do everything in their power to figure out who you are. They are very skilled at these investigations.

While it may seem low risk, if you take to social media to vent about your employer and rely on your anonymity (or even blind items) to protect you, I have some news for you: they can easily find out who you are. Social media teams basically work in customer service. They are skilled at going down the rabbit hole to discover your identity because they do this all the time to match customer profiles.

Typing behind a computer makes us feel powerful, or sometimes too powerful. The impetus to share every thought on your mind is strong. However, if you want to maintain your personal brand at the highest level, resist posting every single thought that crosses your mind. Now, this is where you tell me that you don't care about what I'm saying, that you have a right to say whatever you want, and gone are the days of not having a strong position on politics or whatever your cause du jour is. That's all true, but this is your fair warning.

> **Pro Tip:** If your opinions are the opposite of those of your boss, your CEO, your client, your main investor, or whoever controls your advancement, you're putting yourself in a precarious position.

Someone who doesn't agree with you or, worse, hates your viewpoint will have a hard time erasing that from their brain, and it will influence their impression of you. It's only natural. If these words make you angry, I'm sorry, but I'm not sorry. It's unfortunate, but we have come to a time in our world where people no longer tolerate a difference of opinion. They want you to have their opinion. We have gone to extremes, there is no middle ground, there is no gray, there is only black and white.

That said, ask yourself if it's worth sharing that thought. What would your key stakeholders think? What if it got picked up by the media? Remember that people are always watching, and the more known you are, the more likely it is that someone is out there waiting to take a screenshot of your post. Once it's out there, it's forever. Something that feels important in the heat of the moment becomes much less so when it could mean that you're fired. If you're passionate and you're going to burst if you don't support something or voice something, go for it, but do yourself a favor and run that mental filter before you post. It takes only a second to ruin a career and a lifetime to build it back up, if that's even possible.

THE BRANDS YOU WORK WITH ALSO REFLECT YOU

If you have clients or work with brands, your personal brand is also affected by what they do and say. (*I'm exhausted thinking about this as I type.*) Consider this scenario: You're a content creator, and you've finally landed a big brand deal. It's a six-month contract, and you're obligated to post twice a month. Then said brand decides to go and sell a swastika necklace, and suddenly, you're faced with the realization that under no circumstances and no matter how much money (hint: A LOT) can you work with this brand. You have no choice but to end the contract. Guess what, though? You can only break that contract if you were smart enough to put a mutual termination clause into your agreement. These are the kinds of things that can really harm your personal brand. You must always have an attorney read your contracts. It's the most important investment you can make. Don't get stuck being aligned with a brand that goes against your core values.

NEVER UNDERESTIMATE THE RISK OF DIGITAL CONTACT TRACING

"Kim Kardashian unfollows Miley Cyrus on Instagram after Pete Davidson special." This, my friends, is news. It was actually a *New York Post* headline. I understand that these are celebrities and that the press is watching their every move down to some little intern whose job is to track Kim's followers and figure out who's missing. *Unreal.* But for us normal humans, there's a lesson here.

Pro Tip: Your silent actions on social media speak volumes too.

The minute you hit that like button (even though you didn't say a word), you've endorsed whomever or whatever was said. People can get themselves in a lot of hot water by just liking things. The same goes for the accounts you choose to follow. All these scenarios can be used against you in a court of law. (*Just kidding, not a court of law, but a court of public opinion, which may be worse.*) Your endorsements also contribute as another telling exhibit of your personal brand. It's hard to think about these tiny little details, but that's also why I put them in a book for you. **Your social media timelines are a popcorn trail that leads back to YOU.**

Everywhere you turn, you're affecting your brand, even when you don't realize it or intend to. I'll never forget when a founder I know went on a rant on her private Facebook account thinking she was doing so among her 5,000 closest friends. When you have 5,000 friends or even 500 friends, you can't possibly remember who they are or whether they're actually friends. Unfortunately, one of her "friends" wrote for *Page Six*, and of course, her little tirade ended up in the paper. This person was clearly not a real friend, and it was a crappy thing to do, but that's the point: you just never know who's reading.

SO, YOU MIGHT ASK: WHY BE ON SOCIAL MEDIA AT ALL?

Good question! I haven't made a compelling argument (YET) for why you should build a social presence, but I'd be remiss not to lay out the potential pitfalls first. In addition, if you've never posted before, I'm not trying to push you into doing something that makes you uneasy. But here's where I tell you that getting comfortable and active on at least one platform will be beneficial to you. I am proof of this. My books are a direct result of having a social media presence. To be clear, I did not pitch my first or second book proposals. My voice on social media caught the attention of an editor.

There's a great deal that can come from building an online community. We're not talking about millions of followers here. I don't have that either. You don't have to build a big following at all. **Your goal, should you choose to accept this challenge, is to build the *right* following.**

UNDERSTANDING THE CREATOR ECONOMY

I'm on the board of the American Influencer Council, the only trade organization in the US led by and for career creators. The council strives to sustain the integrity and viability of the influencer marketing industry in America and provides incredible resources for people who want to start in this field. A main pillar of the AIC is education.

There are different levels of influencers or creators (the words are used interchangeably):

More than 1 million followers = Mega-influencers

500K to 1 million followers = Macro-influencers

50K to 500K followers = Mid-tier influencers

10K to 50K followers = Micro-influencers

1K to 10K followers = Nano-influencers

The words *influencer* or *creator* may not resonate with you. You might think you need to be a career-creator (full-time influencer) to be called that. You don't. I want to be clear: anyone who has people following them wields some level of influence. You could have 200 followers on your private account. It doesn't matter. Those people are there because they're interested in what you have to share.

While organic growth isn't as easy as it once was, good content finds its audience. As I write this, Instagram just announced that they will be prioritizing small creators. The landscape changes constantly, and it's something that you need to keep up on.

Not only has my social media presence been instrumental in bolstering my career, but I've also made incredible connections through it. The positives that can come from being on social media far outweigh the negatives. If you implement everything I say in preparation for your social strategy, you'll be set up for success. Regardless, please read my very comprehensive chapter on managing your reputation and surviving cancel culture, just in case. (*I mean, I can only do so much, LOL.*)

Social media provides a medium to establish your voice and thought leadership. It's essential for leaders today to have an online presence. Going back to intention, it's for you to decide who you're trying to influence and where that audience is. When Ross Martin is advising clients on their personal branding strategy, social media is one important part of the medium mix. He recommends that his clients calibrate their personal brand expressions across a variety of carefully chosen social and IRL (in real life) platforms.

"The questions to start with are: Who are you trying to reach? What do you want them to feel and do? Where and how best to engage them? At Known, we think holistically about your brand's communication strategy, and that means: Where are you going to show up? Where's your column? What are you doing on social media? What conferences are you speaking at? Who's in your network? What distinctions are people considering you for? When are you going to write your book? What are you investing in? Authentic personal expression is essential for this generation of business leaders and marketers," advises Ross.

WHAT DOES SUCCESS LOOK LIKE TO YOU?

If you're starting from scratch, I would advise first identifying your goal in embarking on social media. Hint: The answer shouldn't be the number of followers, but it could be something like sharing expertise to amplify your voice or products, land a client, pursue a new role, or network with people in your industry, to name just a few possible reasons.

In the next chapter, I'll walk you through how to create a content strategy, but first let's review a few platforms that I believe are the most useful for growing your personal brand professionally, starting with Twitter (*yes, Twitter*) and LinkedIn, which to me are the most accessible platforms to demonstrate your personal brand through dialogue. These are especially beginner-friendly because you don't have to think about a visual content strategy. Instead, you can jump into conversations relevant to your industry/business that are already happening. You can repost other people's content that is interesting to you or helps convey your expertise or passion about a subject. You can also add your own commentary to begin to establish your point of view. To repeat, growing a following isn't the point here. It's how you contribute to the conversation that matters.

TWITTER

OK, I get it. Most people would argue that Twitter is a toxic environment and a waste of time, but my experience tells a different story. Aside from the DKNY PR GIRL example, the relationships I've formed from my presence on Twitter have led to countless other opportunities. It has given me the platform to connect with very important people that I might not otherwise have had the chance to meet. And I can keep up with my press relationships even though I don't work with the media anymore. It's how I do my research, get my breaking news, and learn about what's trending. It's the first thing I check when I wake up and the last thing I check before I go to bed.

Twitter has its pros and cons, and it's not for everyone, but if you understand how to use it to your advantage, it can be an excellent tool for establishing your expertise and being at the center of what's happening in real time. First, in my opinion, it's for those who prefer writing. Sure, you can share images and videos alike, but the people who rule the Twitterverse are the ones who enjoy the written word and being immersed in up-to-the-minute news and pop culture. It's also why journalists spend their days on it. If you want to have your finger on the pulse of what's happening globally, there's no better platform than Twitter. News often breaks here first, and this one time . . . *wait for it* . . . I broke the news.

When I was DKNY PR GIRL, I was tweeting 24/7. I kid you not, I was glued to that account and, subsequently, the news. It was a Sunday night in 2011, and I was watching TV and flipping channels. As I was clicking through, I caught Geraldo Rivera confirming that Osama bin Laden had been killed. I couldn't believe it! Then I proceeded to have the most off-brand moment of my career. Because his death was so monumental for the entire world, I automatically tweeted it without thinking. Unfortunately, I hadn't considered my brand filters or how widespread the news was. As it turns out, I tweeted it about an hour after the Chief of

Staff of the Secretary of Defense but before the majority of mainstream media. OY! Clearly, this wasn't something I should have done, but it was too late, and it went viral. I got a not-so-friendly call from my company's legal department. Oops.

Pro Tip: Consider your brand filters and think before you post!!

But honestly, how funny are these tweets?!

"I love that I learned about Osama from @dkny . . . NOTHING gets past this girl."

—@k_conran

"When my daughter asks me yrs from now where I was when I heard Osama got dead, my answer will be: 'On Twitter, from @DKNY.' WOW"

—@wicked_chick

"didn't believe that osama was dead at first cause @dkny was the one who tweeted it."

—@per_phat_ion

"May or may not have just gotten an email asking if talking about Osama is 'off brand.' Not sure how to answer this one . . . @dkny thoughts?"

—@WhitBenj

How to Start on Twitter

Your presence on Twitter can be twofold. First, you're a voyeur, there to consume information. Second, your goal is to follow and interact with people for personal or professional use, or both! Again, you don't need a content strategy for Twitter. Everything I tweet is off-the-cuff and in real time. I like to post based on what I'm feeling at that second.

> **Pro Tip:** Always check trending topics before posting to ensure there isn't something globally important happening. You don't want to look ignorant by posting something frivolous during moments of crisis.

For example, during the Osama bin Laden scenario that I just shared, Lady Gaga tweeted "Are monsters ready for me to announce the premiere of *The Judas Video? The Motorcycle Fellini Pop Art Fantasy?!*" She raked in some bad press for posting this and being clueless as to what was happening in the world. That's also the danger of scheduled posts (I'm assuming it was scheduled since it was a Sunday night). You always need to consider the bigger picture and how your messaging works with or against that.

Curate Your Twitter Experience

Use Twitter to follow brands and people that serve you professionally or your interests, watch the ping-pong of conversation, and jump in when it suits you.

> **Pro Tip:** Read the room before you jump into conversations.

It's a best practice to review the thread (tweets connected together) and understand the origination of the discussion. Look at the original person's profile to make sure this is someone you want to engage with.

If you type your interests into the search bar, you'll find people who have included those keywords in their bios. If you know you'll be launching something eventually and want to start curating a list of people who cover that specific topic or area, Twitter is especially useful. While some journalists don't enjoy being pitched on Twitter, it's a great way to research the people you *need* to know.

One of the best things about Twitter is that you can talk to anyone and join any discussion. The downside of Twitter is well known, and it can be horrible if you're the target of harassment. With any online platform, what you say can sometimes yield a reaction that you least expect. Going back to what I advised earlier, make sure you REALLY feel the need to say it. You never know what the aftermath will bring.

Twitter can be extremely effective in building your personal brand if you do it right. As I said, it's not about how many followers you have; it's about defining your voice. How you choose to share your personality on Twitter is a choice that should be made with strategic thought. Focusing on your passions or interests is always a good strategy. If you can be laser-focused on a niche, you can work strategically to become known for that niche. Every person or brand should have a brand filter, which includes a list of topics that you should or should not be speaking about. A clear brand filter will help keep your messaging on track. The more you're seen speaking about your niche, the more you become known for it. This book is a result of me talking about my niche of personal branding and how to build a brand online.

Pro Tip: Make sure the accounts you follow are nutritious, meaning that you've curated a timeline that serves to feed your brain, your contacts, your business goals, or your entertainment.

You don't even need to make the account in your name if you don't want anyone to know you're there. You can create a steady flow of pertinent information on any area of interest by curating your timeline of accounts you follow. You never need to engage, either. I know people with multiple anonymous accounts used to track competitors and people of interest on the down-low.

Pro Tip: Don't take comfort in your anonymity to the point that you feel it's a shield of armor. You're still responsible for what you say.

Conversely, your entire content strategy (or non-strategy) can be participating in other people's content either by replying, retweeting, or liking. For good measure, a mix of all tactics is best. You don't have to share your own content. You can make yourself known by amplifying others or being clever in your replies. If there's someone you're interested in connecting with, engage with that person's content. With enough consistency (not stalking), your name will become familiar. I've hired many people from Twitter, and if you've read *Leave Your Mark* you know that the book's introduction is the inspiring story of my former assistant, Jenna Blackwell, who I met on Twitter. At the time, Jenna was selling artificial turf in Texas and ended up working with me dressing celebrities for the red carpet. We've worked together at three companies. She also met her husband on Twitter! Granted, with Elon Musk now owning Twitter, it's bound to go through a transformation. But as far as I am concerned, Twitter still offers a ton of value, and the relationships you make online can easily lead to offline—and isn't that a beautiful thing?

LINKEDIN

I like to think of LinkedIn as the darling of the pandemic and beyond. LinkedIn went from being a platform where you make a profile and forget about it, to a legitimate place of social connection and personal growth. Callie Schweitzer, Global Creator Programs Lead at LinkedIn, spoke with members of the LEAVE YOUR MARK Community on the platform's power and explained how much it's evolved. "It's incredible to see how much it changed during the pandemic because we are now bringing our full selves to every aspect of our lives. And I think you see that on LinkedIn. You see the generosity that people are leading with, you see the vulnerability, you see people just showing up as humans, and it's so much less of the business façade. I believe it is the greatest place in the world to scale what it is that you know, to mentor and be mentored."

> **Pro Tip:** LinkedIn is a conversational platform. It is a place to have a dialogue. It's not a broadcast platform.

You can post anything from a photo to a poll or ask a question to invite people to share their thoughts on something. Callie believes that you're an expert in something, whether you're 20 years old or a 75-year-old retired CEO. But what if you've never had a corporate job? Callie says, "Have you ever babysat? Have you ever worked in a store? Are you in any clubs in high school or in college? You have so many experiences, and frequently you discount them because you think they don't fit the traditional way. The future of the workforce is not about the traditional way. What makes you unique?"

DO THE MENTAL GYMNASTICS
What Makes You Unique?

Take a luxurious moment to recognize your individuality. We spend so much time focusing on where we fall short and what we could do better. We judge ourselves based on the success of other people and think, "Why can't I be more like . . . ?" We don't ever pat ourselves on the back and say, "Great job!" "Way to go!" "Wow, you killed it!"

Focusing on your strengths isn't a regular occurrence, but even more rare is a deep dive into what makes you, you. You are an original. No one has your experience or your story. How can you tap into that to set yourself apart?

1. What is your most unique skill or quality?

_____

2. What is one adjective that describes your persona?

_____

3. If you had to choose an emoji to represent you, what would it be?

_____

4. Does your current social media bio express your unique skill or quality?

_____

5. Does this skill or quality support what you want to be known for?

_____

POV: Bringing Your Whole Self to LinkedIn Can Be Tricky.

On LinkedIn, we see people on both sides of the coin. People who are super buttoned-up professionally with a profile picture to match or people who have changed the way they present on LinkedIn to their more authentic selves. During our LEAVE YOUR MARK Community event, Callie shared an extreme example of someone during the pandemic whose profile picture was just out of the shower with wet hair. I'm sorry, but this doesn't fly anymore. You should always think about your audience—bosses, direct reports, potential hiring managers, and future colleagues. Even though an authentic picture might generate lots of likes and comments, it doesn't serve your professional goals.

Pro Tip: Don't confuse social engagement with success.

Out of all the platforms, however, it's my opinion that LinkedIn can be the most effective, especially if you're someone who doesn't want to be on social media. The good news for those of you who don't want to post is that the comments themselves are a breeding ground for inserting your personal brand. Callie adds, "Something that I always tell people is that you can build thought leadership, whatever that means to you, in the comments. Just start commenting, following people, and connecting with people. You can begin to build who you are and your personal brand that way. I think these tactics are so underestimated. Your words don't always have to be coming from you on your page to be meaningful. Think about how you can amplify people in your network and help each other build your own brands."

As I mentioned earlier, I have a LEAVE YOUR MARK subscription newsletter on LinkedIn. If you're a fan of writing long-form content, LinkedIn is a great place to do so. Regardless, whether or not you choose to share original content, being strategic with the companies and high-profile individuals you follow says something about you. LinkedIn has a section dedicated to highlighting your interests.

It's important to have an "all-star" profile, which is the rating LinkedIn gives you when your profile is complete. You should keep your experience section updated and include any awards or affiliations, volunteer work, or memberships. LinkedIn is an essential place from which recruiters source, and you just never know when someone is looking. Well, if you have LinkedIn Premium, you do.

> **Pro Tip:** Turn off the setting that notifies your network when you change your profile (before you make the edits). You will want to do this incognito.

Of course, if you have an exciting update, i.e., a new job, an award, or a board position, by all means turn that function on. I also advise you to stay in private mode so people can't see you reviewing their profiles (and vice versa) unless you pay for Premium.

I strongly believe in having a professional-looking profile picture and using your full name in your bio. Canva has a LinkedIn banner template you can use to customize yours. Brand yourself in the way you want people to know you. Start building credibility with your name, not just the company you work at.

But What if You Have Nothing to Share on LinkedIn . . . Yet?

The pressure to come up with experiences to list on LinkedIn is real, and when you're working your way through your career journey, you're not expected to have it all perfectly figured out. Home From College is a career starter site founded by Julia Haber intended to support you during the time when you're not quite ready to play the all-star LinkedIn game. Home From College's tagline is "Where Gen Z Starts Their Career." They understand that you don't have the experience yet to have a robust LinkedIn profile, so instead, they give you the tools to present yourself and your unique attributes in a way that's geared toward that early career stage. It's free to join, and their clients are companies who want to tap into the Gen Z demo for various projects and focus groups while allowing them to present their resumes in a fun and dynamic way. They call these gigs. Per their site, "a GIG is a flexible work experience that allows you to try out as many careers as you'd like before committing to just one. Because getting an internship can feel impossible, we created the place for you to get your foot in the door." Instead of the pressure of a job interview, companies post IQs (interview questions) on the site that allow the users to answer in a way that shows how they think versus what they've done. This is a great alternative to what some people do, which is making stuff up.

INSTAGRAM

Instagram has changed so much since its birth in 2010. I used to think of Instagram as a personal brand's store window, but these days it's morphed into another version of TikTok. Regardless of Instagram's identity crisis (and no doubt it will change by the time this book is published), you need a visual content strategy, and it needs to be centered around video. Your content plan doesn't have to include you at all, but it's always better if you can personally connect with your community, especially if you're a founder or want to become a thought leader. That said, videos featuring people speaking directly to the camera are what Instagram is looking for.

In considering Instagram, the first step is understanding the visual story you want to tell. This can be for you personally, a business you're building, a side hustle, a hobby, or a passion. It can also be for fun! The platforms decide what type of content they prioritize at any given time. We've seen Instagram shift from its early days of perfectly staged static images with some dreamy background to favoring Reels, which is lo-fi (low production iPhone) vertical video made on the fly.

When you're building your presence on Instagram, consider what's important to the platform. Whatever new product tool they've introduced is what their algorithm will prioritize. If Instagram loves vertical short-form video, but you only post static images, I promise you that your content won't have the level of impressions or engagement that it should. This is called *shadow banning*. Instagram selectively decides the type of content it surfaces to others and the type it purposely suppresses. I've tested this theory by posting the same content as an image post and as a Reel, and the difference in performance is incredible.

Instagram is scrubbing your content for visuals, keywords, sentiment, and hashtags that they don't approve of or deem irrelevant, not just the format choice of video or photo. The best way to stay on top of the dos and don'ts of Instagram (or any platform) is to read industry sites like socialmediatoday.com and blogs like later.com. The platform itself will also always share its news and best practices, but they will never admit to controlling your content! Trust me, they are.

When I launched the *Leave Your Mark* podcast in 2019, I knew that I didn't have the energy or desire to build an Instagram following from scratch. I already had my personal account @alizalichtxo, which was hard enough to grow. But what I did want was for my podcast to have a home on Instagram. For example, what would they tag if someone loved listening to an episode and wanted to share it? I created @leaveyourmarkpodcast. But how was I going to do this in the least complicated way? I decided that its purpose should be more like a directory, and I didn't really care if the following remained small because of that (i.e., I didn't follow the format I knew Instagram preferred). Sometimes practicality is the goal versus something grander in scale.

But as my podcast matured and Instagram evolved, I needed to rethink my strategy. With the ever-changing landscape of social media, you must be willing to change also. When Instagram introduced the collaboration tool, I realized it was something I could leverage. The "collab" tool is a function where at the point of tagging someone in a photo or video, you can also add a collaborator. The person added will be notified in their direct messages that they were invited to be a collaborator on your post. If they accept, your post will also appear on their feed. So the same post will be on both accounts, and what's more, the comment feed is shared as well. That function is a great way to cross-pollinate the two audiences.

When this feature was introduced, I realized that a video Reel I was making for my personal account could be shared with the podcast account as a collaborator. This helped me to not only evolve my content strategy on the podcast page but to marry @alizalichtxo and @leaveyourmarkpodcast in relevant posts.

Instagram stories expire in 24 hours and are for the benefit of the people who already follow you. They are not really shared outside your existing base, unlike Reels, which are served up on Instagram's Explore page. Reels are exposed to people who don't follow you and are the antidote to TikTok's For You Page #fyp. Relevant hashtags help drive this exposure.

No matter the changes Instagram has gone through, it's still an incredibly fun and important platform. Leveraging Instagram, especially for a small business, is very beneficial. More to come on this when we dive into content.

TIKTOK

TikTok is the social media cool kid whose algorithm and understanding of what you like is so powerful that it's not even about who you follow or who follows you. It's about seeking out (via hashtag search) or liking the type of posts you want to be served again. TikTok's famous #fyp (for you page) is where all the action is. It's scary how well this app knows you. When TikTok first became popular, it quickly became the breath of fresh air we needed during the pandemic. TikTok is low production value, with people genuinely being themselves. This might sound ridiculous, but there's so much you can learn from following your interests on TikTok. Being on TikTok means you optimally must have a vertical video strategy (aka the direction your phone is normally in) and one where you're either the face or someone else is, but whoever it is, they better be comfortable speaking directly to the camera.

That said, TikTok has started playing the "copying is the best form of flattery" game and borrowed the signature style and call-to-action of Be Real with TikTok Now. The feature prompts the user to share a selfie using the back and front camera at a random time each day to capture a 10-second video or static image each day. I swear these platforms are all at a loss as to what to do to stay ahead and capture and keep our attention!

When you think about building a presence on TikTok, do a deep-dive search into the hashtags that are relevant to you or your business. It's essential to analyze the type of content that's out there specifically in your niche. You should comb through 20 to 40 of the most viral videos by filtering by "most liked in the past week."

Next, strategically emulate the style and format of those videos, down to trending sounds and hashtags. It's also important for you to think about why something popped off. While this may sound boring or make you question why you should mimic these videos, that's in essence the magic of TikTok. Everything is a version of something that came before. Of course, if you're a brand, your music options are limited to commercial music, which makes it harder to go viral. That said, plenty of brands are crushing it by producing the type of content that works well on TikTok in combination with being nimble enough to jump onto a trending hashtag or sound.

Note: The content you post on TikTok needs to be developed for TikTok and utilize all the native captioning and title tools the app has to offer. Taking previously made high-production video content from elsewhere will not perform. For example, a brand that spends millions on a TV commercial must rethink what that same content looks like for TikTok.

The good news is that whatever you create for TikTok can easily be posted to Instagram Reels. Be warned, though, that Instagram knows how powerful TikTok has become, and if you post a video on Instagram with the TikTok watermark, Instagram will purposely deprioritize that content. (*The solution here is to create the video, post it to TikTok, and then grab that post's link and put that URL into one of the many watermark removal tools on the internet.*)

Title cards and on-screen captions are essential and need to be sprinkled throughout the video to hook and grab the viewer. It used to be that the shorter the content, the better, but alas, TikTok is now eyeing the ad dollars of YouTube and favoring long-form video. Their maximum length of video is now 10 minutes. Honestly, these platforms are never happy!

With TikTok, it's about frequency, consistency, and laser focus on your niche. The most successful TikTok stars post every day and often multiple times a day. Unless you're legitimately trying to be a TikTok star, I'd recommend posting at least three times a week. (*This is also hypocritical for me to say since I legit fail at this weekly.*) With TikTok, speed is everything. Your ability to jump on a trending moment could mean the difference between success or not.

THE OTHERS

YouTube is a great but mature platform, which means that it's very hard to grow organically there anymore. In my view, having an effective YouTube strategy is too heavy of a lift for an individual who doesn't want to be a full-time content creator. Even though

YouTube has added short-form vertical video to compete with Tik-Tok, its main offering is still longer-form horizontal vlogs. "How-to" or product review type of content works best here.

I barely use Facebook, and most brands today primarily use it as a paid strategy, not an organic one. That said, Facebook groups are still a thing, and if your brand or product makes sense to be consumed in that type of community, then it can be effective.

Pinterest is your online mood board, and they've been making moves of late, acquiring different companies and perfecting their game of pinned aesthetic. Many people use Pinterest to repurpose content they have already posted elsewhere and then drive organic traffic back to their other accounts (backlinking each post). But honestly, there are only so many hours in a day, so unless you have a social media team handling this for you, it's not realistic.

You can also have a paid social plan on any of these platforms without really having an organic presence. Both Pinterest and Snapchat are great examples of this type of strategy. This means you can run ads on the platforms but don't actually post organically.

There are, of course, other platforms like Twitch, Discord, Clubhouse, Be Real, and the list goes on. Decide where your time and effort are best invested. But if you build your personal brand on one platform, you're putting an incredible amount of trust into that platform. (*Cough, cough MySpace.*) Remember that the more control you give these social media platforms over your personal brand, the shakier the ground you're on. Too many people I know have been locked out of their social media accounts for days, or their accounts have been disabled for some unknown reason. Imagine that you've spent years cultivating a community only to one day have it disappear in a second. Don't risk that happening, so make sure your personal brand on social media is diversified.

9

Ideate Your
Social Media Strategy
and Build a Community

Having a solid online presence can only help you establish your brand. The overwhelming problem I see is people who want to create a social presence but don't know where to begin.

The great news for you is, I'm taking you step-by-step through this thought process. To get started, you need to think about four main areas.

- The Platform(s)
- Your Niche
- Your Content Strategy
- Your Brand Voice

In Chapter 3, I explained the usefulness of creating a Venn diagram. If you didn't do this exercise, do it now before we dive into content. As a reminder, a Venn diagram allows you to create a visual representation of two or more things that you want to compare the similarities or differences of. When you create your Venn diagram, contemplate topics you're interested in talking about on social media so you can examine what their common ground might be. This will provide the framework to take the next steps below, which are aspects to consider when you're embarking on this endeavor.

DO THE MENTAL GYMNASTICS
Plan for Your Strategy

1. Define your goal. Why are you using social media? Here are some thought starters. Choose more than one answer if applicable.
   a. To raise my professional profile and build my network
   b. To become known as a subject matter expert
   c. To share a talent/hobby I'm good at in the hopes that it will evolve into a business
   d. To promote an existing business or a product
   e. To become a full-time content creator

2. If you had to pick one niche to be known for on social media, what would that be?

   _____

3. What are one or two other supporting areas you would also like to highlight as part of your overall brand on social media? (Hint: You can get these answers from your Venn diagram's overlapped area.)

   a. _____

   b. _____

For example, my areas of focus are career advice and personal branding. I'm going to mirror your efforts by adding my own answers in parentheses to help you think this through.

4. Decide which main platforms make sense for you.
   a. LinkedIn
   b. Instagram
   c. Twitter
   d. TikTok
   e. Pinterest
   f. YouTube
   (I post on LinkedIn, Instagram, Twitter, and TikTok.)

5. Depending on the platform(s) you chose above, your new bio will have a limited number of characters. Let's use Instagram's 150-character limit to write a bio reflecting your answers to questions 1 and 2. This exercise will help you center your thoughts.

   _____

   _____

My Instagram bio is currently:

Founder of LEAVE YOUR MARK: Brand builder, author, podcaster @leaveyourmarkpodcast, mentor @leaveyourmarkcommunity.
Speaking: info@harrywalker.com

My future bio might be:

> Founder, brand builder, author of *Leave*
> *Your Mark* & *On Brand*, host
> @leaveyourmarkpodcast, and career mentor.
> For speaking: info@harrywalker.com

We shall see! This will and should change as your priorities for what you want to be known for shift.

6. Determine the frequency with which you want to post (consistency is important).
   a. Once a week
   b. Twice a week
   c. Three times a week
   d. Daily
      (I aim to post three times a week, if not more. I also usually post first thing in the morning because that's when I have the most time.)

7. Will you be creating your own content or having someone else do that for you? (yes/no)
   (I create my own content.)

8. Do you plan to be the face and voice of your accounts? (yes/no)
   (Yes, but I also share content promoting the guests on my podcast.)

9. If you answered no to the last question is there someone else who will be? (yes/no)

Pro Tip: If you plan on having someone else be the face and voice of your accounts, what happens WHEN that person leaves?

(Remember what happened with DKNY PR GIRL. Even if they had wanted to continue with that personality, it would have been hard to replace me. Not because I'm so great, but because I was so synonymous with that persona.)

10. If you answered yes to question 8, are you comfortable doing video? (yes/no)

    (Fun fact about me: While I was always comfortable with someone capturing video of me, i.e., if I was doing a talk, I was uncomfortable speaking directly to the camera. To be honest, I just felt stupid and attention-seeking. Clearly, being able to do this is no longer a choice as TikTok and Instagram have made it very clear that this is what we all must do to build a community. I overcame my hesitation by focusing on my purpose and reasoned that if my videos provided a benefit to others, I'd feel more inclined to post them. So that's what I did. Better late than never!)

11. List three to five adjectives to describe the way you want people to feel when they consume your content.

    a. _____

    b. _____

    c. _____

    d. _____

    e. _____

    (I want people to feel: inspired, educated— like they learned something new—motivated, empowered, and entertained.)

12. Why should people follow you? Describe the benefits people will get by doing so.

(People should follow my accounts for career and personal branding advice from me and my guests. I also couple my mentorship with my other hobby, hair and makeup for #beautyandbranding. You learn something new while I apply my makeup or do my hair. I mean, what could be a better combination? LOL)

13. How much of your content needs to be created versus sourced online? This affects both budget and bandwidth.

(My content comes from me and the videos I capture when recording my podcast.)

A note on borrowed content: Reposting other people's content is a regular occurrence on social media. Generally, it's a best practice to ask for permission (especially if you're a brand/company account).

> **Pro Tip:** If you repost someone else's content, always make sure to tag the source and anyone else who should be credited.

Always attribute any content borrowed to the person you took it from, but that said, also look to see who they tagged in their credits, as finding the original person to credit is always smart (and appreciated!). This is especially true if an artist or photographer was involved, as they are especially sensitive to their content usage.

A rule for celebrity content: Company accounts shouldn't repost celebrity content. As a company, you don't have usage to those images unless you license them from a photo service site such as Getty Images. Even then, the celebrity themselves may not be OK with being featured. A general rule is to remember that you can't use someone else's image for commercial use, i.e., when you are selling something.

A STEP-BY-STEP SOCIAL MEDIA STRATEGY

STEP 1. FILL YOUR CONTENT BUCKETS

Imagine you have a dresser in your room. That dresser represents your brand on social media. The drawers in your dresser represent the different topics or themes that you want to speak to. These are also called your content buckets (or pillars if you prefer). Each bucket serves a purpose in supporting your overall brand and helps you express whatever subjects or niche you want to be associated with. Content buckets help you outline the different ways that you can tell your brand story. While each bucket is unique, they work together harmoniously to support your overall goal and help convey what you want to be known for in interesting and eclectic ways.

Going back to my Venn diagram from earlier (featured again on the next page), everything I listed here could feasibly be a content bucket for my social media strategy. Let's take office culture as an example. As a content bucket, office culture is a general theme, but if I wanted to expand that theme into multiple pieces of content, I could do so easily.

For example, first I would consider what the **educational** expression of office culture could be. I could share some tips

Digital Strategy
Partnerships/Events
Influencer Marketing
Fashion

Social Media

Professional Development
Mentorship
Job Hunting/Interview Tips
Office Culture
Career Journeys
Podcast
Community

Brand Building

Content Strategy

Personal
Branding
Empowering
Women
Books

Marketing

Executive Presence
Thought Leadership
Relationship Building/Network
Social Capital
Reputation Management
Rebranding

ON BRAND

or best practices from a workplace expert. Second, I might ideate an **inspiring** expression of office culture that could serve to motivate people. Perhaps some tips about leadership. Third, I could craft an **entertaining** version of office culture. Maybe use a meme or something else funny. Once mapped out in concept, I would then think about all the different ways to visualize office culture across photo and video in longer and short-form versions depending on where this content was going to live. Do you see how one topic was divided into three different use cases? Think in terms of a flow chart to map out your topics.

> **Pro Tip:** A great way to get ideas for the type of content you might want to create is to search your topic by hashtag.

STEP 2. CONSIDER YOUR CONTENT'S CREATIVE FORMATS

Start saving the formats you like and especially ones where you can picture what your version of that piece of content might be. The bulk of the content out there is simply different renditions of the same thing. You can mirror the same format or put your unique spin on it.

Your content buckets could also be general areas of focus such as 1) Inspiration, 2) Education, 3) Selling products, 4) How-to, 5) Spotlight of the week, 6) My favorite _____, etc.

You might decide that each content bucket has its own look and feel. For example, maybe all inspirational content will always be designed in shades of blue because blue is the main brand color of your logo. Perhaps your educational posts will be in a carousel post format, so each tip is its own image. You can add up to 10 swipes in a carousel on Instagram to share up to 10 educational tips per post. Maybe your spotlight of the week will always be in video format.

> **Pro Tip:** Giving each content bucket a signature look and feel also allows your community to become familiar with it.

DO THE MENTAL GYMNASTICS
Your Content Buckets

List 5 to 10 content buckets (general areas you want to focus on). You can take these from your Venn diagram!

1. _____

2. _____

3. _____

4. _____

5. _____

6. _____

7. _____

8. _____

9. _____

10._____

STEP 3. PLAN OUT YOUR CONTENT PRODUCTION AND CADENCE

Block time to ideate your content strategy and calendar. Next, set aside some time to capture content. Last, plan focused time to edit and prepare your posts and captions. Many people who do this for a living will bulk shoot and bank their content. For example, setting aside a day to shoot multiple videos (changing outfits for each video so it's not monotonous). This is just one way to be efficient and knock out a lot of content at one time. I will add here that I don't do this. My content comes from the gut, in real time. I need to feel it in the moment to post. I have never been an obligatory poster. You should, however, feel free to do this in whatever way feels right to you.

There are many platforms that you can use to lay out a draft of your content strategy, but Canva is the easiest. You can create a template using their image or video placeholders and then drag and drop your content in to visualize how it will look. One note here: people obsess over what their feeds look like from the profile view. The funny thing about that is people don't consume your content from your main feed view unless it's literally the moment they hit that follow button. What's more probable is that they're consuming your content via the timeline of accounts they follow. So don't overthink it. (I know that's easy for me to say after I've rattled off a million things for you to think about.)

> **Pro Tip:** Being successful on social media is really first and foremost about authentic storytelling.

I never had a content strategy for DKNY PR GIRL. Everything I posted was in the moment. I don't have a content strategy for my personal accounts either, but I do give thought to what I want to talk about. This generally happens while I'm doing my morning routine. I do, however, have very robust content strategies for clients that are planned at least a full week out. When there are multiple entities that need to approve a plan, you have no choice but to think about it in advance. **But if you're doing this as an individual, I recommend that you think through your Venn diagram, identify your content buckets, and establish your brand filter or "guardrails"—the topics that make sense for you to post about and those that don't.** Doing these things will give you the needed parameters for your strategy and keep your messaging on point. You don't have to go into excruciating detail or planning. Here's a great example of what I mean.

My Sister Made an Instagram Account and Launched a Business in One Day

One rainy afternoon, my sister Ilana took some old pairs of white sneakers and decided to do a splatter painting activity with my nieces. She splattered a pair of her old white canvas Superga sneakers and then posted a picture of them on Facebook. Her caption was something as simple as "DIY rainy day activity with my girls." Next, the comments started rolling in from friends who said, "I want those!" Ilana thought it was hysterical, and she called to tell me. The minute she shared their reaction, I said, "You need to make a brand! You need to sell these!" She was shocked. After all, she already had a successful career as an attorney, but I saw the potential of this side hustle.

I told her she needed a logo ASAP and that I would make her one. I went on Canva and ideated her brand name and logo. I came up with Splatterazzi, a mix of *splatter* and *paparazzi*. It was cute and felt buzzy. I designed each letter in a fun pop color of pastel and neon.

Next, we crafted the bio, which spoke to the idea that you could upcycle your old, existing accessories or give Ilana your new ones for her to splatter. We landed on her hashtag as #livecolorfully. Her whole brand would be about loving color, and she decided to make a bunch of samples—everything from Uggs to the plastic caboodles the kids need for sleepaway camp. She posted these images, which she took herself on her iPhone, and started taking orders. Fast-forward to today, and not only is she the moms' go-to for kids' personalized accessories that are both splattered and patched to order, but she's also transformed her brand into experiences. She created a brand extension called Splatterazzi To-Go, an at-home splatter paint activity kit. She also does private events. Her @splatterazzi Instagram bio is: One-of-a-kind private event experiences for kids to design! Shop custom splatter-painted styles for kids & adults. NYC based. #LiveColorfully.

Ilana's Instagram is her store window, and her followers expect to see her new designs there. It's simple and effective, and she shoots the product "flat lay," meaning just on the floor or a table. But to keep her brand's integrity consistent in every medium, she also designed the packaging. She makes a cellophane-wrapped item look custom by adding stickers of her logo so that every time she ships her designs, they show up in her customers' homes on brand and perfect for an unboxing video!

The purpose of her Instagram is to sell her accessories and promote her party business, and the people following that account know that from the start. If your social media account is functioning as your online store, then it's completely fine to sell all the time. But if it's not, you shouldn't always be pushing product. That goes for both your business and yourself. If you're a full-time content creator, where it's your job to post yourself and whatever brands you're repping day in and day out, remember that your community doesn't want to be bombarded by sponsored content all the time.

STEP 4. DEFINE YOUR BRAND VOICE

Content strategy isn't just about the images or videos you're posting. It's also about what you say and how you say it. Your brand voice might be that you're someone who values grammar, and your captions include full sentences that are perfectly punctuated. Or you might decide that you're never going to use emojis because you want your brand to give off an air of sophistication. Brands have style guides for both content and voice. When you're creating your presence on social media, it's helpful to think of these guardrails before you embark on posting.

Take Netflix's *Bridgerton* as an example. The show is set in 1813 London. Lady Whistledown is the narrator of the show, and she does so by reading from her weekly gossip newsletter. Her tone and voice reflect her position in society and the time. She starts every newsletter with "Dear Gentle Reader" and then speaks in an Old English vocabulary as colorful as it is biting to those she speaks of. So naturally, when *Bridgerton* considered their social media accounts, Lady Whistledown had to be the voice, and it works.

Take these tweets, for example:

> **"The Viscount's mind has been elsewhere as of late. This author cannot help but wonder what, or perhaps who, may be occupying his thoughts."**

or

> **"One cannot blame Miss Bridgerton for her response to such bizarre rituals."**

You feel as though Lady Whistledown is a real person who is speaking to you. Talk about staying on brand! It's perfect. If they didn't share one image on Twitter and all you had were these words, they would still be communicating their tale in a captivating and brand-focused way. There is nothing more powerful than the proper use of words and tonality to advance a story.

There are so many ways to play with your brand voice. When I was tweeting as DKNY PR GIRL, I was always a little coy. There was an element to my voice that made you feel the confidence of this character I was creating in my mind. She was your BFF but always just a step ahead. She had the closet you dreamed of and the access to the glittering world of fashion shows and celebrities that you only read about. I wanted people to be able to live vicariously through her. This account started a year prior to Instagram's existence, if you can imagine that, so most of my content strategy was truly just written. Through my Twitter and Tumblr (DKNY PR GIRL's blog), I provided an insider's fly-on-the-wall view into a world that was typically closed shut to outsiders.

As an individual or a brand, you can put together a list of adjectives that define you and ones that don't. If you do this simple exercise of listing words that you would never say and the alternatives to those words, you can start to craft your brand voice. For example, DKNY PR GIRL would never describe a piece of clothing as "cute." She would have said "chic." (P.S. I purposely used the word *girl* in her name versus *woman* to convey youth and spirit. That's probably why so many people thought she was a 22-year-old assistant instead of a 35-year-old mom of two!)

In the same way that you never would have guessed that Dan was Gossip Girl, your brand voice can be unexpected. (*Oops, sorry if that was a spoiler, but honestly—you should know by now.*)

For your personal social media accounts, of course, you're not going to make up some fake personality for the internet, but you can decide how you want your personal brand voice to come off. You could, however, create a made-up persona (or model the voice after a famous character) for a business account that is not your personal one.

DO THE MENTAL GYMNASTICS
Brand Voice

1. Is your social media brand voice that of a company or an individual? Will your captions say we or I? Pick a

lane here and be consistent. If you're putting together a
strategy for a brand/company, it's always weird to see
the word *I*.

_____

2. What's the vibe of your brand voice? Think in terms
   of adjectives, for example: *friendly, professional, fun,
   snarky/cheeky, inspiring, motivating.*

   a. _____

   b. _____

   c. _____

   d. _____

   e. _____

3. List adjectives that your brand would use:

   a. _____

   b. _____

   c. _____

   d. _____

   e. _____

4. List adjectives that your brand would never use:

   a. _____

   b. _____

   c. _____

   d. _____

   e. _____

It takes time and energy to come up with a content strategy for one platform, let alone several. These are people's full-time jobs. My recommendation for anyone starting out is to craft a plan that's realistic for you to execute. Consistency helps build a stickier following, because why should someone follow you if you're never going to post, right? But that said, you have many priorities in your life. So commit to what seems doable and see how that goes. If your goal is to build a community, then make sure you're regularly delivering for that community. That also means engaging with your followers' comments. You don't have to respond to everyone, but you should at least like each one (where merited). The more your followers see that you value their participation, the more they'll engage. In fact, the faster people comment on your posts, the more the algorithm believes that your content is worth serving up to other people who don't follow you.

STEP 5. DO A COMPETITIVE ANALYSIS

In the previous sections, you did a lot of internal reflection for what your social media content intentions are. But that's not all you have to do. Just like with anything else, it's important to understand the landscape and know what's already out there. Going back to your goal, find accounts that you admire or are already doing what you want to do. These can serve as examples (to model behavior) or make you aware of your competitors. You could also track accounts of people or brands outside of your industry to cast a wider net of inspiration and comparison.

If you're a founder, research other founders in your space. If you can't readily think of names, you can search by a hashtag like #FemaleEntrepreneur. If you're launching a single product, research other brands with a single product. You want to get as close to apples to apples as possible. For example, how a multibrand store plans its content is very different from how a store that sells one product does. Obviously, as a multibrand store, you have more to work with.

If you're an individual who wants to build a presence to increase your credibility on a particular subject, you'll want to research other people who speak on the same topic. This is not to copy their strategy, but more so that you understand how to make yourself stand out. Again, hashtags are your friends. Take advantage of them to help you research and learn what's out there. I'll share more about hashtag strategy later. . . .

DO THE MENTAL GYMNASTICS
Who Are Your Muses or Accounts to
Be Aware Of?

1. List five accounts you admire:

a. _____

b. _____

c. _____

d. _____

e. _____

2. List five accounts in your competitive set:

a. _____

b. _____

c. _____

d. _____

e. _____

Once you have the list of accounts you want to track, chart your observations by going through a few weeks of each account's content on a specific channel and categorizing their posts. Patterns will start to emerge.

- Notice the consistency (or not) of their content themes and how often they use them. Is there a consistent face of the brand?
- Observe their brand voice and how they speak to their community. Take note of both captions and comments back to their followers.
- Analyze their content mix. How much of their content is brand created versus influencer made or reposted? Note: If a brand is tapping into influencers, you can cross-check the content on the influencer's account. While the brand doesn't have to post a disclaimer on the content they post, the influencer must legally include some version of #ad #partner #sponsored if they were paid (or should be including it!).
- Track how much of their content is image versus video versus text posts.

In doing the above, you'll become crystal clear as to what you like and what you don't want to do. It's harder these days to track the engagement rate of other people's posts since some people on Instagram hide their likes, but you can still see how many comments or views they get per post. I should also point out that for videos, likes, comments, saves, and shares (engagement) tend to be lower because your primary call to action for a video is to watch it. There's only so much we can expect people to do.

STEP 6. MAKE CONTENT FOR THE MEDIUM AND TRACK YOUR PERFORMANCE

Today, with so many platforms to navigate simultaneously, it's essential to understand the content that works for that platform. One size does not fit all. Cater to the format that they are prioritizing.

The answer here is you have to play their game. There's no point in swimming upstream.

> **Pro Tip:** The best way to learn how to make compelling content is to make content. Play with these apps; try all the tools. Test and learn. Pay attention to what resonates and rinse; repeat.

The only way to know what's resonating with your audience is to track your performance. Like you did in that competitive analysis, look at each piece of content you posted, categorize it, and track its metrics. For example, did a video of you speaking to the camera consistently perform better than, say, a video of you giving a tour of something? Do images of people perform better than static images of other things? When you look at your impression volume and engagement, you'll be able to tell the winners clearly. Then you need to do more of that. Always keep your goal in mind, but don't discount your community. Give them more of what they want, but just make sure the content you post serves that goal and is on brand for you. For example, memes perform really well, but a meme may be off brand for some.

The other important factor is the use of hashtags. They matter. I hate them because they make captions look cheap and thirsty, but if you want your post to show up in searches, you must use them. You can space down and put them safely away from your caption or use a few in your caption sentence. Don't overdo it. Make sure the hashtags you use are relevant to what you're posting or you'll be shadow banned (i.e., your content will be suppressed). I loathe the look of many hashtags, but they do work. I try and stay with three at most.

HERE'S A BEAUTY BRAND CONTENT EXAMPLE

To help you imagine what a simple content strategy might look like, let's play with Company X, aka another celebrity beauty brand the world doesn't need. The first step is always a competitive analysis, as mentioned previously. Take notice of what you admire about their content and what you don't.

Here are some examples of the content buckets that I would recommend for this beauty brand. These ideas will get you thinking about what makes sense for you.

Content Buckets:

Mani Monday
Makeup trends
Must-have new product
How-to videos
From this to THIS (makeover)
New color trends
Exploring new beauty treatments
Satisfying makeup application videos
Funny beauty-related tweet (screenshot)
Makeup artist spotlight
We're obsessed with _____
Beauty hacks
What's in your makeup bag?
Self-care Sundays
Love it or leave it (sliding scale Instagram story on beauty trends)
Would you rather . . . ? (Instagram story poll on products)

But if, for example, you saw that your direct competitor had #manimonday as a recurring part of their strategy, that might be an idea you want to skip. It's always smart to become educated on what's out there. You can then decide what makes sense for you.

Think about what you want to convey and the different ways to put that topic through the lens of social media.

> **Pro Tip:** You need to stretchhhhhhhhhhhhh your key themes to have new content ideas every week. If you identify good content buckets, they will allow you to keep refreshing your brand while always staying on message.

STEP 7: DETERMINE WHAT IS TMI

People share a lot of their lives on social media, and it's a personal decision to divulge more of your authentic self online. When you know someone's bedtime routine with their toddler or someone's morning makeup regimen, it creates the feeling that you know them inside and out, despite never having met. This is called a *parasocial relationship,* and you have this with the celebrities you love. We'll dive into how to cultivate this affinity later.

But if you're a senior executive, how much is too much information? How far back should you pull the curtain? I was in a mentoring session one day when a woman shared that at her company, the senior executives were told that social media isn't appropriate at their level and that it's beneath them to partake. She explained that though this was years ago and is still the sentiment, she is now recognizing the importance of having an online presence. I couldn't agree more. If you're someone that people need to follow in real life, meaning you have a management role, it can only help solidify your expertise by sharing your expertise beyond the walls of your office.

Pro Tip: There is no rule that says that to be successful on social media you need to share the personal aspects of your life. *You don't.*

You can find a healthy and comfortable balance between your professional role and who you are as a person. The areas you focus on and strategically decide to leave out are up to you. Admittedly, there's something to be said about human connection. Giving people a glimpse into your life, interests, passions, etc., only makes you more likable. This is especially important for founders. People need to buy into YOU in addition to what you're selling.

To create differentiation between what's public and what's private, decide what is off-limits. For example, if you're a public person and want to maintain a private personal life, don't post pictures of your kids or weekends away with your partner. Don't bring family members to public events where media is covering. Don't talk about those aspects of your life, either. When you decide to show only certain aspects of yourself, you're building a wall between what is for public consumption and what is for you privately. It can be done, but there's one caveat: the people around you, your family members, for example, need to be in on the plan. If you're strict about what you share publicly, you probably want to make sure that the people around you abide by the same rules.

You are in control of the narrative you share, and if you choose to share those aspects of your life, you're making a conscious decision to mix the personal and professional.

For a well-known person, when their personal life becomes part of their social media content strategy, it can be an addictive drug to their followers. It is often the part that people want to see the most, and because of that, it might also be the content that gets the most engagement. That might make some people want to feed the beast, and then soon enough they're looking for ways to incorporate their personal life into their public life.

You see this happen a lot when celebrities or influencers become pregnant. Suddenly, every single thing they do for that baby becomes content.

Once you do that, you can't complain when others make your private life public. An easy example would be if a celebrity always posts pictures of her baby and then gets upset when the paparazzi is following her as she's wheeling her baby around in the park. She's exposed that child already. She's made that child press-worthy. You can't blame the media for doing their job, especially when you've sent a signal that you're comfortable with photos of your baby being public.

As you gain experience and possibly notoriety, people will naturally become more curious about who you are in your personal life. So, while you're working to build your personal brand, think seriously about which aspects of your personal life are on the table for viewing. Of course, the other consideration when making that decision is that sharing some of the personal parts of your life is what makes you, you. Why do we love Jennifer Garner's Instagram? Because it gives you a glimpse into her real life. It's her no-makeup, pajamas, and sometimes messy real life. Seeing that is what makes her even more of the girl next door. This real-life authenticity is also why everyone loves Tik-Tok. There is no filter, no pretense, and nothing is shiny and perfect. It's actually funny watching generally stiff businesspeople try and let their hair down (figuratively) on TikTok. Some people evolve to share this natural side. I bet for some, it's a huge relief to finally be themselves, but for others perhaps it's something that they had to train themselves to get comfortable with.

I'm a big fan of sharing enough so that people around you get a real sense of who you are and what's important to you. I am not a proponent of showing everything. Some things should remain personal and private. But it's not just about what you post that matters here or determines how personal your personal brand should be. It's also what you share verbally.

Divulging information about your personal life with colleagues can be tricky because it's easy to forget yourself and overshare. And once you start tangling your personal life with your professional life, you have crossed a line. If you're sharing with peers, there's not as much risk. But if you're a senior executive sharing with junior-level people, you're changing the dynamic of your relationship. You're starting to unravel something that was previously tightly wound. It's not to say sharing is a bad thing, it's just that once you go down this path, it's hard to go back.

10

Manage Your Reputation and Survive Cancel Culture

Celebrities . . . they're just like us. Well, sort of. Back in the early days of social media (*or shall I say back in the dark ages when celebrities didn't think they needed to have "online" presences*), there were people like Kendall Ostrow. Kendall's college days were filled with internships in radio. She loved the instant gratification of a daily produced show and engaging with listeners who called or texted the program. It was an adrenaline rush. Being able to touch the fans and create content on demand was exhilarating. But as new forms of media were taking shape, sites like MySpace were able to deliver that interactive real-time experience. The capacity to change programming and create impactful entertainment on the fly was incredible, but it also signaled to Kendall that radio might be dying.

Seeing what she thought was the writing on the wall, Kendall decided to move from Seattle to LA, the promised land of television and film. She started in the Page Program at NBC with the goal of wanting to be a talk show producer. Kendall was still after that "daily" experience. She purposely didn't pursue movies because of the lead time those projects take. She landed a job on *The Ellen DeGeneres Show*, hoping it would deliver that real-time, instant experience. But television was much slower than she expected, and she missed the spontaneity she craved from her experience in radio. Recognizing that she wasn't going to change the way shows are produced, she instead decided to try to convince them to join social media. Channeling her college days, she wrote a manifesto, albeit Jerry Maguire–style, on why Ellen needed to be on social media. Kendall was convinced that social media was the future water cooler conversation. Not everyone was convinced. It was 2007.

"I remember writing an essay quoting Cecelia Tichi's book *Electronic Hearth* and FCC Chairman Newton Minow's *Vast Wasteland* speech from 1961. For hundreds of years, families gathered around the fireplace after dinner to share stories and talk about their day, but as new technologies were invented, the 'hearth' changed. With each new technology, the centerpiece of the home and the driving force for popular culture changed too. In the 1920s, families gathered around the radio to hear radio dramas and plays. Then, in the 1950s families gathered around their new 'electronic hearth,' the television. I was convinced that social media would become the new 'digital hearth' that would drive culture and shape the American experience. I wrote a six-page college-style paper pitching the executive producers of *Ellen* that social media was the new water cooler, and that we would all gather around online to talk about entertainment and the things we love. I pushed them to have *Ellen* be the first talk show on social media and use it to engage with audiences—in the studio and out in the world—in real time. I knew that Ellen had to be on social media if she wanted to stay relevant and ahead of the curve," says Kendall.

Umm, I have chills. The truth is that some people are just intuitive. I had the same feeling in 2009 when I started on Twitter. It felt like we were a part of something big, something that would change the way we communicated and connected with each other on a global scale. I remember seeing a video by Erik Qualman, author of *Socialnomics*, on the Social Media Revolution and feeling completely inspired and validated that it wasn't just me who felt that something massive was shifting. Needless to say, Kendall's essay worked, Ellen clearly joined Twitter, and she was even included in Qualman's *Socialnomics* video:

"ASHTON KUTCHER AND ELLEN DEGENERES HAVE MORE TWITTER FOLLOWERS THAN THE ENTIRE POPULATION OF IRELAND, NORWAY, AND PANAMA."

As Kendall became immersed in social media, what intrigued her was really understanding how to convey a person's essence on social media. Being able to tap into someone's personality and understand what drove people to love them was intriguing to her. "I've been a *People* magazine subscriber since I was in fourth grade. I loved contemplating who these people were. What makes them tick? Why do we idolize and fall in love with Julia Roberts, America's sweetheart? What is it about Charli D'Amelio that captivated Gen Z? Why are we interested in them? Who were they in kindergarten? Who were they at their high school lunch table? What is it about them that draws a fandom? And how do you use the digital technologies at your disposal today to make friends and influence people? Even further, how can you leverage them to achieve your long-term or short-term career objectives and monetize your extracurricular activities?"

In her former role at United Talent Agency, Kendall went on to do just that, delving into the core of celebrity talent and building online strategies for artists, as well as brands, corporate executives, and creative intellectual properties. Along the way, celebrities went from shunning social media to valuing the platform it gave them to focus not on their starring role or press tour, but rather on who they really were. Kendall recalls actors sitting in her office crying tears of joy.

"It's not because they were upset or frustrated with what we were doing. The reason for their frustration was that audiences only saw them through the lenses of the characters they had played on-screen or onstage. The work we did together to figure out how they should show up online was the first time they had the freedom or space to have someone truly see them for themselves versus a fictional or exaggerated caricature. **Social media can be the deepest reflection of your public identity. Doing it right means you're sharing content that fans want to engage with, that you feel proud of, and that stands for who you want to become.** One of my real focus areas, and a big part of our secret sauce, was helping people hold up a mirror and see themselves for the first time, and then use social media to impact how the world sees them."

Building someone's social media strategy is a personal endeavor. Creating that authentic connection with your community cannot be undervalued. Making sure that the audience understands who is speaking matters. You might be thinking right now, *Do celebrities actually run their own social media accounts? Or are they ghostwritten?* "It is case by case. I think you can kind of tell when it's not the person. The people who are best at social are usually the ones that are doing it themselves," says Kendall.

This brings me back to my TV live-tweeting of *Scandal* days and #TGIT. Kerry Washington was a prolific tweeter, connecting very personally with her community. When she didn't have the bandwidth to tweet, her posts were signed "KW Krew." I loved this because it was truly respecting her relationship with her fans. Committing to authenticity cemented the trust her community had in her so that even when the "krew" was tweeting, we all knew that whatever they were saying was something that Kerry would sanction.

While social media today might feel like something that should be handled by a team, the impact it has on one's personal brand can't be minimized.

"I think we're at a place where social media managers assist and help their clients—they don't do it all top to bottom. They might help shoot, edit, draft, and optimize, to make sure it's good, but the content should always be personally touched and approved by the celebrity. If you're a public figure, if you're anyone in the world, this is something that's either going to hurt or harm you. And if it's not going to be from you directly and it doesn't at least have your oversight, why are you doing it? I think the most successful celebrities are the ones who have a content production team to help them capture and edit content—not someone to draft the copy, but someone to design the overall aesthetic, help you shoot and edit video, and take the content you're doing and slice it a million ways to make sure you're staying on brand and consistent. The best ones also have an assistant that's with them all the time to assist with capturing content. Some celebrities have rules that every makeup artist, stylist, hair stylist, etc., is supposed to shoot at least three pieces of content that is postable every day. The candid stuff is great," advises Kendall.

The other part that's challenging here is how someone nails your voice correctly. When the public thinks they're connecting with a person, not a brand, whether a celebrity or public figure, there's an expectation of personality. If someone is known to speak a certain way and then their social media voice is something different, it's pretty clear what's going on.

If you're trying to establish your personal brand online, this isn't the sort of thing that you can pass off to a team. Like Kendall says, though, there are many elements that can be supported by team members that already exist. They don't have to be people who work in social media. They could be anyone you train to understand what you're looking for from both a content capture perspective and your voice. Even with support, however, it's you who's being represented, and that's a really hard thing to farm out.

When you represent your brand, it can be especially difficult to allow someone to put together content in your voice, let alone post it. And even if someone is able to put together a content strategy for you, you'll still need to approve it. I've tried doing this for the LEAVE YOUR MARK Community and failed. Not because people who worked on it didn't do a good job, it's more that it felt off brand to me. It wasn't my aesthetic or the way I would speak, and if I'm massively editing someone else's work, I may as well just do it myself.

I pride myself on being authentic and always felt that posting in real time was an important pillar of my strategy, but the truth is, as you scale your business, you do need to hand over the reins to some capable people so you can focus on more important things. That said, there are ways to do it so you maintain that personal brand integrity while being able to get much-needed support. Leaning on people you trust to be thinking one step ahead of you, and looking for those moments that they know you'd want to capture, can become an integral extension of your brand (and brain!).

And that's exactly what Kendall recommends. "You can dictate to someone and have them help you workshop something. You can have someone look at your upcoming calendar and say, 'Is there something you want to say about this event that you're going to?' They can help prepare a shot list and make sure you have all of the correct hashtags and handles for each event. Or they can listen when you're recording a podcast or speaking at an event in order to help you pull out the best clips, quotes, and takeaways to post on social. You need a producer. Jimmy Fallon is still approving his own monologue, but a team of people is sitting in the writers' room to help him get started and shape the final draft. No matter what, the final product needs to come from you and sound like you. Social media is the most public form of your identity," she says.

And she's right. Whenever Kendall took on a new project, she'd sit down with clients to learn about their personalities and values. Who are they? What do they stand for? Who do they want to become? After that, she'd create a North Star strategy that defined what they should post on social media and what their public persona should be. Then she'd assist them in determining how to generate revenue around their passions.

"I love helping people figure out how to monetize their extracurriculars. Everyone else was focused on their acting roles or endorsement deals. I would ask, 'What's the book you've always wanted to write? If you had a podcast, what would that be?' By planting seeds on social media, we can help them achieve those goals. I really enjoyed helping my clients come up with a social media strategy that would help them gain cultural capital, garner influence, and become known in specific categories. **When people learn how to talk about themselves and their dreams online, everything else in their life begins opening up.** And once you have a sizable social following, you can extract insights from your audience that enable you to map the most impactful areas of opportunity for your career growth," says Kendall.

A big part of Kendall's work with celebrities—but also with companies, brands, creative IP, and even corporate CEOs—was heavily reliant on data and analytics. During her time at UTA, Kendall helped establish UTA IQ, the agency's market-leading data, analytics, strategy, and insights division. UTA IQ used more than 30 different commercial and proprietary technology tools to deliver critical insights to clients. This enabled Kendall to go deep into an artist's fan base. How big was the audience? What were the demographics and geographies? What posts truly resonated, which didn't, and why? How could she map talent to the affinities of their biggest fans, to confirm obvious opportunities (an actress that has "brand permission" in fashion and beauty) and nonobvious areas to explore (that same actress might also have real influence in a less obvious category, such as gardening, which could lead to her developing a new venture, nabbing an endorsement deal, or writing a book).

Data-driven insights not only helped Kendall's clients improve their use of social media and grow a more deeply engaged audience, but they also led to more creative and commercial opportunities. "We were using data so regularly, and in such a sophisticated way, that we saw clients beginning to get opportunities that otherwise wouldn't have come their way. Because of the size of their engaged fanbase, we were also able to significantly increase the value of those deals."

I always say social media is exhibit B right after your resume, and if you're someone who is being considered to speak at an event, be interviewed by a journalist, go on TV, or do anything publicly, the first deep dive people will do is in your social media.

Kendall adds, "So how do you write the headline of the future? How do you want people to be seeing you? How do you use social media to reshape those first three pages of Google search results? You really can shape your destiny if you strategically think about the goals you want to achieve and express those on your social media. Or you can phone it in, have someone else do it, and not be strategic."

The truth hurts, doesn't it? But she's accurate. The risk of not having your eye on your social presence is too great whether you're a public figure or not. Understanding how to navigate the treacherous waters when things go south is essential for everyone.

CAN SOMEONE PLEASE CANCEL CANCEL CULTURE?

Damn, it's hard to be on the internet sometimes. There are so many ways to get in trouble. If you're not terribly up-to-date on cancel culture, it's the mass "canceling" of a person in power and the removal of public support by mob culture. While some people would argue it's no more than online bullying, cancel culture has a deep impact on our society. People of course justify this because they believe the high-profile person did something to deserve it, and it's usually something that's socially unacceptable. Depending on the celebrity and the network the person has, their canceling might be short-lived. But it could also be forever and at the onset, dangerous.

In recent times we've seen people get canceled for everything from racism and antisemitism, to sexual assault, fetishes, cyberbullying, and more. If you kept a chart with dates of the offense and the next time the person has a new partnership coming out, you might see that cancel culture isn't dished out equally. Sure, some people have remained canceled, but there are many instances in which people have a very short memory and forgiveness is granted.

There are some good reasons for canceling someone who exhibits any of the aforementioned behaviors, but the punishment is completely subjective. One executive's social media post ended with them being fired, while another popular podcast host was basically left unscathed for making the same comment. That might have something to do with the latter's $200 million contract.

There are two schools of thought on cancel culture. On the one hand, it's toxic; and on the other, it might be instrumental in correcting bad behavior. Cancel culture campaigns are swift and unforgiving. You are guilty and must be proven innocent. There's generally not an opportunity to even explain yourself. The public decides—and they decide quickly and in masses. Because these situations can be so abusive, longtime friends and even family members may be intimidated to speak out on behalf of this person from fear that they'll be roped into the controversy. Those brave enough to support still might opt to delete their statements after the verbal abuse that follows. Cancel culture represents the opposite of freedom of speech. It doesn't even invite debate. It squashes people's ability to engage in a thoughtful and productive way. Being canceled can result in losing jobs, deals, wealth, and even your network, friends, or family. *Gulp.*

People spend years rising through the ranks of their careers, building their reputations, and in one swift move, the house of cards can come tumbling down. In corporations, we've seen that previous exemplary track records don't seem to matter when it comes to weighing whether keeping the person on staff will have greater societal or financial implications than firing them. Oftentimes, the opinions of company employees and/or customers also inform a CEO's decision whether to fire an executive who's slipped up.

We've seen people's pasts come back to haunt them. There's probably no greater example than former governor of New York Andrew Cuomo. During the height of the pandemic, Cuomo's daily briefings and PowerPoint presentations were the saviors of not just New Yorkers, but the American people at large. He also made international news and became a leading Democratic voice as "everyone's governor"; and many would argue his leadership was far superior to the president's. Not only was Cuomo comforting at a time of incredible uncertainty, but he also showed us how human he is. His casual demeanor during his news conferences made us feel like he was just like us and that we were all in it together. People speculated that perhaps this was going to be the spark that catapulted his own presidential career. But just as quickly as Cuomo became a superstar, he was ousted from not only the political elite but from society. Allegations of sexual harassment started swirling around him, and in just a few short months, his career was over.

This was an incredible shift in perception for someone whose personal brand was previously of the highest caliber. There are so many other examples. The lesson from all of them is that you can't rely on your personal brand to counteract bad behavior. The more senior people get in their careers, the more they believe that they can do whatever they want. Power is not a get-out-of-jail-free card. There's a false sense of security that people feel when they wield influence. If you own a company, it's easy to believe that because you're the boss, you can do whatever you want. You can't. Your employees, customers, and perhaps board members and investors will have something to say about that. It's the curse of hubris. It's the misconception that your secret is safe. That people wouldn't dare divulge the truth. But they're just waiting for the right moment.

THE SECRET WEAPON OF PERSONAL BRAND
MANAGEMENT: PUBLICISTS

Founders and executives of major companies today are under constant scrutiny. And for people who have gone from obscurity to having a leadership role and a public persona, the adjustment can be tough. In short, if they're not used to being under the microscope, they swiftly need to get acclimated to the intense analysis that will be made of their every move. And for anyone looking to build their personal brand, there are a lot of lessons to be learned from the experiences—good and bad—of these public figures. The PR pros who covertly help guide these executives are the true unsung heroes, and just like their clients' confidentiality, they, too, operate in stealth mode and stay safely under the radar.

I'm fortunate to have worked with some of the best in the biz, like my friend Jane*.

Jane has seen it all.

CEOs need to be highly effective communicators. This is not optional. In recent years (and this has certainly been escalated by the pandemic), the demand to hear their voices, both within their own companies and outside of them, has risen enormously. A company's culture and employee sentiment can rely significantly on how management communicates. It's not just about speaking well, it's also about being able to connect with people. Employees need to not only understand their CEO's vision, but also feel directly engaged in executing it. The most successful leaders do more than communicate; they inspire and motivate.

Of course, not every CEO or top manager is a natural at this. It takes work. And in some cases, when an executive is promoted to a

---

* I can't disclose who Jane is, but rest assured she's a seasoned corporate communications partner with decades of experience. Her firm positions companies and executives within those companies with the stakeholders they want to reach. She shapes how they're viewed in the outside world because, as we all know, the credibility of the CEO or founder can drive a lot of the public opinion of a company.

leadership role, a founder's business takes off very quickly, or someone gets catapulted to TikTok stardom, the transition from being an under-the-radar person to suddenly being the person whose tweets are screenshot means that this person needs to proactively think differently about how they communicate. The stakes are too high.

When Jane takes on a new executive client, she first must understand who she's dealing with and what they want to achieve in their business, in order to determine how their communication can support it. The main part of this audit is understanding how the person has communicated up to this point in their career. Do the employees know this person? How much does this person speak to the press and about what topics? Is this person on social media and is that a good thing? What does Wall Street think of this individual?

If this person already has a public voice, is it helping the business or not? If how the leader communicates isn't additive to the business, is it because the person isn't communicating enough, or is their style ineffective, unthoughtful, or even damaging? Once Jane has that level set, she can help her clients communicate in ways that reinforce the reputation they want to build and also ensure that all communications decisions made support their strategic goals. This isn't easy. "In high-profile roles, communications decisions require thought and, frankly, self-control. Leaders need to think about everything they say, from speaking directly with colleagues and business partners to what they share on social media, with a reporter, or with their investors—the full spectrum," says Jane.

As we know, there are certain people who can be on social media and those who should never be given a login. Of course, in doing her due diligence, Jane analyzes someone's full history across platforms. When you take that necessary trip down memory lane and find problematic posts, though, what do you do? You might wonder, can you delete old posts? The answer isn't simple.

Pro Tip: If you delete a post that's already had views, once people notice it's gone, the ramifications can be detrimental.

For someone in a high-profile position, you can't assume that deletion will go unnoticed and, in fact, it might draw more attention to something you didn't want to get attention on in the first place. It is something to consider carefully. Either way, you should proactively draft reactive messaging to answer why it was shared in the first place or why it was removed. This response should only be served up if necessary and you're being asked to address it.

Recognizing the scrutiny leaders are under, communications training for executives is an essential part of Jane's services, including for executives who've taken on roles that have put them in the spotlight quickly. **"There are no more bad days, no knee-jerk reactions, no thoughtless comments. People expect leaders to be leaders all of the time.** You're always on, and that's a learning curve. So when you have to climb quickly, we train executives to develop the presence they want to have when they are communicating with each of the audiences that matter most to them. Being able to deliver messages effectively and handle tough questions well and on your toes, are essential leadership skills," says Jane.

While you probably can't hire Jane, you can think through some of the steps she recommends to her clients.

DO THE MENTAL GYMNASTICS
Be Crisis Ready

1. Do your own due diligence:
    a. What is the history of your behavior?
    b. How do you speak to other people?

   c. What's already documented on the internet?

   d. What would colleagues past and present say about you?

2. **Assess your risk.** What you find in your research may yield problematic things, whether bad press or your own posts that are questionable. When thinking about deleting anything, though, you need to consider how many people have already seen it. Sometimes the answer is too many people, in which case you must weigh the risk attached to deleting something.

3. **Come up with a proactive list of challenging questions and answers.** Think about the tough questions someone might ask you. What would you possibly need to explain? Defend? Draft answers accordingly.

4. **Assemble a brain trust.** In times of crisis or any type of stressful situation, our brains can get paralyzed. It's important to know who you can lean on and for what. Think about your network and who might be able to lend counsel, legally or otherwise. Make a list of these people and their contacts, and invite them to be part of this unofficial group.

5. **Get clear on your message.** What do you want to say in response to a situation, and is that message going to help, or make it worse?

6. **Know your blind spots.** Do you have a sense of your weaknesses? Are you skilled at communicating in real time? Under stressful situations? Not everyone is. If you know you're better with prep versus on the fly, don't put yourself in a situation to answer questions without first contemplating the answers. For example, if you're someone who reacts without thinking things through,

a platform like Twitter probably isn't the best place for you.

SO, YOU THINK YOU'RE A THOUGHT LEADER?

"Thought leadership takes communications to the next level because it needs to come from a place of actual thought. If you want your personal brand to convey expertise, especially as the head of a company, you need to express ideas that are both unique to you and matter to other people," advises Jane.

Certain companies are so important to the economy or in society that it's worthwhile and even critical for their CEOs to communicate about topics that matter on a macro level—because people are interested in what they have to say and their views have an impact. They are thought leaders. But other CEOs may want to work to become thought leaders for specific business reasons. For example, is their company trying to attract a certain type of employee? Do they want to reinforce how their business is differentiated from their competitors'? Could a CEO's voice help to excite consumers?

Of course, developing the reputation of being a thought leader takes time, and people often wonder if it's a function that can be passed off to someone else. It can't. While an executive may be able to work with a speechwriter or ghostwriter to get their thoughts on paper, leadership starts with having the thoughts that set you apart. "The reality is that thought leadership essentially equates to someone who knows what they are talking about, bringing new information . . . great ideas . . . smart thinking to the table and garnering attention and respect from others about what they are saying. On the flip side, for people trying to establish their voices publicly, real trouble can start when they comment on things that they don't know enough about and that becomes clear. That is when you lose people's trust and create problems," advises Jane.

And as we've all seen in situations where people lose trust in a leader, that can pretty much be game over.

SHOULD YOU GET POLITICAL?

It used to be that you could keep your personal views to yourself, but the more successful you get, the harder that becomes. If you lead a company, your employees and often your customers want to know what you stand for and if it aligns with their beliefs. But what if your personal views are the opposite of those of your customers? Or the community who follows you? You are taking a risk by sharing them. Be aware that with transparency might come backlash. Half the country may not agree with you. There's more pressure than ever on leaders to say where they stand on issues, but not every company does, and not every leader has to. When major political or societal issues arise, leaders need to make decisions about which ones make sense for them to weigh in on and when. The most critical part of that calculation—for anyone—is that if you are going to weigh in on an issue, you must fully understand it and its impact on you, your company, and beyond. These decisions can never be made lightly.

Part of that decision-making process is whether speaking out is helping or hurting your personal brand. Even if you're not a CEO, consider how your colleagues and clients might react to what you're saying. If there's a cause you're super passionate about, weigh the pros and cons of making your view known publicly. Your voice doesn't need to be heard all the time. You can selectively choose what you speak up about. Says Jane, "The issues that people weigh in on are not always straightforward. More often, they are very complicated. You really need to know what you're talking about. So, I think the way people often get themselves into trouble is to go outside of the areas that they know well because they think there's an expectation that they should be speaking about the topic. But in actuality the expectation is that they've educated themselves enough beforehand to be talking about it."

DO THE MENTAL GYMNASTICS
Learn PR 101

Let me just start by saying this: All press is not good press. Fifteen minutes of fame doesn't necessarily benefit you, nor does it even have a long-lasting impact. Sometimes you can't come back from negative press. When you're rising in your career, it's exciting to get noticed. If a reporter calls you and wants to interview you for a story, you're flattered! But not so fast. Before you engage with a journalist, please consider the following rules:

1. **Rule number one:** Always review the media policy at your company before speaking to a reporter. You should also review your company's social media policy, because it's not only speaking with a reporter that can get you into trouble.

2. **Rule number two:** Reporters are not your friends. I have many close friends who are journalists, but let me be clear: you must remember that if they're contacting you for a comment, they want one thing, and that thing is a STORY. They do not have your best interests at heart; they have the best interests of their story at heart. That's not to say that they're trying to trip you up, but if you say something stupid, they're not going to correct you. The best way to prevent that is to go into an interview prepared, meaning knowing the messages you want to share and thinking through the likely (and tough!) questions and how you'll answer them.

3. **Rule number three:** Everything, and I mean everything, is on the record unless you explicitly discuss with the reporter BEFORE you start speaking that it's not, and the reporter has acknowledged that and agreed. There are three ways to share information with a reporter:

   a. **On the record:** Everything, including what you're wearing, your Zoom background, what you're eating, the expression on your face, and even your tapping foot can be documented. If you're meeting with a journalist in person, you need to know that everything is fair game. If something is on the record, anything you say can be used with no caveats, quoting you by name. When you read articles that say things like "So and so ordered a salade Niçoise and an iced tea, dressed in a crisp white shirt and slacks," that's on the record. When I interviewed Jane for this book, we actually cracked up laughing because the order is ALWAYS salade Niçoise.

   b. **On background:** This is an official term for "I will give you information and you can use this information, but it will not be attributed to me." "On background" is basically a contract. The information can be published only under conditions negotiated in advance. You and the reporter need to agree that the conversation will be "on background" before you start talking. If you're sending information via email, you need to establish this BEFORE you email the information. It doesn't work after.

   c. **Off the record:** This is when you're giving information that can be useful to the reporter, perhaps explaining a certain situation, but the reporter can't use the information in the article or attribute anything to you. It's more like a secret on the DL, FYI. That said, unless you have a good relationship with this reporter, you should always assume that whatever you're saying could end up in their story somehow. And just like with speaking on background, the reporter needs to agree up front to how the information is being shared.

4. **Rule number four:** While sometimes it's unavoidable, saying "no comment" or declining to comment can itself be a comment, as it can come across in a story as defensive or, worse, like you're hiding something. Often, if you get asked a question that you can't answer, the best thing to do is to say, "I do not have anything I can share on that very specifically, but here's what I can tell you about x, y, and z." Steer the conversation away from what you don't want to say, and try to give the reporter something of value.

5. **Rule number five:** Unless you're a seasoned speaker who has experience being interviewed by the media, always try to do any interview via email.

6. **Rule number six:** Don't be long-winded in your answers. The more concise and to the point your answer is, the more likely your responses will stay whole. If you go on and on, it's likely that the reporter will shorten your answers, and the parts they include might not be those you think are most important or might be taken out of context, or worse, make you sound bad.

7. **Rule number seven:** Reporters don't all cover the same things. If you want to pitch a reporter, make sure to research past articles the reporter has written. Nothing makes a reporter more annoyed than when you pitch them something that they don't cover. Don't waste a reporter's time. With quick research, you'll be able to piece together their style, tone of voice, and how they

cover their subjects. If someone is always snarky in their reporting, assume they'll treat you the same way. Make a thoughtful pitch that shows you're familiar with their work and are pitching them for that reason.

8. **Rule number eight:** Reporters have jobs to do. If you're not going to deliver useful information that can add value to their piece, don't pitch it or participate.

Remember that if you're talking to the media, you could very easily get asked a challenging question, one that is totally fair game given the discussion you're having, and you can't ignore it. When that happens, Jane recommends acknowledging what the person is asking you but also answering in a way that enables you to bridge to a fact that is more in line with what you're willing or able to share. You might consider the following types of responses: "That's a good question. I understand why you're asking that, and this is what I can tell you about how we think about the topic. . . ." Or "I cannot give you our specific sales figures, we don't disclose that information, but what I can tell you is that we are very proud that we remain the number one brand in our category according to the XYZ survey that just came out."

Being someone quoted in the media sounds like you've made important strides in your career. While it helps build your personal brand, it's also a very complex endeavor. Just like when you were little and your mother or favorite teacher advised you to think before you speak, the same rule applies. Fame just isn't worth it.

WHAT TO DO WHEN THE SH*T HITS THE FAN

We really never see this coming, so that's why, even if you're reading this and thinking, *This will never be me*, trust me—it can be you and it can happen at any point in your journey. You just never know when you're going to mess up and say or do the wrong thing. If that happens, here's what needs to happen next.

The first thing you should do is take a breath. The number one problem that we see when these things don't go well is that someone has a hasty response. While you may need to be quick, even very quick, in addressing an issue, your chief goal needs to be a measured response, one that helps a situation rather than inflames it. And there are times that can mean no response at all.

To determine what you should do, you really want to assess the damage, recognizing that what might look horrible to you might not look horrible to someone else. It really depends on the issue. And, consistent with that, you don't necessarily want to make big decisions on your own if you're upset or emotional. You want to get smart people on your side. If you're at a company, the PR team, legal, and HR are all resources for you and, for professional reasons, you really have to engage with them to help you determine the right next step. Your job could depend on it.

One route to take is often an apology, but that itself can be complicated (and also sometimes have legal ramifications). You don't want to rush into an apology without proper counsel and consideration. And if you do go on the apology tour, you must do it right. Why? Picking apart apologies is a new public pastime. *Was she sincere? Empathetic? Accurate? Remorseful?* You name it, they'll analyze it. Mean what you say and don't make excuses. You can't say, "I'm sorry, but . . ." You can't say things like "I'm sorry you feel that way. . . ." and expect to be excused. Both examples point blame toward someone else. Says Jane, "The public is really good at dissecting apologies, so they better be sincere. And what you often see is people do more than apologize. They give a sense of what actions they might take, including really learning about an issue they probably shouldn't have ever spoken out about in the first place or getting involved with an organization tied to that issue that helps people. There is no formula for how to apologize, only the reality that how you do it and if you mean it matters."

Then there's the subject of a track record. Does a track record matter? I would hope so. If you have a history of doing great things for a lot of different groups of people, then it makes sense to lean on that track record in your defense when you've said something wrong or that has been perceived badly. The language used, though, needs to be expertly crafted by people who do this for a living, so it doesn't sound like an excuse.

YOU ARE RESPONSIBLE FOR YOUR TEAM

"When in doubt, blame the intern" seems to be on a sign somewhere. Do not blame the intern. As you rise through the ranks, you might start hiring team members to help with different areas of your business. Perhaps you have a ghostwriter for your LinkedIn newsletter or an assistant who helps you with your social media. There are many ways to outsource work, and let's face it, your time might be better spent doing more meaningful things. Even though you're not doing the work yourself, and you're not personally posting, the communication and the message are still coming from your account. *You* are responsible for whatever is said, and like Kendall said previously, you should have approved it. Have people on your team who you trust and are trained to understand what is appropriate and what isn't. But regardless of their experience level, nothing gets shared until you have blessed it.

REBUILDING YOUR PERSONAL BRAND

It's pretty wild to think how long it takes to establish a reputation and how quickly it can all come crashing down. One wrong move, tweet, sound bite, and it can be game over.

You might think a bad decision can be addressed with a heartfelt apology, but that's just the first step. "Rebuilding your reputation is a process. You will want to do things that demonstrate progress, and show that you have learned from the experience and that your actions are sincere. In short, you need to show that you got the message loud and clear so you can start the process of regaining credibility, respect, and trust," says Jane.

Beyoncé and Lizzo shared the same experience (at different times) of fan outrage over the use of an offensive word in their lyrics. The backlash was swift, and they both apologized and immediately removed it. This was an easy fix for them, but worse offenses take a great deal more effort to repent for.

When you're making an apology, sincerity isn't the only thing people are looking for. The other essential factor is speed. Will Smith apologized for that famous Oscars slap in a video to Chris Rock in July when the incident was in March. Chris declined the direct apology and said he wasn't ready to talk. Many think it was too little too late. People are fascinated with how long it takes you to recognize your ways and make amends.

Pro Tip: Once you apologize, people really don't want to see you for a while.

You can't say you're sorry and then just get back on your normal social routine. If you snap back like a rubber band to the pre-scandal "you," they're not going to believe that you were really scathed or sincerely apologetic. You need to start from a bit more of a humble beginning. In truth, though, you need time to self-reflect and figure out how you got to where you are today. What were the missteps? What could you have done better? Noticed sooner?

You need to lay low and take a moment to reflect (or at least pretend you are). It's been years since Matt Lauer got ousted from his star position at NBC in 2017, and we basically haven't seen or heard from him since. People don't necessarily forget the past, but there is always an opportunity to rebuild your future. Unless, of course, you've done something really unforgivable.

11

Rebrand Yourself to Change Perception

You don't have to go through a scandal or social media crisis to need a rebrand. There are many reasons why you might want to shift how people see you. You could be a corporate lawyer who is going out on your own and looking to build your own client list. Or a doctor who's pivoting into medical device sales. You could be a freelance writer who wants to work in-house at a brand. Or a stay-at-home mom who wants to start a business. The scenarios are endless.

Everyone loves a second act. When you think about how you want to rebrand, consider the audience you need to affect. Depending on where you've been, you can strategize the types of people in your network to help get you where you need to go.

Your public interactions leave an impact on those around you. Sometimes we're oblivious to that impression, and part of your rebrand has to start with the reality that you need to change how you interact with others. Here are just a few examples of the kinds of ways this can show up.

POV: YOU'RE STARTING A NEW JOB

Starting a new job isn't only an opportunity to advance your career; it's also a chance to think of yourself in a new way. If you had to name three things you want people to know about you when you start a new role, what would they be? You have a new, exciting chance to shape perception by thinking through how you present from day one in your mannerisms, verbal communication, and visual identity. Yes, you've nailed that interview and have been hired, but the real audition starts when you walk into that office or log onto your first meeting. Good impressions still need to be made.

It's not easy to be the new person, but if you start by making sure you bring positive energy to the team, your transition will be way easier. If you usually take a little bit to warm up and for people to get to know you, consider putting the onus on yourself to be the one who is friendly and open. Make a concerted effort to smile. Be proactive about getting to know people by inviting them to coffee meetings (virtual or otherwise). Start with your team but go beyond it. Consider the different departments and key players you will need to build relationships with. Think of yourself like a talk show host—ask questions, and understand their roles and their history at the company and what they've done previously. You could also prep and do a little LinkedIn research before to see if you have any connections. Being interested in other people makes you interesting. But be prepared for the questions to turn back on you, and here's where strategy matters.

> **Pro Tip:** Get clear on your narrative before your first day.

What do you want people to know about your professional past? Come up with an answer that you rehearse (not kidding) on what to say if people ask you about your experience. What made you join the company? Why did you leave your last role? These are simple questions that can leave you feeling like a deer in headlights if you don't prep for them. While not everyone would stress over a simple question like this, you'd worry if you'd been laid off, fired, or pushed out. You can never be overprepared. The information you choose to share could be a part of or the whole truth. Note: You aren't obligated to disclose anything to anyone that you don't feel will help you succeed in your new professional adventure. I'd never recommend lying, but you could selectively leave out certain things.

Next, for your visual identity: Using fashion to communicate who you are before you've even said a word is a strategic and easy way to set the bar higher. How you show up says a lot about you. Being put together inherently says you mean business, and it also shows that you have your own best standards. It doesn't matter if you're an intern or an executive; when you show up looking polished, it says that you value what you're doing and where you're doing it. Remember how we used to obsess over our first day of school outfit? Well, there's a good reason. That good old saying "Dress for the job you want, not the job you have" still holds value. Bonus, it will make you feel great too.

Also consider what shape your LinkedIn is in. This is the very first place that colleagues will look the minute they learn your name. Of course, this should be up to snuff prior to interviewing, but it's always good to give it a once-over before you start a new role. Is your profile projecting the same image you just introduced to the company? What about your social channels? Do you want new colleagues or your boss to see those? Review them all to ensure that you're presenting exactly the way you want to be, even when you're not physically there.

If you haven't been working for a bit, it behooves you to brush up on some basics. This may sound silly to some of you, but work has changed drastically in the past decade. If you've never worked in a place where the main mode of communication is Slack, get to know how it works. Perhaps the last job you had was a Microsoft Word and Excel culture, but your new job cross-functionally operates exclusively on Google Docs and a never-ending game of "Tag, You're It" in comments. Depending on how old you are, you may not know that the double space in writing has been killed off. Are you aware of the most commonly used acronyms people in your industry employ to simplify their emails? There's a ton you can Google about your particular role and the terms and tools that are important for you to be adept at today.

POV: YOUR PERSONAL BRAND IS DUSTY

I've seen too many people who've held positions for a long time get comfortable with the status quo. They believe that their jobs are secure—after all, they've been there for ages! But the honest and self-reflective people know that deep inside, they were better and smarter "before." When time passes and experience grows, you can get left behind if you don't evolve.

> **Pro Tip:** At the exact moment you think to yourself how good you have it, you should take stock of what you haven't pursued in a while.

When was the last time you networked with new people in your industry? Outside of it? How long ago was your resume updated? Can you recall when you were last invited to attend or speak at a conference? Do you remember when you last learned a new skill? Have you recently shared your expertise in person and online? Presented a groundbreaking new idea? Tried to innovate in your role? Been quoted in the press?

If the answers to these questions are too hard to remember or simply no, we've got work to do. Your personal brand needs some Windex. Immediately start dusting it off by pushing yourself outside of your comfy, cozy, warm bubble. That bubble is going to burst, and you'll be safest if you come outside of it on your own terms. Relying on the status quo is the kiss of death. Everyone is replaceable. Start marketing yourself again to show that although you've been around for a while, you're still full of new, exciting ideas, and you're a force to be reckoned with. But it's not just your position you need to protect here. You need to plan for the future as well.

When you've had a long career, what comes next? How do you position yourself for a new opportunity? A future board seat? Or maybe even something grander? The answer lies in acting like every day is day one. Bring that same curiosity and drive to this new effort, and focus on the areas that have been ignored over time. **Your value hasn't changed; you just got comfortable and stopped protecting it.** It's time to show up again like the star you are. (*Please send thank-you DMs to me when you're done.*)

POV: YOUR PERSONAL BRAND IS "WALK ALL OVER ME"

There's a fine balance between being a stellar contributor who is always the first to say yes to things and someone who's chosen precisely because people know you won't say no. Of course, these tasks are presented as something only you should do because you're "so good at it!" You've always said yes and done the work because you wanted to be a team player, but after a while, you realized that you were the only one being handed the odds and ends projects that none of your peers were asked to do. (*Is anyone reading this always the appointed note-taker?*)

Even if your own plate was full, you still said yes in part because you didn't know how to say no. What if your colleagues got annoyed at you for not doing it? What if your boss would deem your saying no as laziness or being difficult? You mentally reason why you should say yes, even though you sometimes know that they're taking advantage of you.

When your personal brand means that people know they can walk all over you, examine why you're allowing that. When you have time to think your situation through, you might realize that your previous bosses never nurtured your confidence, and because of that, you always felt like you were walking on eggshells. Saying yes to things was your way of protecting yourself and ensuring you never got in trouble for not getting something done.

While being the person who says yes can be a positive in many ways, you need to make sure that you're being handed off meaningful work at least most of the time. I am a yes person also but in a very different way. I've always believed that being accessible makes you indispensable, but I can promise you that if my Spidey sense went off and I realized that I was always being asked to do the things no one else wanted to, I was quick to rectify that. And I'm also not suggesting that you don't have boundaries. There's a balance to the art of being an overachiever.

Once you identify the problem, though, you can slowly start to fix it. Repeat after me: *I am not a carpet. I do not let people walk all over me.*

Next, think about the personal brand you want to have. Of course, you'll still want to say yes when it makes sense for you to because that's your nature, but you can begin to draw some boundaries. Now, you may be thinking that if you say no, it will be unprofessional and aggravate your boss. Here's the trick: you're not saying no to say no. You're saying something like "I'd be happy to do that, but I have x, y, and z on my plate today and wouldn't be able to get to that until at least late tomorrow. Would you like me to switch gears and prioritize that instead?" Or try this on for size: "I've taken notes in the last five meetings. Maybe that's something someone else can do? I would really love to have a chance to contribute in another way." Statements like these show others that you respect yourself and value your time. You're still a team player and are happy to go above and beyond, but you are also making sure you are valued.

POV: YOUR PERSONAL BRAND HAS BEEN ON VACATION

Sometimes your personal brand needs a jump-start after some time off. You could have been burned-out, laid off, or fired; gone on maternity leave; or had to take care of a sick relative or even yourself. Regardless of the reason, it's been on hiatus due to circumstances probably out of your control. Sometimes, when you're so focused elsewhere, the last thing you're thinking about is your personal brand. But then, once whatever you're dealing with is over and the dust settles, you're left there a little less of a person than you were before. Or, shall I say, that's just how it feels?

When you're on a roll, especially in your career, and something halts your momentum, it can feel like you've lost your magic touch. If you've been out of the business, you might not be aware of new advances, tools, or trends important to what you do. Because of this, you might start to feel irrelevant. You are not. But that said, you do have to do a little work to gain back the confidence you lack because of your time off.

> **Pro Tip:** The success of a rebrand starts with your mindset. There are so many ways to count yourself out, but if you focus on your strategy instead, you can push past the self-doubt.

The first thing you should do in a case like this is to start reading. Bring yourself up to speed on what you've missed, catch up on what's happening in your industry, and get familiar with what people are doing and talking about.

Next, decipher if there are some key skills that you need to develop. Is there a course you can take to get them? What holes do you need to plug in your experience?

Then, come out of hibernation and reconnect with people in your network. Reach out to people to see how they are and explain why you've been MIA. If you're usually active on social media and stopped during this time, re-emerge and share your story. Explain what you've been up to, and your community will understand. It's never too late for your sequel, and now more than ever, people are empathetic when real life gets in the way of our regularly scheduled programming. Everyone loves a comeback.

POV: YOUR PERSONAL BRAND REPRESENTS YOUR FORMER SELF

We hear the word *pivot* more than ever. So much has changed since the pandemic, including our priorities. But sometimes, we want to become someone new to the people around us. I spoke about my pivot earlier in this book, but that's nothing compared to the extremes that someone can undergo. What do you do when everyone thinks of you one way and you need to reintroduce yourself as someone else? Maria Brito is a great example of an extreme career pivot.

Today, Maria Brito is an award-winning art advisor with A-list celebrity clients like Sean "Diddy" Combs, but she was once a corporate lawyer in a job that she describes as "soul-sucking." How did Maria pivot? She decided to start paying attention to the people doing the job she wanted to do. Maria grew up in Venezuela and was exposed to art and culture her whole life. She just didn't know it could be a career.

When Maria finally decided to take the plunge and quit her job in law, she didn't know what she would tell her network. She was afraid of what they would say and think of her drastic move. After all, who leaves a high-paying and stable job as a corporate lawyer to pursue a passion for art? She had no experience other than her culture-rich Venezuelan childhood and the affirmation from her friends that she had great taste.

Pro Tip: Don't let the fear of public opinion scare you out of making a big change. Practice telling your story so you can confidently explain what you're doing.

Maria decided that the best way to convey her passion for and knowledge of art was to start casually helping friends with their art selections, blogging, and sharing her finds on social media. By watching other art advisors in the space, she also knew what they weren't doing—and what they weren't doing was social media. When you want people to think about you in a new way, start talking about what *you're* doing that's new. Tell your friends and family and share it. The more people saw Maria conveying her art knowledge, the more she became known for art. But the other thing that started to happen is that people began recognizing her keen eye, and her reputation as an expert followed suit. Maria documents her creative journey and provides the tools and research to turn your creative ideas into success in her book *How Creativity Rules the World: The Art and Business of Turning Your Ideas into Gold.*

Pro Tip: Plans DON'T need to be perfect to share them. You can bring others along on your journey, giving them an insider's view of how you're shifting into this new career.

What's better than hearing a story about someone known for doing one thing and completely transforming into something else? **You need to own it, shape it, and share it. That's how you become it.** There will be a time when you're on insecure ground and when you might feel like a fraud. That's totally normal, but remember that the only person who knows you're not comfortable is you. You might need to fake it a little until the people around you notice your new persona. That's OK. Just know that confidence is contagious. The more confidence you exhibit, the more confidence people will have in you and what you're trying to do.

POV: YOUR PERSONAL BRAND MEANS YOU'RE CONSTANTLY BEING PASSED OVER FOR A PROMOTION

You're probably not going to like this, but if you can relate, you're doing your own PR wrong or not at all. The time has come to up your self-advocacy game. You might be doing a great job and are an essential part of your team, but you're not being valued because you don't value yourself—or at least not verbally. There are ways to rectify this, and it starts by making sure you're aware of all the great things you're doing. Immediately start documenting your wins and accomplishments. If someone sends you an email that compliments something you've done, save it. Compile everything great that is shared about you or that you accomplish yourself. Raise your hand for projects beyond your regular scope that you can own and shine in accomplishing. Then, figure out how to make these wins known. Set up a meeting with your manager at least three months before the typical review time to give her your own State of the Union.

Pro Tip: Everyone wants a promotion. To beat the employee year-end chorus, proactively set up time with your manager early so you can make your case before anyone else.

Then, you need to think like an entrepreneur pitching an investor. Here's what I mean: you need to convince your boss to invest in *you*. Prove that your efforts and results exceed what is expected of you and, therefore, you should be rewarded with money and a new title.

Gentle reminder: your salary is what you get for doing your actual job.

Present your wins in a slideshow deck or however you believe your boss will be most receptive. If you are declined, ask what you need to do in the next few months to get to that next level and be considered.

If you've done everything you've been asked and nothing happens, you might want to try a different strategy. A good pressure test would be to get another offer and take that back to your company for a potential counteroffer. If you do that, though, be prepared to leave if they don't bite.

POV: YOUR PERSONAL BRAND IS ALWAYS THE SIDEKICK

You're your boss's right hand, critical to the well-oiled machine your boss leads. You are empowered right up to the tip-top of your job title, but you've never managed to go beyond that because that was always your boss's turf. To be clear, you're the one on the sidelines listening and letting your boss shine. You carry your weight, but the optics around you are quiet. That's OK, though, because you're happy being number two and your hard work is recognized by your boss. You've mastered this role and can do it with your eyes closed. The skills you've honed are excellent but limited to your job description. There's no real issue here until your boss suddenly leaves unexpectedly, and you're told that you have a shot to take this top spot and prove that you're worthy.

Panic sets in because while you are great at your job, you've never been the frontperson. Hell, you've never even spoken directly to a client. You're the bridesmaid, never the bride. You're in every meeting, listening, taking notes, and diligently plotting the next steps. And now, you must step up and show that you're capable of filling your boss's shoes.

What's the game plan? How do you prove that you have the executive presence to make your stakeholders feel taken care of? How will you cultivate the respect of your peers?

Pro Tip: Managing up starts with you believing that you have what it takes.

After all, you've watched your boss for years. You can picture her voice negotiating with vendors and tackling issues head-on. You just have to model that behavior. The problem is that you're the poster child for imposter syndrome. You're not sure you're worthy, but you really would like that promotion.

Step one is getting comfortable being uncomfortable. Step two is analyzing the difference between your job description and your boss's. Be proactive by telling HR that you'd love to pitch in during this transition, but to do so effectively, you'd like to review your boss's job description. If you don't feel comfortable asking for this and want to be a little more covert, go on LinkedIn and start looking at the job descriptions with your boss's title from other companies. Circle the commonalities between those and your current role. You'll find that there's a lot of overlap and synergy. Once you identify the different areas, you'll know what you need to focus on. I would bet my life that the skills you need are ones you already have. You just haven't flexed them yet on your own. Don't let that scare you. You've got this, and more than anything, your goal is to show management that you can do it.

Everyone feels insecure doing something they haven't done before. It's not easy to have the buck stop with you, but if you break down what's needed into small tasks, you'll see that it's really not that different from what you already do. Don't miss an opportunity to shine! As they say, it always seems impossible until it's done!

POV: YOU'RE FIRED

Or about to be . . .

If we're being honest, your communication and management style has been questionable over the years. You get the job done well, so things have gone on, unchecked. Sure, maybe HR has spoken to you a few times in the past, but in the world today, your management style no longer works and necessitates that you evolve into something more than just results-driven. You need to become a camp counselor, therapist, best friend, and parent to your direct reports because the Employee Engagement Survey isn't painting a pretty picture. It's imperative to lead with empathy, advice, and guidance, but not everyone is cut out for that type of management, and your company decides that your services are no longer needed. You find yourself in the middle of your career, too expensive to land another role quickly.

What do you do first? You start frantically contacting everyone you know to see what new leads you can find. You reach out to countless recruiters and spray and pray your resume all over your industry. What you don't do, though, is take the time to understand why this happened. It's much easier to blame management or the economy rather than yourself. When people make drastic decisions for you that shock your system, first think about *why*. Why were you singled out? Be self-reflective and examine your history of behavior at that company. Is there a pattern to the feedback you've received over the years? Could you have managed your team differently? Extra points if you can ask for retrospective feedback from the people you worked with.

> **Pro Tip:** Honestly assessing your personal brand after a gut blow like a firing is essential to helping you learn and rebrand.

Recognizing your areas of weakness will steer you where you need to focus. Take a course on effective leadership and team building. Spend your free time volunteering at an organization or mentoring college students studying your profession. Arm yourself with activities that build your arsenal of skills and add value to your resume and LinkedIn. Show people that you're investing in your own education while helping others. This is how you change people's perception of you.

Besides the optics of what you're doing, your brand voice also needs to adjust. First, you need to assume that your reputation is known in the industry and the recruiters you're contacting are aware of it as well. Getting in touch with your softer, more empathetic side is an important counterpoint to what people may think about you. Be mindful that you're not slipping back into your old habits when interacting with people. Your tone matters, and unfortunately, once you speak one way, it's easy to make the unconscious mistake of doing it to others. You're naturally dictatorial, and you need to be sure that you're not continuing that practice with others. You especially don't want to do that to people who could potentially help you find your next job. Tap into your humility and recognize that you need to endear yourself to others. Spend your time reconnecting to people in your network and asking about what they're up to and how you can be helpful to them. If you focus on being of service to others, goodwill and opportunities will come back to you.

DO THE MENTAL GYMNASTICS
Rebrand Yourself

There are many more scenarios that might necessitate a rebrand. Whatever your inspiration is, and especially if you're not gaining the exposure and credibility you think you deserve, follow the steps below to self-assess. These 15 steps work exceptionally well in combination with the content strategy chapter in this book.

Try These 15 Steps:

1. **Self-reflect:** Understand where you are today and what your personal brand stands for currently. Answer the following question:

   a. Why do I want to rebrand myself?
      » I want a promotion
      » I need a new job
      » I want to change industries
      » I'm not being respected in my role
      » I have no executive presence
      » I want to launch my own company
      » I was laid off
      » I was fired
      » I'm not attracting new clients
      » I need investors
      » I made a public mistake
      » I want to build a community
      » I want media attention
      » Other

2. **Ask for feedback:** No one ever wants feedback, especially critical feedback, but if you're going to evolve, bite the bullet and hear what people you trust have to say about you.

3. **Put your social media bios to work:** This is the first place where your rebrand gets the spotlight. Make sure they help convey the new you and are consistent across all platforms.

4. **Update your website:** Create an online presence that supports your goal.

5. **Nail down your story:** When you proactively craft your own narrative, you explain what people will inevitably wonder about. This is your new elevator pitch. Tell your story so others don't have to make up their own version. But more importantly, give people the tools to communicate your story on your behalf. If you've done something that necessitates an apology, make sure it's sincere, well written, and critic-proof. Go back to the section on reputation management in this book, and take a deeper dive.

6. **Assess your online reputation:** What is out there? Do a Google search to understand the state of your personal brand online. What are people saying about you? Your business (if applicable)? How can you create content that counteracts what you're seeing? Bad business reviews? Strategically aim to get new, positive ones. Negative press? Pitch a new story to change the narrative. Give Google something else to serve up! Set up a Google Alert for your name to keep abreast of anything else that may pop up.

7. **Clean up your social media:** Do an audit of your channels, and delete anything that doesn't align with your brand filter. Reminder: if you have a following and something questionable or in poor taste has been viewed many times, there is a risk in deleting it. I still believe that if the post reflects poorly on you, it's better to remove

it, but you must think about a statement as to why you removed it just in case someone notices. Go back to Chapter 10 for more on reputation management.

8. **Strategize a plan:** What proactive steps can you take to reinforce your new mission or reverse some of the negativity surrounding your personal brand? Some of the things you can do include volunteering, networking, public speaking, being a guest on podcasts relevant to your business, press, and of course, your own content strategy.

9. **Stage your fake press conference:** Anticipate what people might want to know, and make a list of possible tough questions you could be asked. Proactively draft responses and practice delivering them. This means actually saying them out loud to another human. Thinking of answers is not the same as speaking them.

10. **Refresh your brand voice:** No, I'm not suggesting that you change your voice like Theranos's infamous founder, Elizabeth Holmes, did, but if you're trying to level up, consider how you communicate.

11. **Create a brand filter:** Get clear on what you should align with and with what you no longer should. Make a list of topics that you should be speaking about (they should support your goal) and ones that you should let someone else have airtime on. Your filter should dictate everything you do and say.

12. **Model behavior:** Identify what you want to be known for now. Set your sights on your goal, and study people who do what you want to do well. What do you like about what they've accomplished? How do they present themselves?

13. **Analyze your competition:** While it's great to find muses who can inspire the person you want to be, you still need to stand out and establish your own unique selling points and style.

14. **Tell people:** Reintroduce yourself to your network, and help them understand where you're going in your professional life. Remember that the more you reinforce who you are and what you do, the more you'll become synonymous with that. If your rebrand comes after a misstep, keep in mind that if you don't add your voice to the mix, the only thing people will hear is other people's versions of your story. It's your story. You need to be the one to own it and steer public perception, but do it carefully.

15. **Share your progress:** Rebranding can be scary. Have the courage to stick with it even when it might feel like it's not working. To help you along, make sure to share any positive outcomes with your network. Whether it's landing a new client, investor, or opportunity, let people know that you see results. Doing so helps you position yourself and solidifies your rebrand in the eyes of others.

12

Beware of "Zero F**ks Given" Branding

This book is geared toward people who want to create an impactful personal brand. I hope you're someone with a strong belief system who will do some good—not just for yourself, but for others. But if I'm being accurate, having an effective personal brand doesn't necessarily mean that you're likable or do anything positive in the world. Countless people are excellent marketers of themselves with a personal agenda that we may not admire or aspire to. I like to call this special crop of people the "Zero F**ks Given People," aka ZFGP. While you may assume these people need a rebrand, they are purposely doing and saying whatever they want to and proving that when you don't care what other people think, you essentially live by another set of rules.

ZFGP have decided that public opinion matters less than staying true to who they are and how they want to be heard. They have a laser focus on who they market to and essentially block out all other noise. They have an uncanny ability to completely ignore criticism, and insults just bounce right off them. By the way, there are some positives to being a ZFGP. Sometimes we admire their brazenness and courage to express themselves freely. Other times, we might resent them, and that is usually when we don't agree with what they are saying or doing.

ZFGP are often memorable in their own way, having a signature style or look that they become known for. They're usually people who are very outspoken in person and online. They are not afraid of getting into a war of words with anyone, and they don't back down when things get heated. Sometimes, they are the fire starters as well.

The most interesting thing to note about these people is that, while they are not people-pleasers, they find their audience. On the one hand, the people who admire this behavior usually have a similar disposition. On the other hand, for the people who are opposite and might be appalled by this behavior, the ZFGP are fascinating to watch. Therefore, they tend to build a diverse audience of fans and haters. Either way, they love the attention. You probably have specific examples that come to mind in the public eye or even in your own life of people who fit this bill.

It might appear that these people are those who speak without thinking, that they're erratic and fly-off-the-handle types. But many know exactly what they're doing. They are fueled and empowered by their audience's reaction. In fact, if the audience disappeared, that would be their kryptonite. They need the audience to validate themselves.

It's easier to be a ZFGP if you've already made it in your career. If money isn't a worry, and you're someone who owns your own business, the risks might not be as high. A ZFGP might not have to answer to anyone, making this person feel even more powerful. Sometimes, though, a board or key shareholders may decide that the person is no longer suitable for the company. Other times, it's precisely this behavior that drives the media mentions of this company. Especially when a company might not have the budget to spend on advertising or doesn't want to, the ZGFP does the job of keeping the company in the news. It's really a catch-22.

But then there's also a watered-down version of ZFGP who have taken the "I'm really honest and just being myself" plea, and that in and of itself is permission to do and say whatever you want. Alison Roman is an excellent example of this type of person. If you haven't heard of her, you're probably not that into cooking. She is a Brooklyn-based cook and writer who is a millennial favorite. Alison knows that while recipes are easy to come by, what makes her able to cut through the noise is the decidedly casual, if not ordinary, way she presents herself and her cooking.

As part of her personal brand, she's careful to keep things price-conscious, and while she takes inspiration from travel, she's also quick to point out when she hasn't been to a place. Downplaying her access or wealth seems to be a part of her schtick.

Her book, *Nothing Fancy: Unfussy Food for Having People Over*, became a *New York Times* bestseller and hit the mark with hundreds of thousands of fans. People who follow Alison know that she often says whatever's on her mind, and that habit of saying whatever's on your mind can get you into trouble.

In May 2020, Dan Frommer interviewed Alison for *The New Consumer* in a piece titled "What Alison Roman wants: The cookbook author and writer on balancing business with brand, how she creates recipes, and what she's doing next." In that now-famous interview, Alison shared her thoughts on some of her internet-famous peers, specifically Marie Kondo and Chrissy Teigen. She remarked on how both have parlayed their internet stardom into books, but what seemed to bother Alison more was that those books became a platform to generate brand deals.

This quote about Chrissy kind of says it all:

"What Chrissy Teigen has done is so crazy to me,"
Roman said at the time. *"She had a successful cookbook.
And then it was like: Boom, line at Target. Boom, now she has
an Instagram page that has over a million followers where it's
just, like, people running a content farm for her. That horrifies
me and it's not something that I ever want to do. I don't aspire
to that."*

Ouch. Please note that high-profile brand deals equate to making a lot of money. But this whole time, Alison has been playing the role of "You like me because I'm just like you!" If her personal brand is dependent on relatability, that connection starts to dissipate once we see her rack in the millions in brand deals. Hmm, food for thought (no pun intended).

> **Pro Tip:** There is such a thing as too much honesty. Every person must have a working edit button on the thoughts that pop into their head and weigh the repercussions of expressing them.

It should come as no surprise that Alison got into a very public scandal with both stars and then needed to apologize to them. The whole episode was documented and weighed in on by the stars themselves and, basically, every existing Twitter user. It wasn't lost on many that both stars are of Asian descent, which opened an entirely new angle to the already insensitive thing to say.

This is where saying exactly what you're thinking can really backfire. As a trademark to her persona, Alison's off-the-cuff, almost improv personality was a little too transparent. If we're being honest, some might read it as bitter. What's ironic is that she herself was promoting her own brand collaboration of cooking tools. The aftermath of this was ugly, and while the flames eventually died down, it was brutal for Alison. Her personal brand temporarily became synonymous with cutting other women down. Her apology noted her insecurity and admission of white privilege, but it's hard to come back entirely from these moments. I don't doubt that her brand of "I'm just being me" doesn't feel quite that comfortable anymore. Alison ended up stepping down from her role at the *New York Times*, where she had a popular column.

> **Pro Tip:** Becoming a ZFGP has high risks associated with it and is not for the weak or weary. You have to be Teflon. Abuse needs to be able to bounce off you.

Chrissy, who was previously a fan of Alison's, expressed public hurt at Roman's comments. You might have felt bad for her for a moment—until 2021, when Chrissy, who has always presented as a ZFGP on Twitter, was outed for bully behavior that happened a decade earlier.

> **Pro Tip:** ZFGP are not immune to the collective memory of the internet. Your words will always come back to haunt you.

In 2011, Courtney Stodden rose to fame at age 16 after marrying a 50-year-old acting coach. The internet, including many celebrities, piled on with a vengeance, calling Courtney every name in the book. The online abuse was off the charts. Chrissy joined the ferocious chorus with a series of tweets bullying Courtney. The tweets may have stayed swept under the rug— except that the internet is written with a Sharpie. Courtney came out in 2021 and exposed all of this with time-stamped receipts from Twitter. In just a few days, Chrissy's cookware line, Cravings, was quietly removed from Macy's website.

Pro Tip: Being a ZFGP makes you a liability to brands and may cause you to lose deals or, worse, be added to a "do not partner with" list of people.

The irony of this scandal can't be ignored. The hate was like a boomerang, with both scenarios resulting in loss of credibility and partnerships. Being a bully of any measure will never add value to your career, but then there is a different set of rules for a ZFGP who's also a convicted criminal, albeit one who we are fascinated with.

Enter stage right . . . Anna Sorokin, aka Anna Delvey.

Anna Delvey is a ZFGP in a totally different way. Her masterful execution of personal brand-building was the smoke and mirrors meant to mask the con she was really pulling. In case you missed it, Anna Sorokin pretended to be a German heiress. Anna, however, claims she never actually said she was a German heiress and that people just thought she was a millionaire of their own accord. She swindled some seriously significant people, banks, hotels, and her best friends out of an estimated $275,000, all while raising millions for the Anna Delvey Foundation, an art/social club for which she was fund-raising.

Pro Tip: Carefully plotting your visual identity with the brands and people you associate with and tailoring that to your audience can directly benefit your goals.

Add the above strategy to a ZFGP, and we understand how Anna went full steam ahead with her plan. When she arrived in New York City, her first order of business was immersing herself in the scene. Her desired network was a healthy mix of the fashion and art worlds. When you think about Anna's personal brand, she ticked off all the boxes of a *Gossip Girl* character, including living like Chuck Bass in a hotel. She played the part perfectly, posh and polished, living the life, albeit on someone else's bankroll. While she proved she was adept at swindling, she was building her brand by her own admission.

Her tactics were illegal, but she believed in her purpose, and her personal brand was extremely well defined. When Alexandra Cooper of *Call Her Daddy* podcast fame asked her how she convinced all these influential people at banks to commit millions to her mission, she explained that she actually downplayed her visual identity. She made a conscious decision to look casual, with the mentality that she was so legit, she didn't have to prove it. She didn't need to impress the bankers; they needed to impress her. She believed they were lucky to have the opportunity to invest in something like the ADF, which according to Anna would be huge. Only a ZFGP would do this.

I believe every decision Anna made was calculated. Her clothing, hotel, travel, and restaurant choices all pointed to the reputation she wanted to have as an "It" girl and someone who had an important place in society. Of course, she funded her lifestyle with checks that could never be cashed and fake wire transfers. It was all pretend, and everyone she contacted bought it.

Anna's case was brought to trial in 2019. Staying true to the personal brand she'd built, she even had a personal stylist prep her looks for court. She cared so much about her appearance that she reportedly refused to enter the courtroom because the outfit she was given wasn't up to her fashion standards. (*Have you ever?*) She was convicted of grand larceny and theft, sentenced to 4 to 12 years in prison, fined $24,000, and ordered to pay restitution to her victims. She was released in February 2021 for good behavior but then got picked up again by ICE (U.S. Immigration and Customs Enforcement) due to her expired visa status. She was then moved to an ICE detention center.

That however, did not stop Anna from curating her personal brand on Instagram. She posted a sketch that illustrates her sitting on a giant slab of ice that says "Anna on ICE" in the ICE facility; the illustration appeared in *Cosmopolitan* magazine and is captioned "Me on ICE in @Cosmopolitan by @emilyepalmer." Countless other posts cover her press coverage from both the Netflix series *Inventing Anna* and other interviews she's done. In October 2022, Anna was released from the Orange County ICE facility after paying $10,000 bail. The conditions of her release include 24-hour house arrest and no use of any form of social media. At the time of this writing, her deportation remains to be seen. Is she sorry? Her Netflix income of $320,000 paid off her restitution and legal fees. She is reentering the art world and hopes to ". . . be given a chance to like focus all my energy into something legal," Sorokin explained to NBC's Savannah Sellers. "I'd love to be given an opportunity for people not to just dismiss me as like a quote-unquote scammer and just see what I'm going to do next." On her website, she's promoting and selling her art prints and NFTs. I think Anna knows exactly what she's doing. In her case, you might say being a ZFGP has somewhat paid off.

ZFGP are master marketers. They know how to manipulate the way you think. In some cases, they're so charming that you might be sitting there secretly rooting for them. I mean, I kind of want to be friends with her. Go read the comments on Anna's Instagram feed. You'll find comments such as "ICONIC," "ADF should still happen," and "TEAM ANNA." She's magnetic and people love her, and even if they don't, everyone can agree she was able to pull off the personal brand of a life she didn't have. While I'm certainly not recommending that anyone follow in Anna's footsteps, it's worth noting how she was able to shape perception to suit her needs. And let's face it, she stole from hedge funds and banks with little human capital expense. No one is crying for them, and maybe that's the secret. It will be interesting to see how her story plays out, but for now, Anna will continue to build her brand, proving that a personal brand in combination with being a ZFGP is a potent combination, even though it just might land you in jail.

PART THREE
Sustain Your Brand

13

Develop a Signature Look and Establish Your Visual Identity

Creating a signature look and a consistent visual identity is a powerful and effective way to reinforce your personal brand. Your choices are making a statement whether you intend to or not. Nobody's exempt from this. (*I might add here that you are guaranteed to run into the person you least want to see when you're not put together.*)

Anna Delvey used fashion as a potent weapon in her strategy by both playing herself up and down to suit her goals. While I'm not discounting her criminal behavior, I am pointing out how she leveraged these elements to create an image used to shape perception. Your visual identity is an extension of who you are, and you, too, can leverage it to convey or extend your personal brand and personality. When you do this well and for public consumption, you become an influencer. I'm sure there are many people who bought her thick black signature glasses after watching *Inventing Anna*.

Signature is the key word here. Steve Jobs wore his uniform, a black turtleneck, every day. Anna Wintour has never changed her short bob. Mark Zuckerberg made the hoodie a Silicon Valley staple for tech entrepreneurs. Each of these icons has different motivations for sticking with their well-known looks.

> **Pro Tip:** Whether for convenience, comfort level, or statement, committing to a signature look day in and day out becomes yet another thing you can be known for.

I wear red lipstick every single day. My nails are always red as well. That's simply my preference—it's how I feel the best—but it's inadvertently also become my reputation. It's not an accident that there's a red lip stain on the cover of *Leave Your Mark*.

Your look tells a story and can be used to paint a certain image. Once you decide on your goals, you can use fashion and beauty to support you in playing the part. Just like a character in a TV show or movie, the style you exhibit can help shape your story.

My friend Lyn Paolo is an Emmy Award–winning costume designer for countless shows, including *Inventing Anna*, *Scandal*, *Shameless*, *Animal Kingdom*, *Little Fires Everywhere*, and back in the day, *The West Wing* and *ER*, to name just a few. She and her career are incredible. When Lyn is working on a new show, the first thing she thinks about is how to express this character through what they are wearing. When Shonda Rhimes's *Scandal* was on the air, I live-tweeted the show every Thursday night as DKNY PR GIRL. Olivia Pope, the crisis management PR guru played by Kerry Washington, was the heroine we didn't know we needed. But beyond her stellar "fix it" skills and her ability to handle everything that came her way, her style spoke volumes. I can't think of another character on television who became so respected for their style that she ended up having a *Scandal* collection at Saks Fifth Avenue. That's a credit to Lyn and how she conceived Olivia's wardrobe.

Lyn and Kerry were aligned on Olivia's style, as explained in *Variety*: "Washington's character, Olivia Pope, would be a glass ceiling–shattering heroine from the moment she opened her closet. She would be successful enough to afford Armani, Prada, and, in a nod to Paolo's native England, a Burberry trench." Since Olivia was always on the side of the good guys and seeking justice for her clients, Lyn dressed her in a ton of white. White is the hardest color to light on set, but Lyn's credibility as a costume designer held more weight and the lighting director obliged.

Olivia's success was also evidenced by her signature Prada bags. The first time I saw her carrying a Prada bag, I made a mental note thinking how interesting it was that a Prada bag wasn't pretentious for her even though she was saving the lives and reputations of her clients. She could still have luxury and be feminine. Lyn explains, "I wanted to feel her femininity. Whenever there's a strong woman on any show, it was assumed that she couldn't be feminine. When I was doing *The West Wing*, I would do interviews, and they would constantly say, 'How should a woman politician dress?' I always wondered, why are they asking this? She should dress any way she wants to, and she should ultimately be feminine. In her strength and brilliance, Olivia could be a gladiator in a suit, but there was this thing of 'OK, but does it have to be a masculine suit?' That was my first question talking to Shonda (Rhimes) and Betsy Beers at Shondaland. I said, 'You've cast us a stunning woman (speaking about Kerry Washington). Shouldn't she stand out in a room full of men?'" Lyn also purposely put her in platform heels to ensure that Kerry was stable enough to walk as Olivia with power and purpose. These decisions were strategic and thoughtful.

When I contemplate the thought process that Lyn employs to bring her characters to life, I think that each of us can use it to direct our own roles. How you dress for a presentation, for example, will make an impression on your audience the minute you walk into the room. People can't help but make split-second judgments. Red is known as a power color. If you're doing a presentation and show up in a red dress, you're telling people that you're confident you will succeed. Or perhaps wearing a suit and tie gives you that extra jolt of strength. How we feel when we dress can affect the outcome of how we perform.

When you envision your goal, whether it's crushing a job interview, negotiating the promotion you want, or nailing a client or investor pitch, you must visualize yourself showing up to claim that top spot. What are you wearing? We speak a lot about aesthetics today, and understanding what yours are or should be can only help you. You might tell me that you're more in the Steve Jobs camp, too busy to be bothered thinking about what you wear, or that fashion is frivolous and you're saving the world and don't have time to care. That's your prerogative. Steve Jobs chose his signature look out of utility and reduced the amount of seemingly insignificant decisions he needed to make in a day to make room for the important ones. But even in choosing a repetitive wardrobe, Jobs was making a statement that pointed to his overall personal brand, which came off as stark and minimalist. His turtleneck, by the way, was by designer Issey Miyake. It sold for $175 back then. Today, it's around $270. Choosing that black turtleneck versus one from the Gap is a personal brand choice. Of course, it's one born of privilege, but it showed that Jobs valued great design and luxury. We know this is true anyway, given the products he invented. Of course, this is the same turtleneck that the infamous founder of Theranos, Elizabeth Holmes, chose as her signature, clearly wanting her personal brand to mirror that of Jobs, someone whose career she worshipped.

Style is transformative, and we need look no further to understand that than in some of the best style makeovers we've seen in film. Andrea Sachs in *The Devil Wears Prada* starts her career as Miranda Priestly's assistant, wearing frumpy, ill-fitting clothes. She can't do her job and fumbles every task handed to her. But once Andy gains experience and gets access to the fashion closet at *Runway* magazine, her confidence goes through the roof. Suddenly she's wearing Chanel and rocking her job. It's not a coincidence. Of course, most people can't afford Chanel, but if you take care with how you dress regardless of labels, you're putting your best self forward and reinforcing your brand. When you're visually put together, people will assume you're buttoned-up in other aspects of your job.

My friend Elizabeth Holmes—no, not THAT Elizabeth Holmes—wrote a book on royal style called *HRH: So Many Thoughts on Royal Style.* She dissected every fashion choice that Queen Elizabeth, Princess Diana, Kate Middleton, and Meghan Markle wore and the strategy and meaning behind those choices. You might be thinking, *How would what the royals wear ever influence me?* But taking cues from their strategy is actually beneficial. When a celebrity steps out on the red carpet, their goal is to get press coverage on what they're wearing. They do interviews about what they're wearing. Every aspect of their look is considered and will be talked about. It's different for the royals because, as Elizabeth rightly points out, they don't really speak. Their function is to appear, and therefore their everyday wardrobe does the talking for them.

"It's not celebrity fashion," says Elizabeth. "Celebrities are there to razzle-dazzle and wow. There's certainly an element of royal fashion that is about that, but their fashion is a working wardrobe. These women are stepping out in very publicized engagements regularly, so they have to craft this visual brand. They are not the people who talk to the media all the time. They don't give big speeches. They don't sit down for interviews. They're not sharing their feelings all the time. Certainly, Meghan and Harry have changed the game a little bit because they are more vocal and have been since they've left the royal fold, but by and large, members of the royal family do not do much talking. They appear, quite often, and those appearances are highly publicized and celebrated and covered in every fashion outlet. They use their fashion to communicate without speaking. If their outfit gets coverage, it also helps publicize the cause they stepped out to support. They use fashion to promote their royal work."

At the very base level, they strategically use color to direct their fashion choices. "When you talk about royal fashion, you can talk about color because that's something that requires no fashion expertise to understand. Anybody can see what color someone's wearing. If you close your eyes and think of what the Queen wore, it was usually a bright color so that she stood out in a crowd, whether she was waving on the balcony or when she got out of the car. It served a purpose, and that's so important. When you're getting dressed in the morning, think about the color you put on and what it says about you. And then there's also the idea of choosing a signature color," says Elizabeth.

Elizabeth did this incredibly well with the launch of her book. The cover was a very specific light blue, so she decided that she would also wear that same color for her entire press tour. That color became so synonymous with Elizabeth that people started tagging her when they saw that color in the wild.

You don't have to know fashion to understand that you can choose a signature color based on a company logo or a time in your life that's important to you to create a reputation. My friend and *New York Times* bestselling author, Dave Kerpen's former company logo was orange, and you could always catch him in at least one article of clothing that was orange. He never missed a moment to reinforce his brand. Author, *Money Rehab* podcast host, and my badass friend, Nicole Lapin, was photographed sitting on a wad of cash and wearing a green dress on the cover of her book *Miss Independent*, and you better believe that she wore a green outfit to every press appearance. Consistent color can connect the dots in the way you tell your story or help you decide what to wear. Says Elizabeth, "Meghan (Markle) wore black and white at the Invictus Games, and that is the color of their logo.

She paired her look with a bunch of gold jewelry and picked up yellow, which is another Invictus Games color."

The color strategy is one of the easiest ways to help define your personal brand, but another way is via consistent silhouettes. Elizabeth explains, "With the Queen, there was a real formula, and I think that is so powerful because if you look at what she wore it was not a uniform, like Steve Jobs and his turtleneck. It's not the same thing repeatedly, but she was operating within certain guardrails that kept her consistent and exciting. She always wore variations in colors but usually the same shape. I think that consistency was very key."

Around the time of her wedding, Meghan Markle was often seen in boatnecks, the same style as her wedding dress, which created a visual consistency. "Meghan is an actress who has worked with costume designers. Their whole job is to tell stories through clothes. When her character on *Suits* was falling in love, she was seen wearing blush all the time. And Meghan, after the wedding, wore a series of blush looks, and everyone was like, 'Why is she wearing the same shade of pink?' She was doing the same thing that her character on *Suits* was doing," says Elizabeth.

Pro Tip: Consistency drives familiarity, and then people begin to recognize you.

"All of this is a choice, and whether you choose to lean into fashion and play around with it, or you choose to pick one thing and make that your signature, you are making a choice. You need to choose what you want to be known for visually," advises Elizabeth.

The other thing to consider is the environment and culture you're immersing yourself in. Elizabeth has lived in Silicon Valley. While hoodie culture is popularized there and made famous by Zuckerberg, consider the stage you're in and how your audience will read that fashion decision. I think if you're a billionaire,

you can wear a hoodie to an important meeting. But if you're trying to create a business or a brand, wearing a hoodie might give
the impression that you're not really worried about that meeting
and that you're feeling too comfortable. Elizabeth agrees. "I'm
a big believer in putting your best foot forward and making an
effort in getting dressed. That said, every clothing choice you
make will say something about you. Especially if you're starting out, I would be very aware of that and choose accordingly
because to the people who think that they can just opt out of
fashion, that's not possible."

While women are more likely to be judged on their fashion
choices, especially in the media, men also sometimes feel the results
of their choices. I'll never forget when I was moderating a panel
on social media with several founders. Two male founders were
onstage, one incredibly well dressed in a European-cut (tighter) suit
with loafers and no socks; the other in a more American-cut suit
(looser fit) with loafers and socks. I kept seeing the latter founder
staring at the other man's shoes until I couldn't help myself and
asked him what he was thinking about as he gazed lovingly down
at the other man's feet. He answered, "I wish I had the confidence
to wear loafers without socks." Now you might be thinking, *How is
that showing confidence?* Not wearing socks goes against traditional
ideas of formal dressing, so one can assume that if you're not wearing socks, you're comfortable being a nonconformist, hence the confidence. The audience, by the way, cracked up when I asked this.

Your style choices can fluctuate, and you can choose a personal style that strategically paints a different picture when it
suits you. We see this tactic often in court. Sometimes you might
want to ensure that no one sees you coming, and downplaying
your style will benefit your goals more than looking great. But
the more consistent you are, the more you become known for
that look.

These are all visual brand choices depending on your goals.
Our work-from-home culture has made everyone more casual. Of

course, if you're working from home, there's not as much pressure or reason to be dressed. Most people are dressed on top, sweatpants on the bottom, if not pajamas. And while it may not matter for the job you do, just remember that certain moments require greater presentation and effort. I'm also a firm believer that how you dress changes your mindset and could affect your performance. I'm someone who got dressed up for college exams, so that should tell you something about how seriously I believe this.

Visual standards can change based on where you work. Sometimes a company has higher expectations, and luxury brands have historically fallen into this category. It's common for companies to pluck certain employees out of the masses to help them level up across all aspects of personal branding.

DRESSING THE PART

Cindy Tien is based in Singapore and works for a company that helps individuals communicate their personal brands. I met Cindy on a personal branding panel that we were both speaking on for the *South China Morning Post* "Women of Our Time" conference. Luxury brands hire her company to train their employees, from mid-level to senior executives. The companies hire her because they don't feel these employees are at the level they need to be in order to be influential leaders and communicators. They're not inspiring their employees or customers and need to be able to do so for the team to achieve their desired results. Cindy's primary mission is to help them understand who they are (what they stand for), how they communicate, and how they visually brand themselves. They don't coach on social media presence but rather focus on the in-person presentation of these people.

When Cindy works with clients on their visual brand, she examines how they present in both style choices and mannerisms. She analyzes their ability to influence others in their behaviors and the way they choose to communicate.

From a visual standpoint, Cindy coaches on seven universal styles: elegant, classic, natural, dramatic, creative, romantic, and magnetic. "We first get them to think about what they stand for, and then we ask them, how are you communicating that through your visual appearance and that includes international business standards. Based on their brand attributes, we try and see which style fits them the most and is relevant to their personality and how they want to be seen. So, for example, I had one client who was really sweet and gentle. She was the loveliest person, but one of her goals was that she wanted to be seen as a little more bold. If you went off her gentle demeanor, it would be easy to match her with a romantic style, but she felt that nobody was noticing her. She wanted to step up a little bit more, so we told her to choose bolder colors. We advised her that her hair should be a bit more asymmetrical than classically cut. Every aspect of her style was examined to help her communicate who she wants to be."

Your visual identity is a powerful way to express what's on brand for you—and let's face it, no one ever got in trouble for looking too put together. People notice when you make an effort, and if you take pride in your look and show up with your A-game, I promise you'll feel more confident to take on your day.

14

Earn Social Capital and Cultivate Authentic Relationships

Some people love connecting with other people, while others would rather be alone and enjoy solitude. The one thing I can say for sure is that success is not an individual effort. If you think of networking as an Olympic sport and challenge yourself to achieve a gold medal, you'll ensure that opportunities come your way. For most roles across industries, your ability to work well with others is an essential factor of your success. But more than that, who you know can put you in the right rooms and bring you opportunities that may not have come otherwise.

A staggering 80 percent of jobs get filled through personal connections. If that doesn't drive home how important networking is, I don't know what does. And, of course, it makes sense. People prefer doing business with people they know and like. Peer-to-peer recommendations matter. So even if you're someone who would rather curl up with a good book than meet a friend for coffee, you need to push yourself to make sure that you have an "always-on" networking strategy.

One positive result of the pandemic is that we realized that a virtual coffee is just as effective as an in-person one. But when we're more physically distant than ever before, how can we forge meaningful connections in business and life? We lean on our networks for different reasons. We might need a friend to help problem-solve, listen while we vent, make a connection, or otherwise simply share in a win.

> **Pro Tip:** Networking is not about adding contacts to your phone. It's about building authentic relationships. To create a genuine relationship, you must give as much as you take.

My friend Susan McPherson is the poster child for how to build authentic relationships. Susan is the founder and CEO of McPherson Strategies, a communications consultancy focused on the intersection of brands and social impact. As a serial connector Susan wrote, *The Lost Art of Connecting: The Gather, Ask, Do Method for Building Meaningful Relationships,* which is a much-needed reminder that sometimes more than skills, progress lies in the relationships we build and nurture. The most powerful question you can ever ask anyone is "How can I help you?" And this is the first question that comes out of Susan's mouth, and she means it.

I'll never forget the first time I met Susan. We hadn't known each other for more than 30 minutes, and she asked how she could help me. I was a bit taken aback. No one had ever offered that up to me so quickly before, and it left an incredible impression. But that's Susan, and not only does she offer the help, but she also delivers on it. In her book, Susan recalls growing up with parents who used to clip articles for friends and mail them with a simple note such as "Thought you would enjoy this" or "This made me think of you." Small gestures, but certainly a way to surprise and delight friends. There's nothing lovelier than being thought of, and in her book, Susan teaches some of the simple ways you can endeavor to build meaningful relationships and how that's vastly different than networking for the sake of networking.

"One very easy way to think of networking is counting the number of followers you have on social platforms where it's very transactional, where you don't know many of the people, and you don't engage with them. Now, I'm not suggesting you get on Twitter and start engaging with every one of your followers. But that's the mindset. It's going and grabbing business cards and then typing them into whatever contact system you use on your laptop—and then forgetting about them. Instead, it's about being vulnerable and open and then engaging with others. I mean, to me, that's the difference. Yes, there's synergy. You go to events just like you would with networking. But I do believe the difference is that it's not about walking into a room and meeting as many people as you can, but rather, walking into a room meeting a few people and finding out how you can help them and how they can help you. Inevitably, when you help others, it almost always comes back," advises Susan.

Walking into a room can be terrifying, though. If you've ever gone to an event alone, you know that you grab your phone as a security blanket the minute you enter the room. But if you're clear on what you have to offer, it takes fear off the table. Doing some pre-work will also reduce social anxiety. Think about who might be there and know who is hosting, what they look like, what they do, and what, if anything, you might have in common. Preparing will make you feel more confident in engaging.

Next, think about why you're going and what you hope to get out of going. Are you going to support someone else? Is there a specific connection you want to make? We are all so busy, so when you say yes to an invitation, think about why you're saying yes, how going will be beneficial to you, and consider how you can add value to someone else.

Researching the key players isn't enough, though; you also need to be armed with your story. Many people don't have a succinct and effective answer to "Tell me about you!" How you deliver your introduction will determine whether people will remember you or not. If you talk someone's ear off, starting with where you were born, your career journey, and 20 minutes later bring them up to the present day, I can assure you that they stopped listening 19 minutes ago. People have short attention spans, so give them enough of a sound bite to understand who you are and what you do (or want to do, by the way) but not so much that it's impossible to remember what you said. And make sure to turn the question around to the other person! I've met many people who don't, and it's blatantly showing that person that you don't care to know them at all.

To nail these first-impression moments, practicing the delivery of your introduction is essential. Serve up what you want people to remember and express your value proposition. This is also called an elevator pitch. If someone asked me to introduce myself, I would say, "Hi. I'm Aliza Licht. I am a marketer, author, podcaster, and the founder of LEAVE YOUR MARK, a multimedia brand and consultancy. I advise businesses and mentor individuals on how to build their brands." Depending on where I am, though, and who I'm speaking to, I might remove certain parts or flip the order in which I share this information depending on what I think might be more relevant to the person I'm meeting. For example, if I'm at an industry event and open to new clients, I might lead with consulting.

Whatever way you decide to introduce yourself, don't fall victim to LAST NAME SYNDROME. "Last Name Syndrome" is a term I made up to describe people whose identity is their company. For years I was Aliza from DKNY. I believe that your name should hold importance no matter what you do or where you work. When you introduce yourself, you should be leaning on your name, full stop. You don't need the crutch of your company to define you. This is also why I don't include the company names in my podcast guests' episode title. Each of my guests' names matters more to me than where they work. I try to honor the people, not the companies.

When you focus on making your name mean something versus your title and what company it goes along with, you realize that your true power lies in being comfortable with your name naked. It's like when you're trying to be healthy and order a piece of plain, grilled chicken. No oil, no sauce. Just the chicken. You stare at it and think, *I don't want to eat this. It doesn't taste like anything without the sauce.* In the same way, your name might not feel like anything without the company title, but just like with that chicken, you'll get used to it and eventually realize that you don't need the sauce after all.

When you introduce yourself, be loud and proud of your name and what you do—less so *who you do it for.* That's not to say that you shouldn't share where you work secondarily (and most people will ask). Of course, you can and should, but remember that your experiences and skill set come with you wherever you go.

> **Pro Tip:** Business titles come and go, but if you have a clear sense of who you are and your worth, your name can and will stand on its own.

YOUR STATE OF THE UNION PERSONAL ADDRESS

While I applaud those who make a point of going out, not everyone has the time or energy to do so at scale. We all lead full lives, so being selective with what deserves your physical attendance is essential to not burning out. Another way to connect without doing the heavy lifting of networking is to cast a wider net. If you're pressed for time, trust me, you'll find other people in your network equally as depleted. That's where your State of the Union address comes in.

Tiffany Dufu is the founder and CEO of The Cru and author of *Drop the Ball: Achieving More by Doing Less.* The Cru is a start-up that brings together small groups of women based on values, life goals, personality, and demographics. They help one another achieve personal and professional ambitions. Tiffany has what she calls her village update. She sent her first update after she graduated from college and now sends it every year. "The people on the email are people who supported me at some point or maybe people I worked with. Whenever I left a job, I said, 'Hey, I want to stay in contact with you. Can I add you to my village update?' And it's literally a quick update that tells everyone what happened that year, what I was able to accomplish, maybe what I'm struggling with, or if I need anything, but it always starts with gratitude for my village and thanking them so much for supporting me along the way. Over time they've seen me get married, have kids, get different jobs, and publish a book. As time passes, you'll curate this village of people who are there for you, whatever you need, and the best part of the village updates is that I get to hear back from them."

> **Pro Tip:** Send your State of the Union email to yourself and put all the recipients in Bcc. People don't like having their email addresses on blast.

Another reason why the village update is effective is that sometimes you don't want to feel the awkwardness of broadcasting what you're up to. It's a rhetorical effort. If you hear back from people, great; if you don't, no harm done.

I don't do a group village update—I prefer one-to-one communication—but it's definitely a tactic you could try and see what comes back. That said, I would be obsessed with the unsubscribes. Sometimes you just don't want to know, ha-ha.

BE OPEN TO NEW CONNECTIONS

People who are Olympic gold medalists at networking will tell you that their superpower is their ability to keep their contacts up-to-date and organized. Keeping track of introductions, when someone moves jobs, and updating your contacts is essential. When you do this, you'll see patterns emerge. Alexandra Wilkis Wilson is not only a serial start-up founder of Gilt, Glamsquad, and so many others, but she's also a networking gold medalist. When Alexandra looks back at her career wins, she realizes that her opportunities came from the least likely people and, in fact, sometimes not even via a close friend. That's why you need to be open to all introductions. Yes, they can be tedious, and yes, there are only so many hours in a day, but you never know who you might meet and who might recommend you for something later on. But more than that, it's a chain reaction. One caveat here: If someone introduces me to another person for "advice" and I ascertain that "advice" is really consulting dressed up as mentorship, I decide if the meeting is mutually beneficial—and if not, I send the person my consulting link. I use Calendly (obsessed!) for booking meetings, and one of my links is titled "Consulting hour." This link requires payment for my hour before you can schedule time on my calendar. I give this link to people to protect my time and ensure that I am paid for my expertise. The best part is that it requires no explanation. I say, "I'm happy to meet you! Please book a time on my calendar." If the person doesn't book a time once they see the fee, it's their loss, not mine.

> **Pro Tip:** The more people you connect with and help in their endeavors, the more your name will pop up in people's minds.

People inherently like to problem-solve, so if someone says to me, "Do you know anyone who (fill in the blank)?" the last people I connected with are the ones that will pop into my mind. Steven Kolb, CEO of the CFDA (Council of Fashion Designers of America), landed his role because the relationships he cultivated throughout his career were meaningful. His network understood his value, so his connections put his name forward (unbeknownst to him) when an opportunity opened at the CFDA, even though he had no background in fashion. They knew that his skills and extensive experience in the nonprofit world would be transferable. He put it best when he said, "You know you're doing something right when your name is mentioned for opportunities in rooms you're not in."

SERIAL DOT-CONNECTING

I like to think of myself as a serial connector, and nothing makes me happier than connecting the dots between two people who would benefit from knowing each other. One of my rules, though, is to make sure that I follow through on the promise of saying that I'll make the connection. Many people say they'll connect you with someone, and then nothing happens. This is one of my biggest pet peeves, because it shouldn't be for you to remind the person to make the connection they offered to make. There's no shame in jotting down a few notes, even during a casual social meeting. I also take it further and before it ends, I rattle off my takeaways and next steps from the meeting. Playing back to the person what you've agreed to do also gives them the assurance that you'll deliver on what you said. I often make those introductions directly after leaving that meeting to avoid getting overwhelmed by my to-do list. It's really my safety tactic to ensure that I don't forget.

If you're offering to make a connection between two people of equal stature or experience, you can be confident that they both will enjoy knowing each other. Making a thoughtful introduction includes a proper introduction of who each person is, what they do, and why you thought to introduce them. But you also need to make sure that you believe that the introduction would be mutually beneficial to both parties.

Here's an example:

Hi, Jade, I'm so excited to introduce you to Lilly Z. Lilly is the Founder of X Company. Lilly, as discussed, Jade is the brilliant CEO of Y Company and someone I greatly admire. You're both passionate about helping women, and Lilly is putting together a panel to speak at an event. Jade, I immediately thought of you. I will leave you both to connect!

If the two people I'm introducing aren't of equal seniority, I always ask the more established person if they're open to the introduction. You might be thinking to yourself, *But wait, the more junior person should always get the introduction; they're the one who needs the help!* While that may be true, realize that unlike the above example, where the introduction is mutually beneficial, if the introduction is likely to benefit only one person, that's a different proposition. You must be thoughtful when offering and subsequently delivering on those types of introductions. Make sure that the more established person has the time and desire to meet someone new. When you reach out, be specific about why you're making the ask on behalf of someone else.

Here's an example:

Hi, Jade, I hope you have been well! I know you're so busy, but I just met a really exceptional person who is dying to break into your industry. It would be a dream for him to meet someone with your experience and success. Would you be willing to speak with him?

It's important to note that you're asking for a favor on behalf of someone else in this request. In my opinion, you can't pull the favor card with the same person more than once a year. People are busy; be considerate of that. If you're making this ask, you'd better believe in the person you're asking the connection for. This may sound dramatic, but it's not. Successful people are careful with their time.

But then there's more. Prep the person that you just went out on a limb for. The worst thing that happens way too often is that you do someone a favor by making an introduction on their behalf, and then they have the nerve to ghost the person they were introduced to or waste that person's time by asking mundane questions. Do not do this. Further, the person benefiting from the introduction should make the effort to respond first.

You could say something like this:

Hi, John, I'm excited to share that Jade is willing to speak with you. I will connect you both by email. She is super busy, so being prompt with your response and only asking for a 15-minute call would be appropriate. Jade has had a bunch of press recently. It would be good for you to read about what she's been up to. I'm looking forward to seeing what you learn after speaking with her, so please round back with me. I hope it's a great call.

Pro Tip: Google the person you are about to meet. This goes for any scenario. Don't give off a lazy impression by asking questions you can easily find the answers to.

I will never assume that anyone has the foresight to research the person. Doing your homework goes a long way. I can't tell you how many times I offer up time to someone as a mentorship call, and they ask me things that are easily found online. It's not that I mind sharing my story, but it shows me that you didn't lift a finger to do any pre-work on our call, which tells me that you don't value my time. Worse for you, though, you're trading an opportunity where you could be going deeper and learning something that's not searchable online. Instead, do the research, and then if you determine that you have a question based off that, by all means ask it.

YOU CAN'T BUY SOCIAL CAPITAL; YOU NEED TO EARN IT

Why is one person more likely to be recommended than another? Why does it seem like some people are just lucky and land in all the perfect spots? The answer is their social capital. **Social capital is the direct result of the personal brand you have built.** It's your reputation in the form of human currency, which means the value you bring to those around you, whether socially or professionally, matters. The more social capital you have, the more likely you will succeed. (*Addendum: Sometimes, the more likely you are to succeed despite your skill set.*)

> **Pro Tip:** You build social capital by delivering on your promise time and again, showing your network that you are reliable.

When you say that you're going to show up for something, you do. When you offer to make that introduction, you do. When someone offers you help, you are gracious and appreciative. It's those you-scratch-my-back-and-I'll-scratch-yours type of favors, information, and support.

You also consistently make anyone recommending you for an opportunity look good. You care about the effort people make on your behalf, and you also pay it forward by helping others. If you take a moment to consider the people in your life who have social capital with you, I'm sure they all have the same two things in common: your trust and appreciation.

Your actions can stain your reputation and directly impact your social capital. For example, if you're recommended for a job and leave that job four months later, that diminishes the credibility of the person who recommended you (unless, of course, there's an unusual unforeseen circumstance). It also hinders your ability to call on that person again. When you do that, your network starts to mistrust your accountability to show up and may stop recommending you. That reputation tends to stick. There's a reason they say "don't burn your bridges."

Author and start-up coach Alisa Cohn points to the importance of frequency when aiming to build social capital. "Social capital is the grease that smooths our ability to work together, and when you build social capital with people, you have built a reputation and a track record with that person. They trust you, and they want to do the thing for you that you want them to do. But more specifically, you can quickly get something done with them because they assume that you know what you are talking about and have good intentions. The way you build up social capital is to get to know people and figure out what their goals are. When you help them and do favors for them and show them that you care about them, you showcase yourself as somebody good to work with. This will result in working together repeatedly."

The idea of being good to work with means you will always get the call, especially when people are looking to fill voids, whether on a team or for a project. The speed with which you can fill their hole is usually of the utmost importance. If you've built social capital with a person, they know they can depend on you and have complete confidence in your ability to deliver whatever they need you to do.

THE TRADE ECONOMY

When you're trying to build social capital and credibility, in the beginning, set the idea of making money to the side. While no one wants to work for free, you need to start somewhere if you're trying to build a portfolio of experience in a particular area where you have no track record. You might offer your services free of charge to gain experience or even prove to someone that you know what you're doing. If they agree and you deliver on what you promised, you have now been paid in the form of social capital. Trust in your ability has been created, and you can leverage that. Your first client or project's success is crucial because this is your test pilot.

> **Pro Tip:** If you can satisfy your first client with your work, you can leverage that relationship to secure your second.

The second client never has to know that the previous client got the services for free. All that matters is that you're attaining experience and building a reputation for yourself in this area. That said, how you position favors and trades matters, as it can be a slippery slope.

When Alisa was endeavoring to build her coaching practice, she didn't have a track record. To create one, she coached for free. But Alisa was transparent about her intentions, and her clients understood the assignment. She told them that if the coaching worked for them, she would like a testimonial in return and also for them to share her services with their friends. **This is how you get experience when you have no experience.** As evidenced by Alisa, the key is to make sure both parties understand the expectations.

There are many reasons to consider doing free gigs, and sometimes the reason is simply that it will benefit you in other ways. For example, as an author, sometimes having people buy books versus paying a speaking fee is more valuable. Taking that a step further, sometimes just saying that you spoke at Company X to their 500 employees will help you get the next speaking gig that does pay. Or maybe that company is willing to send a company-wide email and promote the sale of your book.

Pro Tip: Before you say no to an unpaid gig, consider the other ways in which it might benefit you to do it.

Sometimes someone important will ask you for a favor that you'd otherwise never do. It's crucial to weigh the benefits of saying yes or thinking about other ways you could get value out of the experience. Back in my celebrity dressing days in fashion, a stylist might come to us requesting a gown for a client who we really weren't interested in dressing. Our first reaction was to pass on the opportunity, but we would instead consider the stylist's other clients because we didn't want to make the mistake of alienating her. We often did the stylist a favor, hoping that one day she'd come to us with the celebrity client that we actually wanted to dress. **Sometimes the small fish leads to the big fish.**

Not everyone can afford to get experience for free, though, and that's where trading information with people you trust in your network is essential. It's wise to lean on your network to understand what's been done before. The back-channel trading of information and support is called a *whisper network*. Nothing is more important than understanding the landscape you work in and the going rates. For example, if you happen to know someone who's done this gig before, you can easily find out what the payment threshold might look like. Then, if you wanted to negotiate and discount what you know they previously paid just to get the opportunity under your belt, you're going in eyes wide open.

DO THE MENTAL GYMNASTICS
Accepting a Trade

I realize that not everyone can afford to do work for free, and of course I want everyone to get paid for their efforts—but it's often worth weighing the benefits of an unpaid opportunity if the upside can come in other nonmonetary forms.

If you get offered an unpaid opportunity and can afford to take it, ask yourself these questions before you decline:

1. Is this a company I want to be aligned with?

2. Has this company paid other people in the past for the same work?

3. Will doing this allow me to make a connection with someone important?

4. Will this build my credibility and add to my resume or portfolio?

5. Will this experience provide me with great social content that I can share to attract other business?

6. Will this person provide a testimonial about my work?

7. Can I negotiate and do this gig at a lower rate, prove myself, and set myself up for a higher rate in the future?

You sometimes need to be flexible with your rate when you don't have a track record; knowing a historical rate helps. Let's say you're starting your consulting business and a friend of yours previously worked with a brand you would like to work with. If you know that they got paid a monthly retainer of $5,000, you know where to start in your negotiation. You can say something like "I know the services I offer are easily worth $5,000 a month, but because we've never worked together before, I want to be fair and flexible, and I'd be willing to work for $3,500 for the first month. Then, if you're happy with my services, you can meet me at my rate next month."

Pro Tip: Always start higher and negotiate from there, but the terms must be negotiated in advance. It's much harder to go back to the money well after you've already taken the lower fee.

Building social capital is similar to building blocks. You must start with a good foundation and go up from there. It takes time to earn social capital, but even though you might be able to get to a certain level, nothing is permanent.

WHEN SOCIAL CAPITAL GOES UP IN SMOKE

Nothing in life is guaranteed, and maintaining your social capital is entirely dependent on the good standing of your personal brand. No matter what industry you work in, people talk. Unofficial background checks are done cleverly to ensure that what someone thinks they're getting is actually what they're getting. If you're not thinking about your personal brand and the reputation you're creating as you move along in your career, it can backfire.

People, for some reason, assume that these missteps are off the record, but trust me, they always pop up in ways you least expect. Here's a great example: I was once interviewing someone for a role. This person was an excellent conversationalist, and I was confident that she would be someone I considered seriously for the position. (*Spoiler alert: I was wrong.*) In the interview, she mentioned a few people in our industry and referred to them as mentors. I happened to know those people and made a mental note to call on those names for references. After the interview, I called HR and told them how great it went and that they should ask for references. The people that this woman handed over as references were not the same names she had mentioned during our meeting (not that they had to be, necessarily). I told HR to call the references while I would call the people she name-dropped. My first phone call was to her "mentor" Laura. The conversation went something like this:

"Hi, Laura! I hope you have been well. I just met with Christina X, and she mentioned that you were her mentor. I would love to learn more about your experience working together."

Laura: "Hi, Aliza, it's so lovely to hear from you! Unfortunately, I have not spoken to Christina in ten years and cannot recommend her."

[Mic drop.]

The learning here is that perception is a tricky thing. Christina was delusional enough to think that Laura was her mentor, but whatever happened along the way over time proved otherwise. Perhaps Laura was her mentor at one point, but Christina's social capital became null and void. The ability to kill your social capital in such an extreme way shows many other red flags, but you can't assume anything either way. This example is a good reminder of networking frequency as well. Under normal circumstances, if Christina had stayed in touch with Laura from time to time, maybe she could have salvaged the relationship, but in this case, it sounds like something less than stellar transpired. That brings me to another rule of networking: you can't assume that a relationship from years prior will hold the same weight.

> **Pro Tip:** Always reach out to a contact to make sure that they are still willing to be a reference before you submit their name.

Maintaining a document of the people in your network who are invaluable assets to your career is the only way to stay abreast of your relationships. As we get older, there are too many people to remember and keep in touch with. Reaching out to say hello and asking someone how they are and what they're up to doesn't require a reason. You need to do so without asking for anything, though.

You might say something along the lines of this:

Hi, _____! It's been forever. You popped into my mind today, and I just wanted to reach out and see how you are. What are you up to these days?

That's it. This could be in any medium you think this person is most likely to respond to. It could be email, text, DM, whatever.

I prefer text or DM because in those two mediums we expect short chats as opposed to email, where one short exchange almost feels like it's missing the ending. The person is likely to respond and share what she's up to. She'll also ask you what you're up to if she is gracious. You can also offer to support her. She is likely to respond in kind.

If you do this at scale, and I mean with the intention that every week you choose a few people on your list to connect with, you'll ensure that your network is there when you need them and simultaneously build social capital.

Pro Tip: Track your networking outreach, outcomes, and follow-ups.

In your tracking document, record the date of the exchange and anything that transpired. You should note any important projects or dates the person mentioned, because wouldn't it be so lovely if you could reach back out to ask that person how that thing they casually said they were doing went? Again, this is all to keep communication open.

Perhaps in the conversation you shared something that you were looking for. If this person can provide that guidance and make an intro that yields success, you want to be able to thank them in the future. **It's crucial to close the loop.** When you tell the other person how their support helped you, you make them feel good! Never underestimate the power of doing so. People value knowing that their advice or introduction was meaningful.

Closing the loop matters in several scenarios. First, make sure that if someone is taking the time to introduce you to someone else (whether you asked for this introduction or not), you give your friend the respect of a quick response. If you don't respond, you make your friend look bad! Second, if you follow through and eventually meet the person, let the person who introduced you know if anything good comes from it. It's preferred that you do so in a timely fashion, but it's never too late to say thank you. Even if it's years later, the person will still appreciate that you thought to reach out. It's important to understand that, despite the time that's gone by, the ability for us to show appreciation for the connection matters more. It might feel embarrassing, but it's not.

Pro Tip: There's no expiration date on gratitude.

Think about the people in your life who have helped you along the way. Why not reach out and thank them? Here's an example of something you could say:

Hi, _____!

I know it's been a long time since we last spoke, but I wanted to tell you that the introduction you made for me resulted in _____. I should have emailed you sooner, but I want you to know that I do appreciate the introduction. I hope all is well in your world, and please let me know if there is anything I can do to support you.

Not only is this example a thank-you, but it's also a way to reopen the lines of communication with an old contact that you may have lost touch with and offer to return the favor.

If you feel awkward reaching out directly because you haven't spoken to them in a long time, that's OK! You can start slowly by instead using social media to reconnect. I can't overstate the effectiveness of using social media to rebuild a connection with someone.

Another effective way to make yourself seen while doing something good for the other person is to amplify their content by sharing it. This is you complimenting this person without having to compliment this person directly. This is yet another way to build relationships and reconnect with people you might otherwise not be speaking to. I find this very effective, mainly because we don't have the opportunity to work with everyone in our network all the time. You can't always directly reach out or you'll be categorized as annoying or, worse, stalking, LOL. But switching between a like, emoji, comment, and share, and maybe occasionally a DM or text, is a totally acceptable way to stay connected with people.

I talked about how to build your personal brand online earlier in the book, but it's worth repeating here that your content strategy also contributes to your social capital. For example, the content that I produce for the *Leave Your Mark* podcast shows that I'm someone who spends a lot of my free time supporting other people and their career accomplishments. Sharing something positive in the service of others helps me grow my social capital. It's a win-win.

PUT THOSE INTROS ON THE FIRE

Contacting people you don't know isn't the most comfortable thing to do. With the volume of inbound messages people get, it's no wonder that sometimes emails go unread. The most strategic way to connect with someone you don't know is to have someone else make a warm introduction. A warm intro means that the connection you have in common can save you the awkward moment of reaching out cold by connecting you with the person you would like to talk to. The likelihood of the person responding to a warm intro is much higher than if you were pitching on your own or even name-dropping the person you have in common. Note: It's important to give context to the person making the intro as to why you want to be connected. It also gives them something to say in the pitch email.

Here's an example of what you could say to a mutual connection:

Hi, Lisa, I hope you are well! I saw on LinkedIn that you're connected to Megan. I'm really interested in speaking with them about x, y, and z for a project I'm working on. Would you be willing to make an intro? I would greatly appreciate it! Also, please let me know if there is anything I can help you with. I would be happy to!

Then, when your contact makes that intro, thank them as per the below:

Thank you, Lisa! Moving you to bcc to spare your inbox. (then move them to bcc)

Hi, Megan! It's a pleasure to be connected, and I would love to learn more about what you did with x, y, and z. I know you're busy, but I would appreciate it if you had 10 minutes to spare for a quick call. Alternatively, I'm happy to send you a few specific questions via email. Please let me know what works best for you and how I could also be helpful to you!

This is how it's done over and over again. When you strategically think about who you know, you're more likely to achieve whatever you're trying to. Warm introductions are the most effective way to meet new people. Still, you should account for how many you've asked for from the same person. You should not repeatedly ask for introductions unless you're sure you are providing some value in return.

Pro Tip: For every ask you make, make sure you're offering to give.

The reverse also applies, though. **Keep track of how many warm intros you've made and for whom, because your network is your currency and you need to make sure that you don't overspend.**

Everyone is mindful when it comes to spending money, right? Well, except, of course, when you decide that, yes, you really do NEED those shoes even though your rent is due. If you think of your network as a currency, you need to be careful about how you spend it. Even though I'd like to believe that everyone has the best intentions, sometimes people don't. It takes time and energy to build a meaningful network. Over many, many years, you build social capital with hundreds if not thousands of people. So when someone asks you to make a warm introduction for them, consider the track record of the person who's asking. I like to think of myself as a gracious connector—it brings me personal joy to connect people—but sometimes you can begin to feel like a piggy bank that people are constantly making withdrawals from without paying you back or even thanking you. These are the people you need to pay attention to.

DO THE MENTAL GYMNASTICS
Are You Being Used?

1. How often has this person come back to you for an intro?

2. Is this person asking to be introduced to top people in your network, and if so, why?

3. What has come from the previous introduction(s) you made for this person?

4. Did this person thank you? Did they close the loop?

5. Do you need support from this person in the future?

My favorite offense is when someone I made an intro for or recommended gets a job or a client, and I never hear about it again until I see their LinkedIn post announcing their new gig. It's not to say that this is a horrible offense, but it would be nice to be appreciated for the effort I made and the support I gave. Every introduction we make is a reflection of us and our personal brand. If we go to bat for someone who isn't worthy of our recommendation, it also reflects on us.

DON'T LET THE COLD PITCH FREEZE YOUR PROGRESS

If you don't have someone who can connect you to someone else, that's not a reason to not reach out! If you make a thoughtful pitch and you're clear about what you're asking for, being mindful of someone's time and what help you could provide, it's easy to make cold pitches work. My favorite example of a cold pitch is one I once received via Instagram.

One day a woman DMed me and said the following:

Hi, Aliza!

My name is Rachel, and I am the contributing editor at X Blog. I am also a freelance writer for a number of fashion, beauty, and lifestyle publications. You can check out some of my favorite pieces on my website, via my link in bio.

I am writing to you as I sit here on a total quarantine binge of Leave Your Mark.

I am obsessed! As I am a journalist looking to learn more about the podcast space, I'd like to offer my research services and guest questions (this is my specialty) totally pro bono if I can just get some exposure to what working behind the scenes at a podcast looks like. No strings attached—really that simple. I have more time than ever to learn because of COVID, and Leave Your Mark *is inspiring me to be bold and courageous and ask for what I want.*

Looking forward to hearing from you, and while we're at it, if you ever need any freelance writing work, I'm your girl.

Talk soon!

This is the perfect pitch for the following reasons:

1. It briefly shares who this person is and her credentials.

2. She acknowledges my work and how it's impacted her.

3. She immediately and directly positions her ask.

4. She offers to pay back the time I would spend teaching her the Ins and Outs of podcasting with a trade.

I was intrigued and decided to check out her bio and site. Everything that she said would be there was. I told her that I would be happy to have a Zoom call and share everything I know about podcasting (*which, to be clear, is mostly self-taught via Google, LOL*). We had a great call, and I decided to take her up on her offer to do some writing. She prepared the show notes for one of my episodes. The whole exchange was mutually beneficial.

When you open your mind to networking beyond your comfort zone and craft a thoughtful and strategic pitch, you can be successful in expanding your network. The other thing I'll point out here is that being receptive to a cold pitch from someone trying to learn is good karma. A few months later, this woman was writing an article for a magazine that she thought I would be the perfect interview subject for and asked me to participate. In the end, the good deed came back.

Please note that just because you don't get an answer the first time you send a cold pitch doesn't mean that the answer is no. I always do one follow-up before I decide if the ask is dead or not. Of course, sometimes it is. For your mental health, remember that this happens to everyone. Sometimes, the answer *is* no, but if you're resourceful, you'll find another contact who can help you get to where you want to go.

> **Pro Tip:** Check social media before you pitch to make sure the person you are contacting is not on vacation. Not kidding.

GHOSTS DON'T JUST COME OUT ON HALLOWEEN

Giving someone an answer, either way, shows the other person respect and decency. Not everyone does this. That said, some people don't do this for several reasons:

1. They have missed your ask entirely.

2. They saw the ask and didn't have time to respond to it.

3. They saw the ask, and they don't know how to tell you no.

My second example happens with recruiters, and while it feels hurtful to the candidate, it's not personal. The inbound volume that certain people have to manage in their roles isn't always conducive to responding to every email. I get hundreds of pitches a day for my podcast (*I am probably on some podcast list*), and I can't possibly respond to them all. Also, bulk or promotional emails need not be responded to.

If you've experienced the third example, it's equally as frustrating. We've all been ghosted, and we have all ghosted others, whether intentionally or by accident. When you reach out to people, remember that everyone is busy, and like Dorie Clark advised previously, no one is thinking about you.

> **Pro Tip:** Do not take silence personally. Not everyone is as thorough in checking email, text, DM, etc., as you might be. People are drowning in overcommunication, and it's coming from different directions.

We all are guilty of seeing an email or text and thinking, "Ah, I need to respond, but I will later." Then, of course, later doesn't happen because life does, and you forget.

Give people the benefit of the doubt that they are busy, and try pinging them again. Just because you don't get a response the first time doesn't mean you can't reach out once more. You don't even have to acknowledge that you contacted previously. Sometimes it's better to send the same message again. It's also OK to say things like "I know your inbox volume must be off the charts, so I'm resending this to make sure you got it!" or "Putting this at the top of your inbox."

No one ever minds a follow-up. I greatly appreciate it when someone helps me manage my inbox by resending communication. It's hard to keep up. Sending a "gentle reminder" to read your email is completely fine. But don't clock the person by saying something like "I sent you an email three days ago. . . ." Three days may seem like an eternity to you, but you don't know the regular cadence of this person's communication. Don't judge their timeliness. That said, though, the busiest people I know are the quickest to respond. Let that sink in. If CEOs can respond to emails within seconds, everyone else needs to try harder to stay on top of their communication game.

If ghosting is intentional because that person doesn't want to connect, you'll know that after your first follow-up. Again, this can feel personal, but it can also result from someone who doesn't want to have to say no directly, so it's easier to ignore the email. I loathe this tactic. I think it's rude. Declining an invitation or opportunity isn't always comfortable, but it's something that everyone needs to learn to do.

Try something simple like:

"Hi, Carrie! I hope you are well. Thanks so much for thinking of me. I really appreciate it, but I'm going to pass at this time."

I love this response because it's direct and doesn't make excuses. You might think, *Why not add a reason like "due to bandwidth" or explain?*, but that can get you into trouble if you never want to do the thing you're being proposed to do. If you make the reason because you're too busy, someone who really wants you to do something will change the goalposts on you and work around your schedule, so I never say that. The keywords I use in my declines are "at this time," which means I'm leaving the possibility that I might be open to doing something in the future, but it will be on my terms. I'm also not specifying any particular reason why I'm passing. This decline works like a charm.

15

Think Like a Winner and Negotiate Your Worth

It would be nice if we could all press a button to channel the confidence that we need to accomplish our goals, but life isn't that effortless. I've had the benefit of speaking to hundreds of people throughout my podcast seasons, and one thing is clear: no matter who you are or how successful you are, everyone feels unworthy at times. Imposter syndrome is something everyone battles. It can come and go at its leisure, but to ensure that we don't let it get in the way of our hopes and dreams, we need to be more powerful than the thoughts we plague ourselves with.

In particular, there's one question that I think is essential in battling moments of self-doubt. That question is **"Why not me?"**

Asking yourself this simple question opens up a world of possibility. Frequently we bog down our thinking with negativity. We love to list a million reasons why something can't happen.

When I decided that I wanted to do a podcast, I was full of hope that I'd be able to find a production partner to work with. Through my network, I was able to land coveted meetings with every major podcast production company. Most of these people knew my book and had been warm introductions by people they respect. Everything seemed like it was going in the right direction, but then I was met with rejection one by one. The common denominator across these meetings was that they wanted celebrity podcasters with built-in audiences. They were unwilling to spend time and resources building an audience for someone even though the podcast would undoubtedly function as the perfect companion to my book that was still selling well four years later. It didn't matter.

This was an inflection point for me because I could have let all those no's tell me that I don't have what it takes to be a successful podcaster. That would have been easy, and don't think it didn't cross my mind; it did. Naturally, I thought to myself, *Well, if everyone is saying no, maybe this isn't a smart idea, or they're the experts, and if they aren't seeing the potential here, maybe I'm imagining something that just isn't there.* So many thoughts went through my head, but the one that was the loudest became *Why not me?* Why couldn't I do this on my own? Why couldn't I just figure it out? Everything we need to know is on the internet. If you're willing to take the time to find the answers, you can teach yourself to do anything.

The secret to success is feeling the fear, acknowledging it—like literally saying, "Hi, fear, I see you"—and then pushing right through it.

DO THE MENTAL GYMNASTICS
Rebrand Your Fear

1. What's your belief system, i.e., why do you believe you can't do this?

2. Identify what exactly is scaring you. Get specific.

3. Counteract that fear with a reason why you should do this.

Your mindset can be a killer. It's too easy to give up. Who we surround ourselves with has an enormous impact on how we feel. Sure, we all want to have great friends, but professionally, it's important also to have people around us who see our greatest potential. This squad needs to have the ability to see the absolute best version of you and understand what the *future you* could be like. When insecurity creeps in, and it always will, these essential people remind us how far we've come and how much farther we can go. We need them to cheer us on when we feel like giving up and in that vulnerable moment when we doubt we can do it. We need them to remind us that we absolutely have what it takes to get to where we want to go.

CURATE YOUR ADVISORY BOARD

My friend Carrie Kerpen, a seasoned marketer and entrepreneur (and wife to Dave mentioned previously), has a personal advisory board, and if you ask me, I've never heard of anything more brilliant. It's not formal, but Carrie has wisely identified people in her network who are great confidantes and to whom she can go for different things. If it's a personal problem, she has someone for that, and if it's a business problem, it's someone else. When we think about mentors, we tend to think about one magical person.

> **Pro Tip:** One person doesn't have all the answers. You can and should be taking little bits of wisdom from different people.

Identifying each person's superpower is a talent in itself. It was never my intention to use podcasting as a way for me to network or learn about a specific area. Still, interestingly, if you create content and can tap into people as guests, you are, in a way, curating your own advisory board. Whatever you're interested in learning can become an episode or a topic you write about. It's an effective way to ask for help without asking for help.

Of course, your self-worth isn't just the job of others. You also have a responsibility to coach yourself, and we need this self-talk of confidence regularly. I've always been someone who kept a folder of my wins back in my early days of work (in preparation for my year-end review), but Tiffany Dufu takes it a step further. She has a great way of reminding herself who she is and what she's capable of by collecting feedback and flipping through it whenever she needs a mental boost. Any time someone says something of value about what she's contributed or done, she writes it down on a card. When times get tough, or her anxiety levels rise, she takes out these cards and reminds herself of the positive feedback she's been given. It's so easy to forget all our wins when all we do is focus on what didn't happen.

Another way to really count yourself out is to focus on what others are doing. There will always be someone who has more, has done more, and gets credit for more. If you base your accomplishments on the results of someone else, you will never be happy.

Pro Tip: Playing the dangerous game of "Compare and Despair" will derail your goals.

Comparing yourself to someone else is probably the number one way to crush your confidence. Instead, I focus on my goals and track my accomplishments based on what I intended to do and was able to do. There is, however, a counterpoint to this advice and a productive way to use other people's success. It's called *modeling behavior*. Identifying someone who's doing what you want to be doing and who's maybe a few years ahead of you can be motivating and leave you a path to follow. While you can feel pride in figuring out things for yourself, there's also nothing wrong with identifying someone who can show you the ropes.

You should opt for whichever tactic feels most comfortable to you. Your mental health is a priority.

No one becomes a success without the guidance of others, but first you need to believe that you are worthy of success.

IF YOU'RE IN THE ROOM, YOU BELONG THERE

Have you ever thought to yourself, *Wow, I can't believe I'm here*? People have these "pinch me" moments that feel part fan-girl, part surreal. But the truth is, if we're in the room, there's a reason we're there. There are no charity invites. No one includes you because they feel bad for you. You are in that room because you've earned your place to be there, or you're someone on the rise who people have faith will one day contribute. Despite this, sometimes we might feel that we don't deserve to be in that room, and because we're focused on that, we don't make the most of those opportunities.

> **Pro Tip:** Instead of focusing on how you got there, focus on what you can do now that you are there. What contributions can you make? What impression can you leave?

Jennifer Meyer is a successful jewelry designer today with a best friend and client like Jennifer Aniston, among many other A-listers. But when she was just starting out, she landed a coveted interview at *Glamour* magazine to be the West Coast beauty and fitness editor. She had no experience whatsoever. Her friend recommended her, and she didn't even have a resume. Just because she had a connection, though, didn't mean the job was hers. She sat in an interview with the editor-in-chief and made a case for herself as to why she was the perfect person for the role. Advises Jennifer, "Even if you think you don't belong in a room, get in the room. Because if you can be confident and sell yourself, you'll figure out the rest later." We've heard the saying "Fake it till you make it" for ages, but the truth is the only person who knows you're faking it is you.

But you can't get in the room if you don't know that the room exists. Visibility needs to come first, and it's up to every person to make sure that they're leaving the door wide open for those who come after. People need to see what they can strive for, and once they know it exists, access is the next step.

> **Pro Tip:** Giving access to someone else makes you even more powerful than just seizing it for yourself. Don't be a gatekeeper.

For some reason, people don't know this. They think that by sharing intel or opportunities, they're diminishing their power. The opposite is true.

DON'T WASTE YOUR TIME IN THE ROOM

Once you're in the room, your job is to think, *How can I maximize this opportunity? How can I contribute in a positive way? How can I sell myself in a way that's appropriate and adds value?*

No one knows how to negotiate a room better than Lydia Fenet. As the former Lead Benefit Auctioneer and Global Managing Director of Strategic Partnerships at Christie's auction house, Lydia knows firsthand that being an effective salesperson distinguishes top achievers in all fields from the rest of the pack. She's led auctions for more than 600 organizations and raised more than half a billion dollars for 400+ nonprofits worldwide. She's still globetrotting the world as an independent auctioneer.

Lydia's widely acclaimed book, *The Most Powerful Woman in the Room Is You: Command an Audience and Sell Your Way to Success,* equips you with the essential tools of the trade and reveals Lydia's strategies behind her revolutionary sales approach. The biggest lesson Lydia's learned is to sell **as yourself**. Often, we start to question our worth and purpose, especially in the presence of more experienced people, but that doesn't mean you need to act like someone you're not.

When Lydia was first starting in the very male-dominated auction world, she thought that she needed to model the behaviors of the old British auctioneers. She tried out that persona, though, and found that it didn't serve her and didn't make her onstage approach effective. She realized that to sell, she needed to be herself. With that, she started cracking jokes and having fun onstage, and the audience responded in kind.

> **Pro Tip:** Reading the room is imperative. Especially in the beginning, listen before you speak. Being thoughtful about how you contribute will always yield good results.

Another vital tip Lydia shares is that if you listen carefully, the audience will tell you everything you need to know. Meaning that if you're in a room and you engage a certain way, pay attention to people's reactions and adjust accordingly. Your words may not always land to applause, but if you're true to yourself and contribute for the right reasons, it's worth the effort. For example, sometimes you might be sitting in a meeting and hearing a strategy that you feel has risks. You know this because of your area of expertise or vantage point, and the person presenting the strategy doesn't know the pitfalls of your area. Even though it's uncomfortable and you might upset the person speaking by poking a hole in their strategy, you're doing it for the benefit of the company. That is worth the effort.

RUN THROUGH AN OPEN DOOR

It bothers me that I even have to say this, but for those of you in the back who missed this advice in life, please listen. The most successful people make sure to seize every opportunity. When you have the chance to connect with someone with experience, don't blow it off. Unfortunately, this bears repeating because many people waste these opportunities. If someone opens the door for you, you need to run through it.

Every connection you make is a new opportunity for you to expand your horizons, mentality, and impact. When you're lucky enough to be exposed to experiences that add value, don't discount them. Little things like not rescheduling unless you absolutely have to or making sure your camera is on for that first meeting make a difference.

The window of opportunity doesn't stay open for long, so speed is essential. That means not taking days to answer an email and then more time to land on a mutual meeting date. If you're the person who is benefiting, make yourself available when it works best for the other person.

I've seen people ruin credibility by showing others that they don't really value that connection or experience. Demonstrate appreciation for someone's time, as well as for the person who opened the door for you. Maximize the moment and be grateful for it.

ESTABLISH YOUR WORTH

If you had to think of your personal brand as a fashion brand, are you more Zara or Louis Vuitton? If you chose Vuitton, you have a strong opinion of your worth. That means when you're communicating your personal brand related to your rates, you need to maintain a certain level of status. Whether you're trying to land a client, negotiate a raise, or charge someone for a service, getting what you're worth starts with you having a clear vision of what you should be charging.

People value what they pay for and don't value what they don't pay for. It's counterintuitive when you think about it. Technically, if we get something for free or deeply discounted, we should be ecstatic and appreciate it. But instead, we tend to think, *Wow, that was cheap!* That's not to say that we don't like getting a deal, but when we decide our worth, we definitely don't want someone thinking, *Wow, she's cheap!*

We already know that sometimes we need to do things for trade or for free to gain experience and street credibility. Still, once we have what we need in that area, it's imperative to make sure that we're pricing ourselves to align with the image we're trying to convey.

One of the most critical aspects of understanding your value is doing your research and knowing what other people are charging. Historically, people are secretive about their rates, possibly because they think there are too many mouths to feed. The opposite is true. If you create a safe whisper network among peers, you can share information to make sure you're not undercharging for work but also that you're not pricing yourself out of the market. Most of all, though, you need to make sure that you're not being duped.

Lauren McGoodwin is the founder of Career Contessa and the author of *Power Moves: How Women Can Pivot, Reboot, and Build a Career of Purpose.* We had drinks one night, and she shared this story about the time she was asked to speak at a conference. The conference producer told her they didn't have a budget for speakers, but Lauren was smart and did a little back-channel research. She remembered that someone she knew had spoken at the same conference the year before. This wasn't a close friend, but she reached out anyway and point-blank asked her if she'd been paid. The person shared that not only had she been paid, she had earned $5,000!! Hello, jackpot. Of course, budgets and circumstances change from year to year, but it's undoubtedly worth pushing back. Lauren got back in touch with the producer and told her that she would love to speak at the conference, but her rate would be $5,000. They said they would see what they could do. Guess what? They paid Lauren $5,000.

If people, especially women, aren't transparent about money, we all lose. The more information we share, the better off we are. There's enough success to go around, trust me. You're not risking your well-being by disclosing your rates to people you trust.

Cindy Gallop is a brand and business innovator, consultant, keynote speaker, and entrepreneur whose headline of her bio states "I like to blow shit up. I am the Michael Bay of business." As the founder of MakeLoveNotPorn and a woman in sextech (a male-dominated industry), she needs to stand firm on her value. Cindy advises that when thinking about how to price yourself, the amount you ask for should be the highest amount you can say out loud without laughing. Cindy's friends who follow her rule swear by it. After all, you decide your worth. Why not decide that you're worth a lot?

The time you spend doing things for other people is precious. But what's more important to protect is the years of experience and connections you have.

Here's an example from the world of public relations. Successful publicists take years to cultivate their relationships with the media. So when a freelance publicist is deciding her rates, it can't just be an hourly rate, because if she's good, it might take her one minute to pitch a reporter and secure a story. She can do that because she's spent many years building that relationship with that reporter. Anyone she is charging needs to pay not just for the time she spends pitching them but for her years of experience and robust network. When you think about a monthly retainer or an hourly rate, you can't only consider what a particular client can afford; think about what your time and experience are worth. Once you define that number, you shouldn't deviate from it because that is your worth.

When I was building my client base as a consultant, I came up with an hourly rate that I thought reflected my worth, but when I spoke to potential clients, instead of telling them what my rate was, I asked them to tell me what their monthly budget for this project was. As a consultant, you're filling a void on that team, especially if there's an open position that they're looking for you to cover. There's a previous salary associated with that role. Or you're being called in because there's a problem that the existing team can't solve.

> **Pro Tip:** The company already knows how much they are willing to pay for additional support, and that's the magic number you need to ascertain.

If a company's budget is $7,500 a month and your rate is $15,000 a month, you will price yourself out. It's much smarter to know what you have to work within and negotiate from there. By asking them what their budget is, you're allowing yourself to price yourself strategically without compromising your value.

Once I understand a company's budget, I take my hourly rate and figure out how many hours of my week they can afford. Then I prepare a scope of work based on that time commitment. All this means is that the project will take longer to complete, but they'll make it work if they really want you.

Some people in this scenario might have lowered their rate. But you don't lower your rate unless the opportunity has an incredible upside. For example, if saying that you've worked with this client will enhance your professional reputation, then there's a different value on the table besides what's going in your wallet. If you decide to lower your rate for these reasons, you must protect your personal brand by saying something like "My normal rate is x, but I really admire your company and mission, and I know I can help you get to where you need to go. Therefore, I'm willing to compromise to *y* rate." Again, make sure that you're only doing this if the benefit of partnering far exceeds the money. You could also take a cue from Alisa Cohn here and add, "If this helps you, I will ask you for a testimonial for my site."

Understanding your value isn't easy, though. Sometimes we estimate incorrectly. I was once talking to an influencer who, at the time, had 80,000 followers on TikTok. I asked her rate per post, and she told me $50. I don't think you need to work in influencer marketing to know that her post is worth more than $50. I decided this could be a teaching moment and helped her get to a place that reflected her worth (and reach). Needless to say, she caught on quickly. No more than six months later, when her following had grown to more than 360K, she quoted me $35K for a video post. I created a monster, ha! But honestly, good for her. If she can get that rate from brands, kudos. Numbers are fake. They are subjective. If you have the confidence to say that you charge $35K a video, people will believe that you are getting $35K a video. It's as simple as that. Of course, when you quote that high, you run the risk of not getting the gig. But that might be OK. You'll say yes to fewer opportunities, but they'll be worth more. (*Doesn't sound bad to me.*) To close the loop here, that influencer passed on that project. She didn't even negotiate, which shows me she really was getting that fee. Bravo for her.

Sometimes you learn your worth by accident. I try to be a clear communicator, but sometimes I miss the mark. I was once emailing a client and in haste typed "$3,000 for both." They read that as my rate for each deliverable and sent me a contract for double what I had asked for. It was a lightbulb moment of realizing that I could charge more. Of course, every project is different, and it's important that you understand the realm of what is possible. For example, a start-up typically has a limited budget, so quoting an outrageous number won't yield success. However, a big, established brand probably wouldn't flinch at a high number.

Pressure-test your rates in a logical way. You won't always nail the magic number, but experimenting to see what sticks is worth it.

> **Pro Tip:** Make sure the rates you quote relate back to the specific project scope as opposed to being abstract. DON'T quote different rates to different people for the same work.

As you endeavor to figure out what you're worth, keep track of your thought process and what you quote people. Staying true to your number and fluctuating on the scope of work will ensure that you keep your integrity and consistency among projects. Also, always remember to take meticulous notes of your discussions and keep records of your proposals so you have something to reference and look back on.

Understanding the correlation between your personal brand and your rates helps solidify the overall messaging you want to communicate. Knowing you're good at what you do and being able to charge for it is sometimes an imbalanced equation. It's not always easy to channel the confidence that Cindy Gallop's advice requires. I mean, what if we do laugh out loud when naming what feels like an inflated price? Like anything else, though, it takes practice saying it.

LEARN HOW TO NEGOTIATE

Alexandra Carter is the bestselling author of *Ask for More: 10 Questions to Negotiate Anything*, as well as an award-winning negotiation trainer, keynote speaker, and clinical professor at Columbia Law School. Throughout her career, Alexandra has trained thousands of professionals on how to negotiate with confidence, driving massive, immediate results for leaders and teams. Even though her book will give you the tools to do so, she admits that it's really about steering relationships. Alexandra advises, "You don't wait until once a year to go into your boss and say, 'Hi, I'm Alex. Keep me in mind when you're making your salary decisions.' It means that you are teaching people to value you in every conversation you have. When I made that shift, it was tremendously empowering because I realized there was a different way to be a great negotiator. I am great at steering my relationships, which has been the building block of my success. How do you teach people to value you every day? Well, multiple ways. I'm intentional about how I frame my experience. It's not just numbers when you're teaching somebody how to value you. It's how you describe yourself. It's the words you use, and it's how you paint a picture of your overall worth and experience. Internal self-awareness is the key to negotiation. Internal self-awareness is how well you know yourself. How well can you accurately look in the mirror and see yourself, your strengths, areas of weakness, and your needs, concerns, and accomplishments? Internal self-awareness is the secret sauce that makes leaders and great negotiators. When you know who you are, you know how to go out and speak about yourself in a way that invites people to join you as a partner, whether personally or professionally."

Alexandra doesn't recommend throwing out an arbitrarily inflated number, though. She believes in the importance of building a network to make sure that you're benchmarking yourself appropriately. "Your ask should be as follows: 1) Optimistic, so you're making the best case for yourself. 2) Specific and concrete. 3) Justifiable. So, I don't just throw out a number that's 20 percent more. I think about how I can frame that number. What does that number mean? How can I find some version of reality that makes it easy for them to understand why I am charging that number? When in doubt, if you max out on the money, I would just say, 'All right, what else can we do to get this deal done?'"

Becoming a skilled negotiator takes practice, and getting in touch with our most powerful selves isn't easy. Many things can derail your confidence. But one way to feel more powerful is to connect with your mission. When you're clear on your vision and what you're trying to accomplish, people can feel that energy, and they respond to it.

> **Pro Tip:** Connecting with your purpose bolsters your ability to have those tough conversations.

Mindy Grossman has had a stellar career as CEO and board member for some of the best organizations in the world. No matter what company she has helmed, she was always consistent with having a laser focus on her purpose. "You can't do anything until you've established the purpose, the vision, and the strategic underpinning of what you're doing. You need a purpose filter for your company. You need a purpose filter for your decision-making. You need a purpose filter for you as an individual. And if you think about it in terms of career, create a purpose filter, which is a series of questions that you must ask yourself before you make any decisions."

This is especially essential if you are managing other people. People will follow your lead when they know that you have integrity in your decision-making. Being decisive and having a strong point of view is powerful. But the most impactful thing you can do is believe in your ability to do whatever you set out to, and others will follow.

No matter whose negotiation advice you follow, the real lesson here is TO NEGOTIATE. Always and forever, negotiate. You will be respected for doing so. Fun fact: If you're interviewing for a sales job and don't negotiate the salary, that is a red flag to a potential employer because negotiating is a core competency to your role!

Embrace Your Potential
and Feel Seen

Is there anything better than watching an epic makeover movie scene? The reveal usually happens in slow motion, cascading down a winding staircase. It's not just the makeover, though, that we obsess over. It's also how the love interest finally sees the other person, sometimes for the first time. Ironically, she's been there all along.

These films, of course, put a lot of emphasis on fashion and beauty, but one thing that ties them all together is the person's boldness once they've stepped (literally and figuratively) into their new persona. It's a visible mental shift that has radically transformed their confidence just as much as it has their look. They now believe that they can take on the world.

Not to be dramatic, but that's kind of how I want you to feel right now. Hopefully, your perspective has widened a little (*or maybe a lot!*). It's my intention that you have not only immersed yourself in the pages of this book but have started to think about how the advice relates to you and your potential. I hope you begin to uncover areas of immediate opportunity and that the possibilities are endless. (*Because they are.*)

While this book runs through many different scenarios, there's one common thread that connects whatever stage you're in and the future of your personal brand: **If you don't do the work to position yourself and share who you are with intention, you're missing an opportunity to be seen in the way you deserve to be.** Remember, in the absence of your story, people will happily create their own for you. Without hearing your voice, people might not be able to view you or the value you deliver clearly.

We don't often have the luxury of introspection because life gets in the way. It's up to us to carve out the time in our week to make sure we're leaving space to dream about what we want to achieve, not for a company, but for ourselves as individuals. Sometimes that's easier said than done. Dedicating time to building your personal brand will support the advancement of your career. This isn't a wouldn't-it-be-nice-to-have, it's a must-have. No one will do this for you.

There are so many tactics in this book that you can adopt immediately. While you probably didn't recognize yourself in every example, you might stumble upon these scenarios in the future. (*Hopefully, not any of the crisis ones.*) Either way, this book will prepare you for however you want to be seen. I purposely added those pro tips and the mental gymnastics exercises in bold so that you can easily come back to them over and over. I want *On Brand* to be your long-term reference and companion.

Before you get overwhelmed by your personal brand's current and future states, I want you to realize a fundamental fact: **You've already impacted those who know you. Now it's time to think about what that impression is.** How do people feel when they see your name or when you walk into a room? What do they think about when you leave? Have you left the room better, worse, or unchanged?

Too many people shy away from doing this work because it's uncomfortable or they assume people know who they are and what they stand for. They don't. This entire book is an exercise in self-discovery so that, in turn, others can see you the way you want to be seen. This must be a conscious and continuous effort. If you haven't achieved what you want to just yet, allow people to understand your goals and help you get there. I want you to find your voice and be proud of it. We all need to feel seen, heard, and valued.

At the beginning of this book, I asked you what you want to be known for. While I believe that creating an online presence will only help you reach your goals faster, I want to remind you that being known doesn't have to mean on a public-facing level. It could simply mean that the people around you understand you and your talents. Those closest to you are there not only for the journey but to be your biggest cheerleaders. You just need to tell them what to root for.

As you start to work on this, please remember that there are no wrong answers here. But more than that, what you come up with won't be final. Your story will continue to evolve, and you now have the tools at your disposal to communicate those changes. You can go back into these chapters every time you need to tweak or reassess. This is a process, and it takes time to see the results. But if you're dedicated and consistent, it works. Not only that, but if you make the effort to share your purpose and passions thoughtfully, and especially if they're in service of others, the energy you put into the world will come back to you.

I have experienced this firsthand. In 2013, when I was using the platform I'd built for DKNY PR GIRL to dish out career advice, that effort was rewarded. I was approached to write my first book, *Leave Your Mark*. Through the *Leave Your Mark* podcast, I've been able to extend my brand further and amplify the journeys, successes, and learnings of people I admire. I've also used my platforms to convey my thoughts on how marketing and communicating your story, passions, and beliefs can serve your goals. In doing so, I've also been able to solidify these principles as part of my own personal brand. Those efforts have resulted in this book, which I am grateful to have had the opportunity to write.

On Brand has allowed me to merge my experience in marketing and communications with my passion for mentorship. Teaching people how to brand themselves has become the mission I was never looking for; it found me. I am now able to clearly see my "why," and my "why" is to help people build their personal brands. Nothing brings me greater joy than hearing from people who have put the advice into practice.

I'm not done, though. My personal brand continues to evolve. I embrace the ebbs and flows of my story, and I believe that the key to success is being open to sharing your wins, losses, and learnings. All these elements contribute to who I am. Just like me, you're going to need to invest the time into thinking your brand through. It's something that you must strive for. It doesn't happen overnight. You might even have to rebrand a few times before you get it right. Don't beat yourself up about that. It's all part of the exploration process, and no one is immune to it.

While we would all love to be given this profound sign that we're on the right track in whatever we're doing, progress doesn't always show itself that way. Creating a personal brand takes strategy, consistency, and time. To keep yourself motivated, you must celebrate the small wins. The signs that you're making headway come in many forms, and if you're not paying attention, you could miss them individually. But if you start tracking each win, you might notice that the tide is changing. Perhaps you've been asked to speak on a panel, or you've gotten a response from your pitch that you would never have expected. Maybe you've been chosen to represent your company at a conference, or that piece you wrote has received some notable attention. Any example that shows you that people are starting to observe what you bring to the table matters. These are signs of validation. They are faint whispers that you should hear cheering you on.

Don't compare yourself to other people. Focus on yourself and force yourself to answer the hard questions that stand in the way of your momentum. I'll ask them here again: What do you want to be known for? What North Star goal is your personal brand in service of? You have to know. You're likely just scared to admit it. If you say it out loud, and you don't achieve it, you might think you're a failure. The truth is, if you don't verbalize it, you will never do it. It will be your best-kept secret.

If you take the time to truly understand yourself and what you stand for, you will solidify your brand foundation. Doing everything I recommend in this book will shape their perception of you, but the most important judge of your personal brand is YOU. You need to be happy with yourself. You need to recognize your true worth.

As you endeavor to build this for yourself, remember that what's on brand for you is your secret recipe. No two people are the same. Lean into your unique qualities, and double down on what makes you, you.

Don't try this on a Monday morning. Don't self-reflect after a bad day at work. Do head to alizalicht.com/personal-branding when you're feeling motivated so I can continue to guide you through your personal branding journey.

There is no shortage of judgment in this world. You can be made to feel small, unsuccessful, unworthy, unloved, and unseen at any given moment of the day. Hell, you can do that to yourself just as easily. You don't need to accept this as your reality.

Instead, you can choose to embrace your potential. Listen to the voice in your head that asks, "Why not me?" Because the answer is, it can be you.

No matter what stage this book finds you in, I can promise you one thing: the tools to create, communicate, or reimagine your personal brand are at your disposal. *On Brand* provides your canvas, brushes, and paints, but the masterpiece you create will be all up to you.

Acknowledgments

Never say never should be on my tombstone. I say *never* a lot. I promise I'm not a negative person, I'm just decisive and make split-second decisions wholeheartedly, believing in the path I have chosen.

After I wrote *Leave Your Mark*, I said I was one and done. That's not because it was a bad experience—on the contrary—but because unless you've written a book, you don't realize how much excruciating work and dedication it takes. It's also unnerving at times. Authors wear their hearts on their sleeves. We put it all out there for the taking and the judgment and hope we get back the reaction we intended.

I can only compare this process to childbirth, where every mother knows that delivery is a nightmare, but the payoff is why you do it. When you get that baby in your arms (I have two kids, by the way), you forget the pain you went through, and then it's easier to do it again. Similarly, the readers' response is worth the pain of the process, especially when they share how the advice has helped them via social shares, DMs, and emails.

Despite all of this, I said *never* again. Until one day, seven years after the publication of *Leave Your Mark*, I was on the phone with a former colleague who also happens to be a psychic. She asked me out of nowhere if I was going to write a second book, and I quickly and decisively answered, "No!" She pushed back and said, "No, I think you will write one." I challenged her and asked, "Just for fun, what would it be about?" She didn't pause for even a second when she answered, "PERSONAL BRANDING." I got off the phone, tickled by the conversation but quickly let it pass out of my mind.

Cut to about three weeks later when Amanda Englander, my original editor for *Leave Your Mark*, texted me. She asked me if I would be willing to meet a literary agent. I was confused and asked her why I would need one, and she answered, "So you can sell your second book." I couldn't quite believe what I was reading. I responded and told her I was not writing a second book, but what would it be on if I did? The three dots started moving, and when she was done, the text said: PERSONAL BRANDING.

This is a true story. The universe told me I had no choice but to write *On Brand*. The concept of being on brand has always mattered to me. You can't work in brand marketing and communications and not have this run through your veins. Personal branding has always been the topic I'm most passionate about because I genuinely believe that when you strategically work on your brand, unbelievable things can happen.

I said yes to writing this book to do my part in abolishing gatekeeping. It's up to all of us to share what we have learned. I hope you walk away from this book feeling empowered to build your personal brand and see yourself in a new way. If you do so successfully, pay it forward.

No one gets anywhere without the support of others, and I'm incredibly grateful to be surrounded by people who see the best in me and want the best for me. I'm fortunate to have a network filled with brilliant and sincere people who have always supported my growth and work. I couldn't manage all the things I take on without the help of so many people. Granted, I'm not someone who understands being bored, ha! When I think I can't take on one more thing, I do.

First, to my entire family: David, Jonathan, Sabrina, Mom, Ilana, Steven, Serena, Micah, Uncle Leo, Aunt Andi, Michele, Aden, and Josh, my biggest cheerleaders. Thank you for your love and support and for understanding every time I said, "Sorry, but I have to write!" or "Maybe later, I have to edit!" I'm annoyed for all of you just writing those words, but you all understood my passion and know that once I commit, I do it 100 percent!

To my amazing husband, David: While I know this whole side hustle world has never been your thing, you have always held my hand on this journey. From corporate jobs to consulting and back again multiple times, to writing books, podcasting, and trying to build a community, you have always understood and supported my creative passions. Thank you for being the best husband, best friend, and best dad to our kids. I am so lucky to be married to you.

To my incredible children, Jonathan and Sabrina: You're my most significant accomplishment and what I'm most proud of. I can't wait to see how you use this book one day. I love you more than the world and know that you both will do extraordinary things in the future.

To my beautiful (inside and out) mom, Madelaine: You are my shining star always. Thank you for leading by example and being the best and most selfless mother ever. I'm so grateful for your unconditional support and insightful advice. I love you so much!

Though he's not with us anymore, my dad, Michael, had an enormous impact on who I am today. My greatest memory of him is that there wasn't a person he wouldn't offer to help. He never asked for anything in return. I know I got my mentor mentality from him, and I feel he's with me every step of the way. I know wherever he is, he's proud.

To my other half, my sister, Ilana: We are so lucky to be each other's ride or die. I can always count on you to tell me exactly how it is or should be. No one is quicker than you with a gut response that's always spot-on. You're the best, and I love and appreciate you always.

To my uncle Leo, who is the smartest person I know: Your wise counsel is so valued and appreciated. I love you and thank you for all you do for all of us.

To my mentor and perma–sounding board, Patti Cohen: Thank you for believing in me from day one and supporting my growth. You have been the most wonderful boss and teacher, always by my side through thick and thin. You are family, and I am so lucky to have you in my life. None of this is possible without you, and I am forever grateful.

To my dear friend and mentor, Lori Krauss: We've shared two decades of friendship and collaboration. Thank you for always being there for me, bringing me opportunities, and supporting my projects with your clever insights and advice. No one appreciates something on brand more than you.

To Donna Karan: Thank you for building the most creative and unforgettable work environment. I'm grateful for my nearly two-decade incredible experience; its impact and memories will stay with me forever.

To my editor and friend, Amanda Englander: Your vision never ceases to amaze me. Thank you for being someone who doesn't take no for an answer and always pushes me beyond where I believe my limits are. I appreciate the platform you've given me and am grateful to you for recognizing what I'm capable of, even when I didn't know.

To my agent, Alyssa Reuben: Amanda knew what she was doing back when she introduced us, didn't she? Who knew we would cross paths again years later and be able to work together. Thank you for having my back and always protecting my interests.

To my editor, Jennifer Lancaster: Wow, I hit the jackpot! To have such a talented author as your editor is no small thing. Plus, you are so on brand for me. Every one of your comments was spot-on. Thank you for the value you've added to these pages.

To my friend Jillian Straus: You took this book on as a gracious gesture and never had to. I'm so grateful you did! Your keen eye and expertise are so appreciated. Thank you for always thinking about the sound bite and taking the time to immerse yourself in this manuscript. Your feedback and insights were invaluable.

To my partner in crime, Eliana Meyer, Founding Director of the LEAVE YOUR MARK Community: Thank you for sending that first DM and inspiring me to take the pages of that book and bring them to life. I can't wait to see what we continue to do together. Thank you for also being my first reader of *On Brand*. I value your opinion so much.

To LEAVE YOUR MARK Community member Despina Soubassakou: Thank you for your support and hard work on the research and preparation for this book and for all you do behind the scenes for the podcast. I am so grateful for you and could not have balanced this without you.

TO MY INCREDIBLE CONTRIBUTORS & FRIENDS

You are all truly rock stars. Thank you for supporting me and this book and lending your expertise and experience for others to learn from. When I asked you to contribute your insights, every single one of you responded, "Yes!" without hesitation, which means the world to me. You are all an inspiration to me, and I feel lucky to call all of you friends.

Alexandra Carter	Alfredo Hurtado
Alexandra Wilkis Wilson	Alisa Cohn

Barbara Barna Abel

Bevy Smith

Callie Schweitzer

Carrie Kerpen

Cindy Gallop

Cindy Tien

Corey duBrowa

Dave Kerpen

David Yi

Dorie Clark

Elizabeth Holmes

Eve Rodsky

Jamie Gutfreund

*Jane

Jenna Blackwell

Jennifer Meyer

Jillian Straus

Kendall Ostrow

Lauren McGoodwin

Lydia Fenet

Lyn Paolo

Maria Brito

Meredith Fineman

Mindy Grossman

Nicole Lapin

Ross Martin

Steven Kolb

Susan McPherson

Tiffany Dufu

TO MY WONDERFUL READERS

Thank you for being here. Your support and feedback mean so much. Nothing makes me happier than seeing and hearing how my advice has helped you. I hope you will "close the loop" with me and let me know how you've implemented these lessons. As my *Leave Your Mark* readers know, I am very accessible. I can't wait to engage with you on social media. If you haven't read *Leave Your Mark*, you'll get a lot out of that one too!

GET ON BRAND WITH ME

alizalicht.com/personal-branding

CONNECT WITH ME ON SOCIAL

Instagram: @alizalichtxo

Twitter: @alizalicht

TikTok: @alizalichtxo
LinkedIn: Aliza Licht

SUBSCRIBE TO MY NEWSLETTER

alizalicht.com/newsletter

SUBSCRIBE TO MY PODCAST

Listen to the *Leave Your Mark* podcast wherever you listen to podcasts.

Instagram: @leaveyourmarkpodcast

JOIN THE PRIVATE LEAVE YOUR MARK COMMUNITY

Apply: alizalicht.com/community
Instagram: @leaveyourmarkcommunity
LinkedIn: LEAVE YOUR MARK Community

FOR SPEAKING INQUIRIES

The Harry Walker Agency: info@harrywalker.com

Index